Read the
Bible in a Year

A Daily Devotional from Words of Hope

Harry Buis

Words *of* HOPE
Good News. No Boundaries.

Read the Bible in a Year

© 2011 by Words of Hope

Published by Words of Hope
700 Ball Ave. N.E.
Grand Rapids, MI 49503-1308

Email: woh@woh.org
World Wide Web: www.woh.org

All rights reserved. No part of this publication may be reproduced, stored in a retrieval system, or transmitted in any form or by any means—electronic, photocopy, recording, or any other—without the prior written permission of the publisher. The only exception is brief quotations in printed reviews.

Unless otherwise indicated, Scripture quotations are from the Revised Standard Version of the Bible, copyright 1952 [2nd edition, 1971] by the Division of Christian Education of the National Council of the Churches of Christ in the United States of America. Used by permission. All rights reserved.

Scripture quotations marked ESV are from The Holy Bible, English Standard Version, copyright © 2001 by Crossway Bibles, a division of Good News Publishers. Used by permission. All rights reserved.

How to Interpret the Bible

The Bible is the Word of God in human language. God led the authors of its various parts in such a way that it is God's completely reliable revelation to us of himself and of his plan for human beings.

On the one hand, the Bible is unique, no other book is like it, it stands in a class by itself. On the other hand, written in human language, it must be properly interpreted using rules for interpretation similar to those used for interpreting any human writing. The main rules are:

1) Context—A verse of the Bible is part of a passage. It must not be read out of its context. The question must be asked, "What is the intention of the author in what he says here?" Each passage is also part of a book. What is the purpose of this particular book and how does the verse under consideration contribute to that book? There is also the historical context. If possible, it is helpful to know who wrote the book, to whom it was written, and under what circumstances.

2) Type of Literature—Some parts of the Bible are historical narrative, some poetry, some what is called apocalyptic literature. An illustration of that latter is the book of Revelation which describes truth in terms of vivid imagery. The historical narratives must be taken at face value as describing what really happened, but poetry and apocalypse use figures of speech.

But it is also helpful—and it has been the practice of many great Christians—to read the whole Bible, straight through, from Genesis to Revelation. This book is designed to help you do that, and to do it, as the title says, in a year. Harry Buis, a beloved pastor in the Reformed Church in America for many years and the editor of the Words of Hope devotional for over 20 years, wrote this study guide to set the pace and offer helpful explanations for each day's reading. Finishing it is a marathon, but I think you will find it is well worth the effort.

~David Bast

Preface

The year 2011 marks the 400th anniversary of the publication of the King James version of the Bible, one of the most important events in the history of English-speaking Christianity. In an address to the Reader from the translators published as part of the KJV's original introduction, Miles Smith wrote,

> *It is a fearful thing to fall into the hands of the living God; but a blessed thing it is—and will bring us to everlasting blessedness in the end—when God speaks to us, to hearken; when he sets his word before us, to read it; when he stretches out his hand and calls, to answer, "Here am I, here we are, to do thy will, O God."*

What John Bunyan said of *Pilgrim's Progress* is equally true of the Bible: "This book will make a traveler of you." And the journey of Bible-believing, Bible-following pilgrims brings them to "everlasting blessedness in the end."

But first we have to read it. The blessing doesn't come just at the end of life; it comes here and now to those who listen to God when he speaks, and read the book he has given. There are many ways to do that, all of them useful. We can read a few verses each day, and reflect on their meaning. Words of Hope's daily devotional guide is designed to assist in that type of Bible reading. We can read and meditate upon the same passage—a psalm, say, or the Beatitudes, or Ten Commandments—over and over until we have it by heart.

Scripture quotations marked KJV are from the King James Version of the Bible.

Scripture quotations marked Phillips are from The New Testament in Modern English, revised edition—J. B. Phillips, translator. © J. B. Phillips 1958, 1960, 1972. Used by permission of Macmillan Publishing Co., Inc.

Italics in biblical quotations represents emphasis added by the author.

Cover design: Josh Leo
Image Credit: iStockphoto.com

Words of Hope will proclaim Jesus Christ through broadcasting in the languages of the world's peoples, seeking with our partners in ministry to build the church by winning the uncommitted to faith in Christ and by encouraging Christians in the life of discipleship.

Printed in the United States of America

16 15 14 13 12 11   10 9 8 7 6 5 4 3 2 1

Day 1   Read Genesis 1–3

CREATION AND FALL

Scripture begins with God. "In the beginning God." This should be our starting point—in all the endeavors of life. Life today is in trouble because it is human-centered, but we can determine, by God's grace, to live God-centered lives in such a world.

God created the whole world out of nothing. With one word of power he brought it into being. And he created us. Therefore we belong to him. He made us for his good purposes, and it is for us to discover those purposes and to fulfill them. The rest of the Bible reveals those purposes to us. When God finished the creation it was very good. All of the evil in the world is not his doing, but rather the devil's and ours.

How tragic that the human race at the very beginning fell away from wonderful fellowship with God. Adam and Eve chose their own way rather than God's way, and as a result, the good creation was spoiled. We have inherited that rebellious nature and therefore continue to seek our own way instead of God's way.

But there is hope. Immediately after the fall, God confronts Adam and Eve and the serpent, which represents the devil, and speaks of One who will be of the seed of Eve and will conquer the devil. This is the first hint of a gracious plan that climaxes in the coming of Jesus Christ.

Prayer   *Father, we praise you for your creation and for your re-creation through your Son, Jesus Christ. Amen.*

Day 2   Read Genesis 4–7

TRAGIC RESULTS OF SIN

These chapters describe the consequences of the rebellion of our first parents. The very first person born into the human race became a murderer—of his own brother! He was motivated by jealousy concerning a religious question. Yet God was gracious even to Cain, marking him in some way so people would not kill him.

There follows a listing of the descendants of a third son of Adam and Eve named Seth. People in those days lived very long lives, perhaps because the physical consequences of sin had not yet done as much damage as they do at present.

Sin has its further tragic consequences. The whole human race, with the exception of one family, was living in sinful ways so repugnant to God that he decided to give the race a chance for renewal by wiping out sinners through a flood so extensive that none would survive.

But again, grace is mingled with judgment. God instructed Noah to provide a refuge from the flood. Noah spends a long time building the ark. One can imagine the ridicule of Noah's unbelieving neighbors as he proceeds to obey God. Following the instructions of God, Noah gathers his family and the animals into the ark, and the flood comes.

Prayer   *Father, we grieve as we see the tragic consequences of sin. May many turn to you for refuge. In Jesus' name. Amen.*

Day 3 Read Genesis 8–11

MORE RESULTS OF SIN

One can imagine that life aboard the ark became less and less pleasant as the weeks rolled on. Yet how much better than the only alternative—drowning. The ark is sometimes used as a symbol of the church. Sometimes life in the church is far from ideal, but again, how much better to fellowship with God's people than to be living in a doomed world.

Note that the first thing Noah does when he emerges from the ark is to worship God. Our deliverance through Christ should produce in us a desire to worship the Lord. Also note that as God had told Adam to multiply and fill the earth as well as have dominion over it, these commands are repeated to Noah. To this is added the concept of capital punishment: because human life is so precious, anyone who takes human life forfeits his or her own life. And again there is the grace of God, shown in the giving of the rainbow as a sign of promise.

Although rebellious sinners have been destroyed in the flood, sin remains in the human heart. Noah gets drunk, and his son Ham ridicules his father, a serious sin in the light of God's plan for the family, which includes respect for parents. Sin manifests itself further in the building of the tower of Babel. Perhaps men thought that if they built high enough, they could escape the consequences of a future flood.

Prayer *Father, man's rebellion in our generation also produces tragedy. Forgive us for Jesus' sake. Amen.*

Day 4   Read Genesis 12–16

THE PLAN OF GOD UNFOLDS

Here we have a very important turning point. Out of sinful humanity, God chooses Abraham to begin to build a special people. Abraham is called to leave the comforts of home and move out into an unknown future as God leads him.

Although Abraham is a man of faith, he too falls short. To protect himself he commanded his wife to tell a half-truth, lest the Egyptians slay him to obtain her. A characteristic of the Bible is that it is so honest in portraying its heroes; it pictures them "warts and all."

God's blessing on Abraham produces great material wealth. But this in turn, as is so often the case, leads to interpersonal conflict. In that conflict with Lot, Abraham who was the senior and therefore had greater authority, graciously lets Lot choose what he wants. Tragically, Lot gradually moves his tent in the direction of wicked Sodom. In time Abraham is compelled to take drastic action to rescue his nephew from the consequences of moving into Sodom.

God has promised Abraham that he will have a multitude of descendants. But he remains childless. Instead of trusting God completely, Abraham resorts to questionable means to produce an heir, which in turn produces tragic consequences within the family.

Prayer   *Father, convince us so thoroughly that decisions made contrary to your will bring sad results, that we may always seek to do what you say. In Jesus' name. Amen.*

Day 5 — Read Genesis 17–19

SODOM AND GOMORRAH

Here is the first use of a very important biblical word: *covenant*. God makes a covenant, a contract, between himself and Abraham in which he makes certain promises to Abraham and commands faithful obedience on Abraham's part. The Old Testament is the story of the old covenant that God made with Abraham and his descendants. The New Testament is the story of the new covenant that God made with the church of Christ.

Names have great significance in the Bible. Abraham's name (which up to this point was actually Abram, meaning "exalted father") is changed to emphasize God's promise to him that he will have many descendants, even though there was then no evidence present for this.

The three men who appear to Abraham are apparently two angels and God, who takes upon himself human form to relate more meaningfully to Abraham, even as he later took upon himself human form in Jesus Christ. God revealed to Abraham that he was planning to destroy Sodom because of its sin. For the sake of Lot, Abraham pleaded with God to spare Sodom if enough godly people are found there.

The sin of Sodom is great, and one of its sins was the practice of homosexuality. Because of such great sin, God destroys Sodom after warning Lot to flee. Sadly, his wife loves Sodom so much that she perishes with it. Though rescued from Sodom, Lot's daughters show that Sodom's sinfulness clings to them through inducing their father's drunken incest with them.

Prayer *Father, have mercy upon our sinful world and keep us from sharing its spirit. For Jesus' sake. Amen.*

Day 6   Read Genesis 20–23

FAITH TESTED

Again Abraham is brought into a situation where he is tempted to tell a half-truth (which is a lie). We are all so slow in learning a lesson. Again, the result of sin is tragedy. Yet in spite of sin, God graciously fulfills his promise and finally the long-awaited son is born to Sarah. And again the consequences of a lack of faith bear their bitter fruit. Tension in the home results from the mistake of the past: Abraham took Sarah's servant to himself in hopes of bearing the son of promise. Sin never pays! When will we learn that lesson?

Despite failing smaller tests, Abraham passes the great test of faith. God had commanded the unthinkable, that Abraham should sacrifice Isaac! Abraham goes forward in obedience, and when asked by Isaac where the sacrifice is, he replied that God will provide. And he did. As Christians we cannot help but think of the ram available to die in the place of Isaac as a symbol of God's provision of his own Son as a substitute for us. Abraham had proved that he loved God so much that he was willing to do as much as pagans did who even sacrificed their children to idols. God showed that he loved his faithful servant so much that he provided a way out for Abraham. That is the God whom we deal with every day. Let us be grateful for his mercy and express our gratitude by obedience.

Prayer   *Father, give us the faith to do what you want, even when we cannot understand. In Jesus' name. Amen.*

Day 7 — Read Genesis 24–25

FAMILY LIFE

If the Christian faith is to be passed on to the next generation, strong family life must be developed. This can only occur when both husband and wife are believers. Likewise, Abraham in his day was rightly concerned that his son should marry someone who believed in the one true God. He therefore took steps to do what he could to cause this to happen. What an important lesson for us.

The servant Abraham sends to find a wife for Isaac is a great illustration of how faith is caught through observing someone else's life. What a wonderful prayer for guidance the servant prays. And God answers that prayer in a remarkable way.

One is also impressed with Rebekah's willingness to agree to what is obviously God's will by leaving her family behind to go to an unknown place and to become the wife of a man she has never met. Oh that all believing young people would seek God's will carefully in the choice of a marriage partner. How much happier they would be. How much stronger would family life be.

But we also see mistakes in family living. Abraham lives among pagans who practice polygamy. And Rebekah, having twins, plays favorites between them. That is something parents should be careful to avoid. We should strive to love all our children equally but not the same, for love responds according to each one's need.

Prayer — *Father, guide Christian young people to choose fellow Christians to marry and with whom to build solid Christian homes. Help them to be wise parents. In Jesus' name. Amen.*

Day 8 — Read Genesis 26-27

MORE HEROES WITH WARTS

Can you believe it! Abraham told a lie concerning his wife because he didn't have the faith to believe that God could take care of him. Then he does the same thing again. And now his son does the very same thing. Again the results are tragic. Will we never learn?

But when it comes to conflict with the neighbors, Isaac takes the high road. Instead of fighting, he moves elsewhere to try again. And in response, God gives him new assurance by repeating his promises. And his ornery neighbor has a change of heart. Let us do everything possible to live at peace with our fellow human beings.

But the old problem of parents showing favoritism between their children again raises its ugly head. Jacob's mother encourages him to cheat his own brother. They take advantage of an elderly blind man to do so. The result is bitter hatred between the brothers. Strife within families is so common. Is there trouble in your family? Are you seeking to solve it in the spirit of Christ?

Besides the deceiving of Isaac, there is a mother-in-law / daughter-in-law problem. So Rebekah suggests a good idea for the wrong reason: let Jacob go back to the family to seek a wife who is a believer. That way he will be where his brother cannot kill him.

Prayer *Father, help us to be honest about the tensions in our own family circle. Help us to take steps to rebuild bridges of love with others. In Jesus' name. Amen.*

Day 9 — Read Genesis 28-30

POETIC JUSTICE

What a price Jacob pays for his cheating. He must now leave the home he loves and sleep in the wilderness with a stone for a pillow. But how gracious is God, who appeared to this scoundrel and promised to bless him. This is a deeply moving experience for Jacob, who calls the place Bethel, that is, the "house of God." Yet how imperfect Jacob's response. He begins with the "if" of doubt. If God will do what he has promised, then he will worship God and give a full tenth of all God gives him.

God in his love leads Jacob to a good wife. But his uncle Laban cheats Jacob as Jacob had cheated his own brother. This is one of many cases of poetic justice in the Bible. Think, for instance, of Haman dying on the gallows he had built for Mordecai. God is a God of justice—in the end justice will prevail. "Though the wrong seems oft so strong, God is the ruler yet."

Again we have an illustration of the tragic results of polygamy. God's will is one man for one woman for a lifetime. Whenever we fall short of that ideal, we bring heartache to ourselves and to others. If you are having marital problems, do everything you can to work them out with God's help. Seek the advice of a Christian counselor.

Prayer — *Father, help us to learn from the mistakes of these biblical characters, and as a result not make the same mistakes. For Jesus' sake. Amen.*

Day 10   Read Genesis 31-33

RELATIONSHIPS WITH OTHERS

Sensing that Laban's sons are growing angry with him, Jacob hears the voice of God calling him to leave. However, when Laban pursues him, Jacob works out an agreement with Laban. They are both conscious of the fact that though they cannot really trust each other, the fact that God is watching their actions will help to keep them from breaking their promises to each other. In our society, relationships of trust have broken down in many ways because there is no longer a strong consciousness that we all live our lives in the presence of a holy God.

Going back home, for Jacob, means facing his brother whom he had cheated. He wrestles with God as he faces this experience. But while Jacob is changed, he is not changed completely, for he sends ahead those members of the family for whom he cares least, willing to sacrifice them if necessary to spare those whom he loves more. It turns out that Esau is willing to forgive him. Even then, Jacob is not completely honest, for he says he will follow Esau back home, but then heads in another direction. It is important that we, like Esau, are willing to forgive those who have hurt us in the past. It is also important that, unlike Jacob, we deal with others with utmost integrity.

Prayer   *Father, as we consider how much you have forgiven us, give us grace to forgive others. Help us to be utterly honest in our dealings with others. In Jesus' name. Amen.*

Day 11   Read Genesis 34-36

BACK TO BETHEL

Outward circumstances may be very different, but the problems of every generation are similar. Here was a case of rape. This is certainly a terrible way for one person to sin against another. We also find a case of revenge. Revenge only leads to more sin. And we find a case of fear. Jacob is afraid of the consequences of the sin of his sons, and rightly so.

Once again, problems with the people around him prepare Jacob to hear the voice of God. God told him to go back to the place where he had such a meaningful spiritual experience. Go back to the place where you made promises to God. Have you had a "close encounter" with God? Since then, has the passage of time dimmed your vision and caused you to forget your promises? Perhaps you need to go back to Bethel.

People must prepare themselves to meet God. If a new Bethel experience is to be a blessing, the members of Jacob's family must get rid of their "foreign gods"; these were the idols they had cherished during all these years when they were supposed to have been serving the one true God alone. What do you need to get rid of in your life if your fellowship with God is to be a great blessing?

Jacob receives a new name, Israel. No longer is he to be a cheater; now he is to be a prince of God.

Prayer   *Father, we thank you for spiritual experiences in the past. May our fellowship with you be even more real in the future. In Jesus' name. Amen.*

Day 12   Read Genesis 37–39

JOSEPH THE SLAVE

The Bible is a constant story of humanity's sin and God's grace. Once again we see tragedy resulting from the sin of parents showing favoritism toward one child over another. Joseph's dreams were from God, but one must ask whether Joseph was not guilty of "rubbing it in" to his brothers. The brothers were certainly sinful in the hatred they allowed to grow in their hearts toward Joseph and in the way they expressed that hatred. The interlude of chapter 38 deals with the recurring theme of sexual sin, plus a terrible double standard, one for men and another for women, which has been practiced throughout history.

Yet God's grace has a way of overruling evil for good. The result is that Joseph is in the right place at the right time to save God's covenant people from extinction by starvation. In the meantime, Joseph has much to suffer. He is a faithful steward, but due to the false accusations of Potiphar's wife, he is put in prison. His resistance to sexual temptation by fleeing from it is a powerful example to us. He is away from home, but he knows that God is with him, and to sin anywhere is still to sin against God. Wherever we are, we live in the presence of the God of love and holiness.

Again, in prison, the Lord was with Joseph, and the Lord caused him to prosper. Let us so live that the Lord will be with us and cause us to be successful as he measures success.

Prayer   *Father, give us grace to flee from temptation and cause us to succeed as we seek to serve you. In Jesus' name. Amen.*

Day 13   Read Genesis 40–42

JOSEPH THE RULER

Notice Joseph's sensitivity to the feelings of his fellow prisoners. Notice also how he gives all the glory to God for being able to interpret dreams. And notice how easily the chief butler forgets about Joseph. What a realistic description of human nature we find in these ancient inspired writings. How important that we learn from them what to do and what not to do.

God in his mercy reveals the future to Pharaoh so that wise steps can be taken to deal with those future problems. We may not know much of what the future holds, but certainly God expects us to make wise plans to deal with the future, and he promises to give wisdom to those who ask him for it (Jas. 1:5).

What an outstanding person Joseph is. Wherever he goes, people are impressed by his character and ability. So he is put in charge of the program to store food for the coming time of need. Now Joseph's boyhood dreams are fulfilled. His brothers bow before him. It is not surprising that they do not recognize him. But he must test them to see if they have changed after all of these years. Change is difficult, but people can change. We must constantly pray that God will change us and that we will be patient with people as we pray that God will change them as well.

Prayer *Father, change us more and more into the likeness of your Son, for we know this is the goal of our salvation. In his name. Amen.*

Day 14   Read Genesis 43–45

FROM ANXIETY TO EXHILARATION

What pressures we must sometimes live under. Consider the predicament of Israel (Jacob). He was between a rock and a hard place. After losing Joseph, he didn't want to let Benjamin go lest he lose him also. But if he didn't let him go, they would all starve. Consider how much better the situation was than he thought it was. So often we are in a similar situation. Things may be difficult, but God has promised that all things will work together for good if we love him (Rom. 8:28).

And consider the predicament of Joseph's brothers. They are in a foreign land playing a game they don't understand, with rules that seem constantly to be changing. Yet just around the corner, everything is going to look brighter. We need to be realistic about our problems, but we also should be optimists, for if we are on God's side, he is on our side, and his plans for us are wonderful beyond imagination.

Joseph believed in providence. Looking back, he could see the hand of God in all that had happened. This enabled him to be gracious to his brothers who had hurt him so deeply. You may have serious problems. You cannot see the hand of God in them now. But trust God, seek to obey him, and the day will come when you will be able to look back and see that he has done all things well.

Prayer   *Father, give us faith to believe that your hand is in all that happens to us. In Jesus' name. Amen.*

Day 15   Read Genesis 46–47

DO NOT BE AFRAID

Why are the words "Do not be afraid" found so often in the Bible? Because Bible characters were just like us. There were many times when they were afraid. But God tells us that we need not be afraid. Usually, when God tells us this, he gives us this powerful reason: "I myself will go down with you" (46:4 ESV). When we consider the great power of God who could bring the whole vast universe into being with one word, surely we are foolish to be afraid. He is with us. He has promised to help us. He always keeps his word. So whatever your situation, here is God's Word to you: "Do not be afraid" (v. 3).

Joseph was a good man, but his governmental policies were questionable. When he gathered the food from the people during the years of abundance, there is no evidence he paid them for it. But when he distributed it, he sold it. The result was that everything ended up belonging to Pharaoh, and from then on there was to be a 20 percent income tax.

In many passages of Scripture, it is evident that God is on the side of the poor. God really owns the land and all the resources with which he has filled this world. We must develop policies that will provide for a fair distribution of those resources to all people. This takes a wisdom and love that only God can give us.

Prayer   *Father, take away our fears. Help us to work for justice for all people, both in our own country and throughout the world. In Jesus' name. Amen.*

Day 16   Read Genesis 48-50

LOOKING BACK AND LOOKING AHEAD

As Jacob nears the end of his life, he looks back and speaks of "the God who has led me all my life long to this day" (48:15 RSV). God is always willing to lead us in ways that are good for us. The only question is, are we ready to follow?

It is good to look back and gratefully see the loving hand of God in all that has happened to us. It is even more important to look forward to the future. Both Jacob and Joseph speak of the time when their people will return to the Promised Land. They are keeping their eyes fixed on the promise of God that their children will inherit the land of Canaan. Things were going well, but they knew that God had something more important in store for them. So with us, no matter what our situation is, let us remember that God has promised far better things for us in the future.

Here there is even a farther look ahead. The blessings of Jacob on his children include the one to Judah which promises that the symbol of rule will be in the hands of his descendants "until he comes to whom it belongs" (49:10 RSV). This is seen as a promise that Christ will come of the tribe of Judah, and so it was. Our future is in Christ's hands. That's great. Faith in that fact should give us an inner peace available in no other way.

Prayer *Father, we look back with thanksgiving and forward with trust in you and your wonderful promises. In Jesus' name. Amen.*

Day 17   Read Exodus 1-4

GOD CALLS MOSES

Exodus is the book that contains *the* great event of the Old Testament: God's deliverance of his people from the slavery of Egypt. In a sense, the book of Genesis is a prelude preparing us for this event.

The Egyptians forget the great blessing Joseph, the Israelite, had been to them. They see his family, which has now grown into a great nation, as a threat instead of an opportunity to enrich their land. They engage in one of the most disgusting practices, making slaves of other human beings. And the Israelites cry out to God.

God hears their prayers and sets in motion a method to rescue them. To do so, he chooses a man, Moses. God often works through people. To be used of God one must have certain qualities: integrity, humility, faith. Let us seek to develop qualities that will make us useful to God as he continues his work of rescuing people from the slavery of sin.

Consider the excuses Moses makes. They are so flimsy. So are ours. If God wants to use us, he will give us what we need to be used by him. Away with excuses. While Moses is the main person God will use, there is also another player on the team – Aaron, his brother. Are you willing to team up with others to accomplish what God wants to be done?

Prayer   *Father, we praise you that you have made the way for us to be rescued possible through Christ. Give us the grace to take that way. In his name. Amen.*

Day 18   Read Exodus 5–7

NO ONE SAID IT WOULD BE EASY

Moses' attempt to do what God wants runs into stiff resistance from Pharaoh. He has an arrogant attitude toward Moses but also toward God. There are people like that today. From this biblical story, we see that such people are in big trouble. How do frail human beings dare rebel against Almighty God. Yet they do. Let us be sure we are not one of them.

Things often get worse before they get better. So it is for the Israelites. Instead of being let go, their situation worsens. Who is ahead at the end of the first inning in a baseball game is not very important; it's who is ahead at the end of the ninth that counts. Never forget that.

God told them he is "the LORD," that is Yahweh, the God who is the constant One, who has made a covenant of grace with his people and who will keep that covenant. Things may be difficult, but you can depend on God. You may not be able to depend on yourself or on other people, but you can depend on God, the faithful One who keeps his covenant promises to his people.

Meeting with the ruler of Egypt comes next. Pharaoh hardens his heart. What is the punishment? God further hardens his heart. Often God does not hurl thunderbolts against sinners; he just lets them harden in sin, which brings sure punishment.

Prayer   *Father, no matter how difficult things may be for us today, give us faith to know that in the end all will be well as we trust you. In Jesus' name. Amen.*

Day 19 — Read Exodus 8–10

HARD HEARTS

Again and again we read of Pharaoh hardening his heart. We need to realize that the Bible teaches we were born with hearts as hard as stone. Only by the gracious work of the Holy Spirit, the divine inner work of regeneration, do our hearts become soft and submissive to God. Let us realize that were it not for the grace of God, our hearts would be as hard as Pharaoh's heart, and we too would suffer tragic consequences similar to those that befell him.

Pharaoh's hard heart is the reason one plague after another falls upon him and his people. Some of these plagues were similar to ones common in Egypt. The miraculous element was the intensity, the timing, and the fact that in some cases they fell on the Egyptians but not on the nearby Israelites. People today don't like to think of it, but the fact is that God punishes sin. He does it in many ways. Sometimes the punishment falls not only on the individual who sins but also has adverse effects on those around the sinner.

It is important to confess sin. But sometimes such confession is shallow and ineffective. Pharaoh "confesses" his sin but then goes right on sinning. He also begins to try bargaining with God. He will do what God wants though only with certain ifs, ands, or buts attached. That accomplishes nothing.

Prayer *Father, we believe that we are saved only by grace, because you have produced a miracle in our naturally hard hearts. Thank you! In Jesus' name. Amen.*

Day 20   Read Exodus 11–13

I WILL PASS OVER YOU

Nine plagues struck Egypt and still Pharaoh hardened his heart and would not let Israel go. One more plague was to strike, but before this Israel was given instructions regarding the Passover meal.

It was to be a family affair. There was to be unleavened bread, since leaven apparently symbolized sin. Likewise, there was to be bitter herbs, symbolizing the bitterness of the slavery of Egypt. But the main course was a lamb. They were not to break any of the lamb's bones even as the Scriptures foretold that the Lamb of God would not have his bones broken when hanging on the cross. But most important of all, the blood of the lamb was to be smeared on the doorpost of the house so that when the Lord went by, the destroyer would pass over that house. Every house not protected by the blood of the lamb would lose its firstborn, but every home so protected would be safe. So also we are saved if the blood of Christ has been applied to our hearts through faith.

With a dead child in each home, finally Pharaoh was ready to let the children of Israel go. Every year they were to celebrate the Passover as a reminder of this marvelous deliverance from the slavery of Egypt. For Christians, the Lord's Supper takes the place of the Jewish Passover.

Prayer   *Father, we praise you for a greater deliverance than you provided Israel that Passover night long ago, for you have freed us from sin's penalty through Christ's blood. In his name. Amen.*

Day 21   Read Exodus 14–16

GOD WILL TAKE CARE OF YOU

Pharaoh's repentance was short-lived. That slave labor was too good to lose. The pursuing Egyptians filled the Israelites with fear. While Moses told them to stand still, God's order was to go forward. Miraculously, the Red Sea or the Sea of Reeds opened before them. Sometimes God uses ordinary physical phenomena to accomplish his miracles; in this case it was a strong wind. Let us accept God's help when he chooses to use ordinary means and simply believe. It was a miracle, for when the Egyptians entered the sea, the water flooded in and drowned them. As a result, the people worshipped God with a song of praise. God takes care of us in so many ways; let us always be ready to praise him.

God not only takes care of the children of Israel by protecting them from the Egyptians; he also provides them with water and food in the wilderness. He does this in spite of their constant complaining. Before we criticize them for this, let us examine our own lives to see how often we complain in spite of God's abundant care for us.

The way God provided the manna has some good lessons in it for us. He gives bread one day at a time. He provides enough for all of us. And he wants us to take a weekly day of rest. Notice that this Sabbath is prior to the giving of the law at Sinai.

Prayer   *Father, thank you for your provisions for all the necessities of life. Forgive us for complaining. In Jesus' name. Amen.*

Day 22   Read Exodus 17-19

WHEN YOU HAVE YOUR HANDS FULL

Moses had more than his share of problems. Notice how he handled them. When the people complained, Moses cried to the Lord. When you have a problem, "take it to the Lord in prayer." When people cause you difficulties, look to the Lord and ask him for wisdom.

Now comes the attack of the Amalekites. Here the answer is a combination of prayer and the help of others. As long as Moses holds his hands up to God, Israel prevails. But his hands grow weary, so others hold them up for him. Let us be ready to work cooperatively with others in the work of the Lord.

There is the task of administration, of dealing with the problems that arise when people live together in a community. Here the answer is to take the advice of someone who can look objectively at your problem and also to be willing to delegate responsibility. We must not think we are the only ones able to do something. God provides people with a variety of gifts so that the household of faith may function effectively.

Finally, we must learn how to give clear instructions, as Moses did when the people approached holy Mount Sinai. Clear communication is essential to prevent misunderstandings, which can do so much damage.

 *Prayer*   *Father, as we are beset with a host of problems, give us wisdom from on high to deal with each one in a way that will honor your name. For Jesus' sake. Amen.*

Day 23 — Read Exodus 20–22

THE TEN COMMANDMENTS

The introduction to the Ten Commandments is very important. God begins by saying what he has graciously done for the children of Israel. He has rescued them from slavery. The commandments are to be their response to his gracious initiative. The old covenant was a covenant of grace.

The first commandments deal with our relationship to God and those that follow with our relationship to our fellow human beings. The great commandment is love, but love expresses itself in specific ways. For instance, if we really love God, we will have the deepest respect for his name and his day. And if we really love people, we will not hurt them by stealing from them their lives, their spouses, or their possessions.

The commandments in the chapters that follow further define what is involved in the Ten Commandments and point out the penalties that enforce these laws. There are so many ways we can hurt our fellow human beings. God wants us to realize that hurtful actions carry with them very negative consequences. Because there is a God in heaven, sin does not pay. Notice how again and again God's Word says "when" this is done, then this will be the result; "if" we do this, then this will be the penalty. This is not legalism; it is the protection of the rights of our fellow human beings.

Prayer *Father, we praise you for our deliverance through Christ. Help us to show our love by obedience. Amen.*

Day 24 — Read Exodus 23-25

OBEDIENCE AND WORSHIP

In these chapters, God concludes the giving of commandments that are to regulate daily life and begins to give instructions for constructing the tabernacle, Israel's portable place of worship. So also in the Christian life, there are two aspects: living godly lives day by day and offering our worship to God. The two must go hand in hand. Neither one ought to be neglected. What we do on Sunday should affect what we do on Monday through Saturday.

Among the commandments for daily living are those that tell how we are to treat the poor. We must not have just a personal piety; we must also have a concern for social justice. Because God cares how the poor are treated, so must we. We must not only say we care; we must do what we can to correct situations.

Connected to the call for obedience are promises of what God will do as a result of such obedience. God said to his people of old, "If you carefully obey" what I say, then I will bless you (23:22). God treats us, his New Testament people, according to the same principles he used in treating Israel.

In chapter 25, we also find descriptions of some of the furniture that is to be built for the tabernacle. The ark is to symbolize the very presence of God in their midst. God dwells in our midst in a far more immediate way—the Holy Spirit is in our hearts.

Prayer — *Father, may our Sunday worship affect how we treat people the rest of the week. In Jesus' name. Amen.*

Day 25　　　　　　　　　　　　Read Exodus 26–28

HOLY TO THE LORD

This passage completes instructions for building the tabernacle and describes the garments to be made for the priests. In doing so, it introduces one of the key concepts of Scripture, that of holiness. These are to be "holy garments" (28:2) and the plate of pure gold, which is to be fastened to Aaron's forehead, is to have on it the engraving, "Holy to the Lord" (28:36).

Holiness means "separated unto." Anything holy is to be totally dedicated to the service of God. Being separated to God includes being separated from sinful purposes. As Aaron's garments were to be holy, so we are called to be holy, that is, so separated unto God that we continually separate ourselves from sin.

The Urim and the Thummim (28:30) are of special interest. They were apparently two objects, something like dice, which were used in the casting of lots to determine the will of God. They were kept in a receptacle in the breastplate of the high priest and were only used to determine God's will for matters that dealt with the national affairs of God's people. It was fitting then that they were kept in the breastplate which was adorned with 12 precious stones representing the 12 tribes. We can be thankful that through Scripture and the Holy Spirit we can determine the will of God in a much more mature way.

Prayer　　*Father, help us to live holy lives of seeking to know your will and, led by your Spirit, to do your will. For Jesus' sake. Amen.*

Day 26   Read Exodus 29–31

PREPARATIONS FOR WORSHIP

These chapters are part of a section describing ways in which to prepare to worship God. The New Testament pays less attention to externals but continues to emphasize the importance of worship. God's Word teaches not only that we must take time to worship but that we must do so with hearts prepared for this sacred event. Jesus said that those who worship God must worship him in spirit and in truth (John 4:24). Are you doing that?

The high priest, the leader of worship, was ordained, or set aside for this sacred task, with an elaborate ceremony. While elaborate ceremonies are not required by New Testament teaching or example, certainly to set aside persons to lead in the worship of God is an important matter. Both the leader and the people should be impressed with the importance of what we are doing when we worship Almighty God.

But who among these Israelites in the wilderness had the skill to produce this beautiful tent and furnishings and garments? God's Spirit filled certain persons, giving them the needed skills. The Bible teaches us that in a similar manner the Holy Spirit gives various abilities to each member of the church so that the work God has given us to do may be done well. God wants each of us to ask ourselves, "What gift or gifts has God given me?" and then to use those gifts for his glory.

Prayer   *Father, help us to worship regularly with hearts carefully prepared. In Jesus' name. Amen.*

Day 27 Read Exodus 32-34

INTERCESSORY PRAYER

While Moses is on Mount Sinai, receiving the commandments of God, the people are on the plain below involved in the very serious sin of idolatry. When Moses discovers this, he prayed fervently that God will not punish the people as they deserve. While this is what God had intended to do, he changed his plan in answer to Moses' prayer!

Notice what Moses does not do. He does not separate himself self-righteously from the sinning people. Instead, he said to God that he was willing to be lost rather than that God should not forgive these people, utterly unworthy though they be. What a different spirit from what is so common among us today.

In reply God said that because of the sinfulness of the people, he would send an angel to accompany them on their journey, but he himself would not go with them personally. Again Moses pleaded with God, and again God changed what he said he would do, in answer to Moses' prayer! If we would pray as fervently and unselfishly as Moses, what great things God would do for his church.

While God is willing to be gracious to Israel because of the prayer of Moses, he is yet a God who will punish sin and who requires obedience. In our emphasis on the grace of God, we must not forget that.

Prayer *Father, cause us to be so concerned for the spiritual welfare of your people that we will pray for them fervently and unselfishly. In Jesus' name. Amen.*

Day 28   Read Exodus 35-37

GIVING IN THE RIGHT SPIRIT

Having been given clear instructions how to build the tabernacle and its furnishings, two things were yet needed: the material for the work and the actual accomplishing of the project.

Though in the wilderness, the people had personal possessions, part of which had been given to them by the Egyptians, who after the plagues were glad to see them go. Pooling their resources, the material was thus furnished. In spite of their faults, the Israelites set a good example for us in how to give for God's work. They gave with a "generous heart" and with a "willing heart" and gave so much that they had to be told to stop.

They had a worthy cause; we have a more worthy cause. They were to build a material building for God's glory; we have the opportunity of investing our resources so that people everywhere may hear the good news of Christ. Let us then give with a generous heart, glad for the privilege of leading people to eternal life. There is no end of opportunities to do so.

Having the plan and the materials, now they actually did the job. It is not enough to have high ideals and great opportunities. We must determine to serve the Lord in the specific ways and opportunities he has given us. Let us not just talk about what needs to be done—let's do it.

Prayer   *Father, work in our hearts so we may want to give and work joyfully. For Jesus' sake. Amen.*

Day 29 — Read Exodus 38–40

COMPLETE OBEDIENCE

Did you notice how the words "as the LORD had commanded Moses" are repeated over and over and over again in this passage of Scripture? God had given a detailed description of how the tabernacle and its furnishings were to be made. He had commanded that they produce these articles exactly as he had said. They had done so. In his Word, he has also given a description of what we ought to do.

God has given us many commandments also, not only in the Ten Commandments, but in describing for us the qualities that are to characterize and fill the Christian life. Having been saved by grace alone, we are called to obey God in all we do. Such obedience leads to great blessing. Carelessness regarding obedience means we will miss many blessings God is ready to give us.

Having been made in obedience to the command of God, the articles of the tabernacle were consecrated to their purpose by anointing. The English word *anointed* is connected to the Hebrew word for *Messiah*, which in Greek is *Christ*. All Old Testament symbolism finds its fulfillment in Christ. He is the One anointed to be our prophet, priest, and king. To be a Christian is to share in that anointing, and therefore we each have a prophetic, a priestly, and a royal task to do.

Prayer — *Father, give us the grace to be completely obedient to all you have told us to be and to do. In Christ's name. Amen.*

Day 30   Read Leviticus 1–4

SACRIFICES

Here is where your determination to read through the Bible in a year will be severely tested. Leviticus consists of detailed ceremonial laws that God gave to the children of Israel. These first chapters deal with various kinds of sacrifices that were to be made on different occasions.

All the sacrifices of the Old Testament are fulfilled in Christ. These laws point forward to the perfect sacrifice he would make. The people were made to realize that there must be great sacrifice to approach God, so they would understand the purpose of Christ when he came. We can be thankful that "Jesus paid it all." Pagan religions also included sacrifices, sometimes even the sacrifice of one's own children. Within the heart there is the realization that one cannot approach a holy God without great sacrifice. How liberating to know that because Christ died for sinners, there is nothing left for us to pay. Trusting in him, we can be sure of salvation.

The hymn reflects biblical truth when it says, "Jesus paid it all, all to him I owe." We owe a great debt of gratitude that we can never fully pay. In gratitude we are to sacrifice and serve for the cause of his kingdom. Not to save ourselves, but with a desire that others should know Christ, trust him, and also be saved, we ought to give most generously for the cause of missions.

Prayer   *We praise you, O Lord, for the perfect sacrifice which assures us of our salvation. Amen.*

Day 31   Read Leviticus 5-7

DEALING WITH SIN

From this passage and many others in the Bible, it is obvious that God takes sin seriously. In a generation that takes sin lightly, we must evaluate it as God does and not as society does. In the description of offerings the Israelites were to make are three principles which apply to us today, even though the perfect offering for sin, Christ, has already been presented to God.

There is to be confession of sin. We must not make excuses for ourselves. We must not make light of our sin. We must honestly acknowledge our sin to God, and where appropriate, we must also confess it to our fellow human beings.

Second, we are to relate our sin to the sacrifice. In our case the sacrifice has already been made for us, but it is important to realize that we receive forgiveness not because God winks at sin but because Christ paid a high price for it. Looking at the cross, we see how serious our sin is and at the same time we can be assured that we are truly forgiven by God.

Third, though the sin has been forgiven, there are many cases where restitution is required. Sometimes we cannot undo the consequences of our sin; on other occasions something can be done. If we have cheated someone, we must repay them.

Father, we measure our lives by your requirements and we see how far we fall short. We confess specific sins to you and ask for forgiveness. For Jesus' sake. Amen.

Day 32   Read Leviticus 8–10

LEARNING TO OBEY

Once again we have a passage where the constant refrain is "as the LORD commanded Moses." Moses was careful to do exactly what God said he was to do. Some people have the idea that the Old Testament emphasizes works while the New emphasizes grace. But we are to remember that God's Old Testament people had been saved by grace. It was to a people whom he had rescued from slavery that God gave the Ten Commandments. Obedience in the Old Testament was to be a response to grace.

And the same thing is true of us today. We are not saved by our works but by the perfect work of Christ. We are not saved by our perfect obedience, for then none of us would be saved. But redeemed by grace, based on Christ's perfect obedience, we are to seek to do what God tells us to do.

We are called to a life of obedience, even as God's Old Testament people were thus called. To that end we are to study the Scriptures that we may learn what God's will is.

In Leviticus 10:11, we learn that teaching was to be one of the functions of the priests. Elsewhere we learn that all of the Levites were to be dispersed among the people to teach (e.g., Deut. 17:8-11; 18:6-7). Yet in the narratives about Israel, we do not see this happening. Could this be why Israel failed to do God's will?

Prayer   *Father, show us your will as we study Scripture. Give us grace to be more obedient. For Jesus' sake. Amen.*

Day 33   Read Leviticus 11–13

SEPARATION FROM UNCLEANNESS

It is helpful to divide the laws God gave Israel into three categories: ceremonial, civil, and moral. Ceremonial laws deal with sacrifices. Christians are not to obey them, for Christ has fulfilled them by his perfect sacrifice, and to continue to obey them would be to deny Christ. Civil laws dealt with community issues. Because our society is so different than that of Israel, they no longer apply to us. But the principles they teach of being concerned for the effect of our lives on that of others still hold. The moral laws no doubt still apply to us. It was wrong to murder before the commandment was given at Sinai, and it will always be wrong to murder.

The laws described in this passage fall under the civil law category. In a time when there was apparently little medical knowledge, these laws of uncleanness helped to protect people from the spread of illness.

But there was more to it. God wanted his people to be distinguished from the pagans around them. He knew that giving his people specific directions in practical matters would help in this. Dietary rules would help to set his people apart from their unbelieving neighbors. The explanation God gives in Leviticus 11:44-45 is significant. The word *holiness* contains the idea of separation. Because he was their God and he had brought them out of slavery, they were to be separated to him and apart from paganism. The same is true of us.

Prayer   *Father, give us grace to live holy lives. Amen.*

Day 34   Read Leviticus 14-15

CLEANSING FOR THE UNCLEAN

The previous chapter described leprosy. The problem was that with the lack of diagnostic tools, leprosy could not be immediately distinguished from other less serious diseases that caused lesions in the skin. Therefore, unlike what we call leprosy today, some of these diseases would clear up or could be cured. How thankful we should be for modern medicine which can diagnose and cure so many diseases.

In this passage, we find how the unclean was now to be declared clean. This was not without blood offerings. We are reminded that sin causes us to be unclean in the sight of a holy God, but he has provided a way through the blood of Christ whereby we who are unclean can be made clean. In several ways leprosy can be compared to sin. In leprosy, the germ is present long before the first symptoms appear. So with sin. We have a sinful nature that produces individual sins as symptoms. Leprosy is contagious, although not nearly as contagious as many other diseases. So also sin is passed from one generation to the next, and individual sins are often engaged in because of close association with other sinners. But most important there is now a cure. Modern medicine has a cure, and Christ is the cure of sin. Finally, those cures must be brought to the people who need them.

Prayer   *Father, we praise you for the good news that Christ can cleanse us of our sins. Cause us to be zealous in spreading that good news to other sinners. In his name. Amen.*

Day 35 — Read Leviticus 16–18

ATONEMENT FOR SIN

This section of the Bible emphasizes the fact that we cannot approach a holy God lightly. No one could enter the Holy of Holies, the most sacred part of the tabernacle, which was separated from the rest by a veil—no one except the high priest and then only once a year, on the Day of Atonement, and only with the blood of an animal sacrifice.

Significantly, at the time of the crucifixion of Christ, the veil was torn from the top to the bottom, teaching that God is now approachable through the blood of Christ. Now, through the name of Christ, all of us can come boldly to God's throne of grace.

It is important to realize that for Israel there was only one day of fasting but a number of feast days. The emphasis is on rejoicing at being God's people, while at the same time realizing this is possible only because God has provided the way.

But we only appreciate grace when we realize the seriousness of sin. Many of the ways of the world are an abomination in the sight of God. Sin can never be taken lightly, and we must recognize that God's people are not to worship the false gods of the people around us or to live the way they live. The sins of the world around us are an abomination in the sight of a holy God and can only lead to tragic consequences.

Prayer — *Father, help us to take sin seriously so that we realize the marvel of your grace, and may that realization give us the courage to live aright. Through Christ. Amen.*

Day 36   Read Leviticus 19–21

WHY DO WHAT IS RIGHT?

Again and again in this passage God states what his people should and should not do. Then the statement is made over and over again, "I am the LORD your God." In other words, act in this fashion for this reason: because I am your God. Here also is our motivation for righteous living. God has entered into a covenant of grace with us. He is a God of righteousness and therefore he expects a high standard of morality from his people—*his* standard.

The reason for not stealing, for not oppressing other people, for not hating our brother or sister, and a host of other things is this: God has been gracious to us, making us his people, calling us to obey. We are to act as he wants us to act.

The reason for much immoral and unethical conduct today is unbelief. Sound theology leads to sound ethics.

In the midst of this passage are the words, "You shall love your neighbor as yourself." When Jesus spoke these words, he was quoting from Leviticus. He was reaffirming the teaching of the Old Testament. He said that this commandment, coupled with the great and first commandment to love God supremely, led to all the others. We are not only to love people; we are to love them as much as we love ourselves. This love is not sentimentality; it is a determination to treat other people in a way that will be helpful to them.

Prayer   *Father, we hear your call to ethical behavior, and we know the reason for such living: you are our God. In Christ. Amen.*

Day 37   Read Leviticus 22–23

HOLY DAYS OR HOLIDAYS

Human nature is such that we need special days to break up the routine of life. God recognized this need by giving the children of Israel several annual feast days as well as the weekly Sabbath. These days also were times to recall the mighty works of God which he had done on their behalf.

While the emphasis of the New Testament is that all of life is to be dedicated to God, and that we are to continually remember the great events in which God acted on our behalf, it is helpful to set aside certain days to remember what God has done for our sake.

Long before the giving of the Ten Commandments, God gave his people the weekly Sabbath, a time to rest and reflect on his goodness to them. It is of great value to make Sunday a special day of rest and worship. One of the factors leading to the problems many people have today is that they live from weekend to weekend rather than from Lord's Day to Lord's Day.

It is also helpful to set aside days like Christmas, Good Friday, Easter, and Pentecost to remember the events in the life of Christ which have produced our salvation. Sadly, some of these special days have become commercialized while others are forgotten. Many people have become spiritually impoverished as a result. Let us focus on Christ on these special days.

Prayer   *Father, help us to use Sunday and special days of the year to lead to our spiritual growth. In Jesus' name. Amen.*

Day 38   Read Leviticus 24–25

ALL BELONGS TO GOD

This section mingles directions for worship with directions on how to treat people. The common thread is this: all belongs to God. God is holy, and his name must not be blasphemed. In the Old Testament the punishment for misuse of the name of God was death. Exodus 20:7 is still true: "You shall not take the name of the LORD your God in vain, for the LORD will not hold him guiltless who takes his name in vain." Cursing has become common, but in the sight of God it is a terrible sin.

The Year of Jubilee was given by God so that the rich would not constantly become richer while the poor became poorer. To start with, each family had a plot of ground to provide for its material needs. If they lost that plot either because of poor management or in spite of their best efforts, the land was to be returned to the original family every fifty years.

In the meantime, if someone had a poor relative, he was to help that person. There were specific regulations to provide for those in need. The Bible constantly emphasizes God's concern for the poor and therefore teaches that he who would be godly needs to share in that concern.

Every part of life was to be regulated with this in mind: the whole world belongs to God.

Prayer   *Father, in this secular society in which we live, help us to have an entirely different outlook on life, one which will affect how we treat people. In Jesus' name. Amen.*

Day 39 — Read Leviticus 26–27

IF YOU WALK WITH GOD

This passage reflects a principle stated throughout Scripture, that God will respond to us depending on how we have responded to him. The word *if* is prominent. If we obey God, he will bless us. If we do not listen to him, he will chastise us.

There is a danger that we take such passages and allow them to lead us to a work-righteousness religion. The New Testament reminds us that our best efforts fall so far short that we must trust in God's mercy and grace alone, a grace revealed clearly to us through our Lord Jesus Christ. Yet it is true that obedience will bring blessings, although not always of a material nature, and that disobedience will lead to God's disciplinary action against us.

This disciplinary action is spelled out in detail here. To disobey is to walk contrary to God. This will lead to trouble. The purpose of this trouble is to lead to repentance. If this does not happen, yet greater trouble will come. The final trouble would be exile, something which actually took place in the history of Israel. If this would finally lead to confession of sin, God would receive them again in mercy. These biblical principles are still at work today in God's dealings with us.

The last chapter talks about voluntary dedication of oneself and one's possessions to God, a practice reported among God's people in the early chapters of the book of Acts.

Prayer *Father, give us grace to be obedient that we may experience your blessings. In Jesus' name. Amen.*

Day 40   Read Numbers 1–3

WE BELONG TO GOD

One purpose of Genesis is to show us how God's people arrived in Egypt. Exodus tells us the story of God's people journeying from Egypt to Mount Sinai. Leviticus takes place at Mount Sinai, and Numbers tells the story from Mount Sinai to the borders of the Promised Land.

The book is called "Numbers" because it begins with God commanding a census to be taken. The census was of men of fighting age, and they numbered 603,550. When one adds men too old or too young to fight, women, girls and the Levites, the total number of people must have been over two million. It was surely difficult to control such a large group in the middle of the desert. Therefore there had to be organization, just as any such group today would need.

The Levites were a special tribe, assigned to the care of the tabernacle. The place of worshiping God was so important that it was given this kind of attention and personnel. The idea that the firstborn of each family belonged to God in a special way was a reminder that all belongs to God. All of God's people were to worship, but it was impractical that all should spend their full time at it. So payment was made that the Levites might take their place. The lesson for us is that we all belong to God and should spend time worshiping him and serving him. We too have been redeemed, but at a far greater price—the blood of Christ.

Prayer   *Father, help us dedicate ourselves to you.*
           Through Christ. Amen.

Day 41   Read Numbers 4–5

COVENANT FAITHFULNESS

An important biblical concept is that God has entered into a covenant with his people. He has made a commitment to them and they to him.

Therefore sin is thought of in terms of unfaithfulness. To sin is to fail to be faithful to covenant promises. It is to break faith with the Lord. Therefore there must be both confession and restitution. Confession brings forgiveness, but this doesn't mean that the consequences of the sin are to be ignored. One must pay back God or neighbor for what one has taken from them. Our present legal system would be far more just if this Old Testament principle were put into practice. This would be much more fair to the victim of crime and would also cut down the tremendous cost of imprisonment. Obviously such a principle would need to be adapted to today's societal needs.

Marriage is a covenant between a man and a woman. To violate that covenant is to break faith, to be unfaithful to vows of commitment. We must not allow the strange way of trying to determine the guilt of the unfaithful spouse in this chapter to cause us to lose sight of the great concept set forth here. Today marriage is taken far too casually by many people. We need to reemphasize the idea that it is a covenant; it is a matter of commitment to be taken seriously by us because it is taken seriously by God.

Prayer   *Father, we thank you for your faithfulness to us. Help us to be faithful to you and to each other. Through Christ. Amen.*

Day 42　　　　　　　　　　　　　　　Read Numbers 6–7

BLESSING AND RESPONSE

The Bible moves back and forth from blessings God gives us to ways in which we are to respond to those blessings. It is a blessing to belong to God's covenant people. Beside the ordinary response of obedience, an Israelite had the opportunity to spend a period especially dedicated to God by taking a Nazirite vow. While all of life is to be dedicated to God, there is real value in making a special response to grace, always being careful to avoid self-righteousness.

Chapter 6 concludes with the benediction the priests were to pronounce upon God's people. It climaxes with *shalom*, "The LORD . . . give you peace." The benediction is threefold, looking forward to the time when God would reveal himself as triune.

Then comes the giving of offerings for the utensils to be used in the tabernacle. While we need to maintain our church buildings in good condition, our offerings can also be used to spread the gospel to the ends of the earth. Oh that each of our churches was mission minded and willing to make sacrifices so the Word can be heard everywhere!

After the offerings were brought, again we have God speaking, as Moses heard the voice of God from above the mercy seat that was on the ark. We too can come to the place of worship and hear the voice of God through sound biblical preaching.

Prayer　　*Father, we praise you for our blessings. Help us to respond by dedicating ourselves and all we have. Amen.*

Day 43 — Read Numbers 8–10

LEAD ON, O KING ETERNAL

Now it was time to leave Mount Sinai and head for the Promised Land. God kept them constantly aware of his presence by inhabiting a cloud hovering over the tabernacle by day and a pillar of fire by night. We too are on a journey through life on our way to heaven. We travel not alone. We are God's people together and we are assured of God's presence. The cloud and fire may have been more spectacular, but Christ in our hearts through the Holy Spirit is much more important.

They set out after partaking of the Passover. So also our journey is periodically interrupted by the Lord's Supper, a reminder of who we are and of what Christ has done to make us his people.

They set out when God commanded them. We are to be constantly seeking to discern the will of God as he leads us each step of the way through life. Prayerful reading of Scripture is the most important way of knowing God's will. Another important way of knowing when he wants us to move forward and when he wants us to stand still is to be alert to ways in which he opens and closes doors of opportunity. Yet another important way is to consult with those wise people in our lives who love us and who love God.

The tenth chapter closes with a reminder that there are enemies who would hinder our progress, but adds the assurance that God will give us the victory over those enemies.

Prayer *Lead on, O King eternal. Through Christ. Amen.*

Day 44   Read Numbers 11–13

PROBLEMS, PROBLEMS

If you haven't noticed, God's people have their faults. The people grumbled. Paul writing to the Corinthians urges us to learn a lesson from what happened to them. God was providing their daily bread, and they weren't satisfied. They remembered the variety of food they had in Egypt, forgetting the bitterness of their slavery there. God gave them what they wanted, but as the psalmist commented, with it "sent leanness into their soul" (Ps. 106:15 KJV). It is a frightening thing that if we insist, God may give us what we want even if it is not good for us.

Moses also had to contend with the criticism of his brother and sister. Moses was involved in an interracial marriage, and his family objected.

Finally, when the spies came back from looking over the Promised Land, they had a bad attitude. They saw all the difficulties, forgetting that God is sovereign. Because they forgot they were the people of God, they had an inferiority complex. They said that they felt like grasshoppers in the presence of the giants, and that those giants also looked down on them. Never have an inferiority complex; you are a child of God purchased with the precious blood of Christ. When you have a low estimate of yourself, others will also have a low estimate of you, making you ineffective in the service of Christ.

Prayer   *Father, in the midst of problems help us to look to you and to have courage. In Jesus' name. Amen.*

Day 45   Read Numbers 14–15

FORGIVEN BUT . . .

Ten of the spies came back saying that the task of conquering the land was impossible. This showed lack of faith in God. When the people sided with those spies, they also showed their lack of faith. God was ready to destroy them. God is love, but this doesn't mean that he will accept any kind of behavior.

Moses now shows his greatness by turning down God's offer to replace Israel with only the offspring of Moses and instead pleads in intercessory prayer on behalf of this people who had treated him so poorly. He bases this intercession not on the worthiness of the people but on the name of God. If the people perished and the other nations thought it was because God could not take care of them, God's name would be dishonored. He asked God to forgive them.

God accedes to the plea of Moses and forgives the people. But that is not all; he also told them that the present generation would perish in the wilderness. They will be forgiven. They will remain God's people. But there will be tragic consequences resulting from their sin. They will miss the blessing they could have had. So with us. How wonderful to be forgiven! But sin results in our missing many blessings God wants to give us. Never forget that in the midst of a generation that takes sin so lightly, God does not take it lightly.

Prayer   *Father, forgive us and also give us grace to keep us from sinning and missing the blessings you are ready to give us. In Jesus' name. Amen.*

Day 46　　　　　　　　　　　Read Numbers 16-18

POWER STRUGGLES

God had appointed Moses as the leader of Israel. He had appointed his brother Aaron to be high priest. However, people like Korah wanted greater power in the community of God's people.

The people of Israel were confused as they listened to the claims of both groups. It was necessary for God to take drastic action to make it clear whom he had chosen for leadership.

Sad to say, in the church today such power struggles continue. People forget that Jesus said that the one who wishes to be great should be willing to be a servant to all the others. We must all recognize that our spirit should not be one of insisting we must have our way or we will not cooperate.

On the one hand, we must recognize that God has ordained that the church today should be governed by pastors and elders. On the other hand, these office bearers must realize that they are called to be unselfish, sensitive, godly persons. Leadership decisions must above all be made considering God's will as it is revealed in Scripture. Such leaders must be sensitive to the desires and needs of all the people of the congregation. Then there needs to be cooperation on the part of everyone, although things may not be done in just the way we would like them to be done.

Prayer　　*Father, may there be peace and harmony in your church so that the world may be drawn to Christ. In his name. Amen.*

Day 47　　　　　　　　　　　Read Numbers 19-21

LOSING YOUR TEMPER

What a great man Moses was! How much he had to put up with in leading Israel through the wilderness. How often he interceded for the people when God was ready to destroy them. Once he lost his temper, with tragic results. The people needed water and God told Moses to speak to the rock. Instead, in anger, he struck it with his rod. The result was that in losing his temper, he lost the opportunity of entering the Promised Land.

That doesn't seem fair, does it? But the fact is that a person may live as he should, yet one burst of temper can have irreparable results. What permanent damage can be done if we lose our temper just once with a spouse or a child or an employee. Let us ask for God's grace always to be in control of ourselves. Self-control is one of the fruits of the Holy Spirit.

After his mistake, it was necessary for Moses to go on dealing with the problems of life. The damage was done, but he still had responsibilities. When we fail, we ask for God's forgiveness and go on.

Moses had to lead the people as they fought the enemies around them. He had to deal with the fiery serpents and make a bronze serpent to which the people needed to look in order to be healed, even as we need to look to Christ in faith in order to be saved.

Prayer　　*Father, fill us with the fruit of the Spirit, self-control, and where we fail, forgive us and help us to continue serving you. For Christ's sake. Amen.*

Day 48   Read Numbers 22–24

THE LURE OF MONEY

What a story! The prophet Balaam is offered a large honorarium by Balak if he will curse Israel. Oh how he wanted to go, for the sake of that money, but God said no. Balaam is not ready to give up so easily. He tells Balak he will see what else God might say. He is not satisfied with God's answer, so God does what he often does for us: he gives us what we want if we insist, but at what a price.

God tells Balaam that if he insists on wanting to go, God will let him go. But he is ready to destroy Balaam for disobedience, something even his donkey realizes and talks about. Balaam is so absorbed in his desire to collect that fee that he doesn't even seem surprised that the donkey speaks!

Balaam acknowledges that he has sinned, but he still wants to go on, and God allows him to do so. What a warning to us. Try as he might, over and over again, still hoping for that big payment, he is unable to curse Israel but only to bless him. Seeing the whole picture, we can see that his prophecy that "a star shall come forth out of Jacob, and a scepter shall rise out of Israel" (24:17) was fulfilled in Christ.

Are you tempted to take a high-paying job which may not be God's will for you? Are you tempted by questionable business practices because of the financial gain involved? Remember Balaam!

Prayer   *Father, help us to realize that there is no profit in gaining the whole world if we lose our own soul. In Jesus' name. Amen.*

Day 49   Read Numbers 25–27

THE DANGER FROM WITHIN

Balaam could not harm Israel by cursing her. But he knew how he could harm her and perhaps yet get the pay he wanted so badly. According to Numbers 31:16, it was the advice of Balaam that caused the young women among Balak's people to lead the young men of Israel astray, luring them through illicit sex and leading them to worship the idol Baal.

It was only decisive action on the part of Phinehas, the grandson of Aaron, that turned back the resulting plague. Let us pray that God will raise up godly leadership in church and state, and let us inspire our own children to be such leaders.

Now a second census is taken, from which the book of Numbers gets its name. The purpose of the census this time is to begin to prepare for the division of the land when the children of Israel will move into the Promised Land. The totals disclosed by the census are about the same as those at the beginning of the book; no growth had taken place because so many had died as a result of disobedience. We grieve as we see many churches that are not growing in number even though they are in the midst of growing areas. True, there is growth which cannot be measured by a census. But sadder yet is the fact that some churches don't even want to grow, even though the Lord calls us to reach out with the gospel.

Prayer   *Father, cleanse our churches and give them the desire to spread the gospel beginning in their own neighborhood. In Jesus' name. Amen.*

Day 50 Read Numbers 28–30

PUNCTUATING TIME

Can you imagine what life would be like if our time was not divided into weeks and months and years? There would be a dreariness about it. God knows that human beings need time broken up into segments. So to Israel he gave a religious calendar which broke life down into manageable segments. And all these segments were occasions for worship.

God gave Israel commandments to worship each day, each week, each month, and on special occasions throughout the year. What was meant to be a blessing, however, became a burden as the Pharisees in Jesus' day weighed down these times, especially the Sabbath, with a host of rules and regulations.

On the one hand, for Christians, every day is the same. Every day we worship Christ, every day belongs to him. But Jesus himself said, "The Sabbath was made for man." One day in seven, celebrated in a special way, through rest and worship, is of great spiritual and physical benefit. We hurt ourselves and others if we do not set one day each week aside to encourage each other in the faith and thus develop and pass on our spiritual inheritance as we worship God.

It is also helpful to celebrate the church year. Every day we rejoice that Jesus came in the flesh, that he was crucified for our salvation, and that he rose from the dead victorious on our behalf. But celebrating these events with your church family once each year keeps them in focus.

Prayer   *Father, we recognize Jesus is to be Lord of every day of the week. We praise you for him. In his name. Amen.*

Day 51   Read Numbers 31–32

THE LORD'S BATTLES

The idea that God commanded the children of Israel to slay their enemies, men, women and children, is highly offensive to many people, and understandably so. It has caused some people to reject the Bible and others to reject parts of the Bible such as this. The problem needs to be faced honestly.

If Israel was to be a blessing to the whole world, she needed to be a holy people. The nations around her were terribly ungodly; their worship of idols led to many immoral activities, things which were abominable to God. If Israel lived among them, many would yield to these temptations. Therefore the source of the temptations itself had to be removed, even if that required drastic action. Only a people pure enough to be an instrument in God's hand could bring great blessings. In fact, Israel failed to destroy the enemy; she yielded to their temptations, and therefore never did carry out her mission of blessing. Her rebellion made her unusable, although out of her God brought Christ to accomplish the needed salvation. There are some things more important than life itself, and God who is Lord of life and death can choose to give life as well as withdraw and take life into his own hands.

We live in a different age. But God's goal is still to have a holy people who will be a blessing to the whole world. We are called to serve, not by destroying, but by giving of ourselves unselfishly.

Prayer   *Father, help us to put the cause of your kingdom ahead of our personal interests. In Jesus' name. Amen.*

Day 52   Read Numbers 33–36

CITIES OF REFUGE

The Levites were not to have a separate area for their inheritance as did the other tribes. Rather, they were to be given 48 cities and the surrounding territory to live in. The idea was that scattered among the tribes they would be available to teach the law of God to the people. There is no historical evidence that such a program was practiced; perhaps that was one reason for the downfall of Israel. In contrast, may all in the church, young and old, be involved in Bible study.

Of the Levitical cities, six were to be cities of refuge. We must remember that the Israelites were a primitive people. As with most such people, it was the responsibility of the next of kin to repay anyone who killed a member of the family. But what if the killing was accidental? Here was a provision for such a situation: the killer could flee to the city of refuge. One can picture such a situation, where the killer is running for his life. Oh what relief when he entered the gates of the city of refuge. If, however, the killing was deliberate, the killer was to die. Sincere Christians differ on the question of the death penalty today. Note that in this passage it was considered that for murderers to live caused the land to be polluted.

Though our sin is not accidental and we deserve death for it, still the gospel urges us to flee to Christ to escape the penalty of sin. How this magnifies the grace of God offered to us through the cross of Christ!

Prayer   *Thank you, Jesus, for escape from sin. Amen.*

Day 53 — Read Deuteronomy 1-2

LEARNING FROM OUR HISTORY

Genesis takes us from creation to the people of Israel being in Egypt. Exodus is the story of their escape and journey from Egypt to Mount Sinai. Leviticus takes place at Mount Sinai. Numbers tells the story from Mount Sinai to the borders of the Promised Land. Deuteronomy takes place at those borders.

Deuteronomy means literally "second law." It consists of the farewell messages of Moses in which he reminds the Israelites of their history and of the law which had been given to them to keep as God's covenant people.

Someone has said that if we do not learn from the mistakes of history we are doomed to repeat them. We too have a history as did Israel. Our history is rooted in theirs but goes on. We are a people who have been redeemed with a greater redemption than being freed from the slavery of Egypt. We have been redeemed from sin by the precious blood of Christ. There is a sense in which we share in Jesus' death, resurrection, and ascension. We are the people of the New Testament. We are also children of the great Reformation. We have Luther and Calvin as spiritual forefathers. We are part of a people which includes martyrs and missionaries.

Let us avoid mistakes of the past and be inspired by those who have done great things for Christ.

Prayer   *Father, keep us from the errors of the past and help us to be inspired by the victories. Through Christ. Amen.*

Day 54　　　　　　　　　　Read Deuteronomy 3–4

THE LORD ALONE IS GOD

Having finished rehearsing their history, Moses said, "And now, O Israel, give heed to the statutes" (4:1). The message from God always ends with "and now." This is the truth, "and now" this is what you should do about it. Sound doctrine is never an end in itself; it is always a call to sound action on our part.

These people not only knew what God had done in dealing with their ancestors in the past; they also had seen the recent punishment for sin at Baal-peor. Therefore as they enter the Promised Land, they are to keep God's commandments. They were told "keep your soul diligently, lest you forget" (4:9). We constantly need sermons like those of Moses. We need to be reminded over and over again how God deals with his people, giving us blessings as we obey him and causing us to suffer the consequences when we disobey.

We are likewise to tell these things to our children and our children's children. God's truths are for them as well. They stand in danger of forgetting and thus losing the blessings God intends for them.

Again and again there is the reminder that the Lord alone is God. There will be temptations to serve other gods which are no gods. Such temptations must be resisted. A god is something in which you center your life or from which you think you can find ultimate happiness. Remember, the Lord alone is God!

Prayer　　*Father, keep us from forgetting the truth so we do not lose our spiritual heritage. In Christ's name. Amen.*

Day 55   Read Deuteronomy 5–7

THE LORD *OUR* GOD

The people are to realize that even though it was their forefathers who were literally present, the Ten Commandments have been spoken to them. So now the Ten Commandments are repeated with the emphasis that this generation is to obey them, for they are the commandments of the Lord *our* God. So also the Bible is to be the living word to us; through it our God is speaking to us, calling us to trust and obey.

Following the Ten Commandments, we have the Great Commandment, to love the Lord *our* God with our whole being.

These commandments are not only for the present moment; they are for the future. They are to be taught diligently to our children. They are to stimulate questions from our children which will give us the opportunity to explain how our God is our Redeemer. The commandments are not the way of salvation. Obeying them is the response to God's grace that he desires.

God's people are to be a holy people. To be holy is to be separated unto, to be dedicated to, the service of God. God is the faithful covenant-keeping God, but we are to respond with a love which proves itself in obedience.

Prayer   *Father, we rejoice that we are saved by grace. We also rejoice that we are called to a life of loving obedience. Through Jesus Christ our Lord. Amen.*

Day 56   Read Deuteronomy 8–10

BY GRACE ALONE

The Israelites had spent years in slavery and then 40 more years literally depending on God for their daily bread as they went through the wilderness. Soon, however, they would enter the Promised Land described elsewhere as a land "flowing with milk and honey." They would suddenly experience prosperity and that would be dangerous to their spiritual life.

It was important therefore that Israel should constantly focus on the fact that they were saved by grace alone, and therefore humility was the only fitting attitude to have in response. So Moses reminds them of their former poverty. He warns them that the new prosperity carries with it the danger that they will forget that God alone is the source of all of their blessings. He points out that they were chosen to be God's special people not because of their righteousness and power, but in spite of their stubbornness and weakness. Moses reminds them that they would have all been destroyed in the wilderness if it had not been for his intercessory prayers on their behalf.

The same is true of us: we are sinners saved by grace. The bottom line is not that we have chosen God but that he has chosen us in spite of our sins and failures. And our material prosperity is also a gift far beyond our deserving, though it likewise endangers our spiritual life.

Prayer   *Father, constantly remind us that since we are saved by grace alone, humility is the only fitting attitude for us to have in life. In Jesus' name. Amen.*

Day 57 — Read Deuteronomy 11–13

OBEY

The constant theme of Deuteronomy is that God's people should obey his commandments. But isn't this one of the major themes of the entire Bible? We are saved not by works but by trusting in Jesus Christ. As saved persons, however, we are called to good works.

Just as with the Israelites, God promises that blessings will flow from obedience. "Trust and obey, for there's no other way to be happy in Jesus, but to trust and obey." And disobedience brings heartaches. It can be no other way (Deut. 11).

Obeying involves worshiping the way God has told us to worship. He showed the Israelites how to worship and how not to worship (Deut. 12). We too must worship God from the heart, responding to the way in which he has graciously dealt with us in his Son Jesus Christ.

Obeying is also a matter of daily living. Things go wrong for individuals, for families, and for nations when everyone does "whatever is right in his own eyes" (v. 8). God has given us not minute rules, but great principles of love and justice which we are to obey.

We must recognize the danger of others trying to lead us astray (Deut. 13). The section ends with the words "doing what is right in the sight of the LORD your God" (v. 18). We must make our goal not to please ourselves, not to please others, but to please God. The result will be that we will be richly blessed.

Prayer   *Father, give us grace to obey you. In Christ. Amen.*

Day 58   Read Deuteronomy 14–17

LIVING AS GOD'S CHILDREN

This passage begins with the words, "You are sons of the LORD your God." Following this there are a number of things which they are to do and are not to do. If we are children of God, this calls for a certain lifestyle. Like father, like son. Being made in God's image, we are to reflect God's nature in daily living. Salvation can be thought of in terms of the restoration of the image of God in us.

Because the Israelites were God's children, there were certain things they were not to eat. In a primitive society, some of these rules served hygienic purposes. We can be thankful that in the New Testament era there are not dietary regulations. But there are still "don'ts," for Jesus says that although it doesn't matter what goes in your mouth, it matters a great deal what comes out.

You are children of God; you should tithe (14:22-29). The New Testament also teaches proportionate giving. When we consider the marvel of grace in Christ and the tremendous missionary opportunities today, we should gladly give more than 10 percent of the abundance that God has given us.

There were also provisions made to help the poor help themselves (Deut. 15). Christian principles are to be applied to the life of our society. Creative ways must be found to help the poor.

Prayer   *Father, we praise you that we are your children through Christ. Help us to act accordingly. In his name. Amen.*

Day 59   Read Deuteronomy 18-21

LIFE UNDER GOD

One lesson we can learn from this passage is that God is interested in every area of our lives. There is a tendency today to restrict God to our private lives and to say that in our pluralistic society, public life is to be governed by humanistic principles. A governor or other elected official will say, "I am personally opposed to abortion, but that has nothing to do with the laws which I favor." No, Jesus Christ is to be Lord of all.

Many of the laws in this passage do not apply to us in the present age, but from them we can still glean principles we can use today. The person who gives himself or herself to a life of Christian ministry is to be provided for by the church (18:1-8). We are not to try to be like those around us who are not Christians (18:9-13). We are to discern between those who are God's spokesmen and those who are not, and we are to obey the word God gives us through those whom he has chosen (18:15-22). We are to have laws which will properly punish those who take the life of another human being (19:1-13). We are to guard property rights (19:14). Our system of justice must be administered with great care (19:15-21). We are not to be afraid of our enemies (20:1-20). Children are to be obedient to their parents (21:18-21).

The New Testament applies the final verse in the passage (21:23) to Jesus' crucifixion for us.

Prayer *Father, keep us from ignoring your rightful claims upon every part of our lives. In Jesus' name. Amen.*

Day 60   Read Deuteronomy 22-24

CARING FOR OUR NEIGHBOR

The common theme running through the various laws in this section is that we must be careful to protect the rights of our fellow human beings, especially those in situations that put them at a disadvantage. We are to reach out to help people whatever their need (22:1). Even animal life must be protected. Care must be taken for a mother bird "that it may go well with you, and that you may live long" (v. 7).

The Old Testament laws can be divided into three types: ceremonial, which are fulfilled in Christ; civil, which for us today provide principles as we seek to live with each other; and moral, which are just as much for us today as when they were first given. The laws in this section are civil laws, and the law of the parapet (22:8) shows us one of these principles. In Israel, houses had flat roofs. If a parapet was not built around such a roof, a neighbor child might climb up, fall off easily, and be injured. The parapet was to be added to protect against such accidents. In a culture where flat roofs are not so common, the literal law is meaningless. But the principle is abiding. We are to do what we can to keep a fellow human being from being injured.

Special concern must be taken in the area of sex. The Bible teaches that sex is neither cheap nor dirty. It is a precious gift of God which must be carefully guarded against misuse. It is meant to be fully expressed only within the bonds of marriage between a man and a woman.

Prayer   *Father, in all our actions help us to be careful to protect the rights of our neighbors. In Jesus' name. Amen.*

Day 61 Read Deuteronomy 25-26

JUSTICE AND GRATITUDE

Deuteronomy 25 deals with the subject of justice. A society must have a judicial system that determines guilt and innocence, but the punishment must not be so severe as to degrade the guilty. One of the high priorities in our society is to call for judicial reform. Christians should unite with others to demand a better system of justice.

Justice includes economic justice (vv. 13-16.). In many ancient societies, a balance was used for measuring goods to be sold. Secretly using two sets of weights, one when you buy, another when you sell, was a way of cheating people. Christians need to realize that we are called to absolute honesty in all of our business dealings.

Deuteronomy 26 deals with gratitude. When bringing offerings to the Lord, we must remind ourselves who we are—people who have been rescued by God, purely because of his grace. If we are those who live in a land that produces riches, this is simply because God has caused it to be so. Therefore we are to bring the firstfruits of our labors to God as an expression of our realization that we have what we have because God has given it to us.

Here we are shown the spirit with which we are to worship. A danger is that we go to church with a heart filled with anxious concerns for the week ahead instead of with gratitude.

Prayer *Father, help us to be utterly honest all week and to worship you with a heart filled with gratitude each Sunday. In Jesus' name. Amen.*

Day 62   Read Deuteronomy 27–28

CURSES AND BLESSINGS

If you stand at Jacob's tomb in Samaria you can see before you Mount Ebal and Mount Gerizim. Moses commanded the Israelites, when they entered the Promised Land, to go to this place and have a ceremony solemnly reminding them of the tragic results of disobedience and the wonderful blessings flowing from obedience.

This passage is first of all addressed to Israel as a nation. She had been graciously chosen by God, but her continuance as the people for special blessings depended on her obedience to him. In fact, she was disobedient, so disobedient that God made a new covenant with his people in Christ.

Israel was to be a people so blessed of God that she would be a testimony to the world. Now the church is in that place of privilege and responsibility. Paul in his letters as well as Jesus in his letters to the churches in Revelation remind us that we too could lose that privileged position if we fail in our responsibilities to God. Are you all wrapped up in your own goals of personal pleasure or is your top priority that you as part of Christ's church will carry out his mission?

God's people are called to a life of joyful worship (28:47). When you enter the church sanctuary, can you honestly say that you are there worshiping God with "gladness of heart, by reason of the abundance of all things"?

Prayer   *Father, enable us to worship you aright.*
               In Jesus' name. Amen.

Day 63 — Read Deuteronomy 29–31

COVENANT

The concept of covenant is a key idea in the Bible. The Bible consists of two parts: the story of the old covenant God made with Israel and the story of the new covenant God has made with his church. God began unfolding his plan of salvation by making a covenant of grace with Abraham. On the basis of this, God entered into covenant with Abraham's descendants, the Israelites, at Mount Sinai. Now at the border of the Promised Land, this covenant is renewed. The covenant is an agreement whereby God promises he will be our God and we promise to trust and obey him.

You must not think, just because you are a part of God's covenant people, "I shall be safe, though I walk in the stubbornness of my heart" (29:19). To grow up in the church is a great privilege, but it carries with it the responsibility of faith and obedience. Baptism is the sign of the privileged position of covenant membership. Woe to the covenant breaker!

Moses is pessimistic as he renews the covenant. He told the Israelites that if they rebelled when he was with them, how much more would they do so after he dies. And so it happened. The Israelites squandered their spiritual privileges. God has made his new covenant with us. Let us learn from the mistakes of Israel. Let us love the Lord our God and express such love by obedience.

Prayer — *Father, thank you for entering into a covenant of grace with us. Help us to be faithful. In Jesus' name. Amen.*

Day 64   Read Deuteronomy 32-34

THE SONG OF MOSES

Moses is about to die but he has a song in his heart because of his relationship to God. His song is about God. He speaks in his song of God's greatness and of his faithfulness. Over and over again, he calls God the "Rock." The New Testament tells us that Christ is the Rock, the foundation upon which we are firmly established.

When we think of God, we also think of his work. Moses thinks of how God had graciously made Israel his people. But Moses also describes how Israel had failed to respond in love and obedience. This is the story of the entire Bible: God's grace and man's response. Let us be sure that we respond in faith, living a life that pleases God.

Moses also pronounced his blessing on each tribe, even as Jacob had done before he died (Deut. 33). As we grow older, let us not think only of ourselves. As aches and pains increase, it is easy to grow more and more self-centered. Let us be concerned with the future of God's people. Let us pray for revival in the church. Let us pray more and more for the spiritual welfare of our children and grandchildren.

The book concludes with Moses standing on Mount Pisgah, seeing with his own eyes but not entering the land which his people will possess. With the reins of his leadership turned over to Joshua, Moses the servant of the Lord dies there in the land of Moab, and he buried him there in an unmarked grave.

Prayer   *Father, raise up deeply godly men and women to be spiritual leaders in the next generation. In Christ. Amen.*

Day 65   Read Joshua 1–4

THE GOD OF THE PAST IS PRESENT

The book begins with God assuring Joshua that he will be with him just as truly as he had been with Moses. But Joshua must be sure to use the spiritual resources provided for him; he is to meditate on the Bible day and night. It is important for us to realize that the God who helped the great men of the Bible will help us today! But we must not neglect the means God has provided for us. Joshua had the five books of Moses. We are faced with new challenges in our generation. We can cope with them if the completed Scriptures are our daily source of inspiration.

To assure Joshua and the people that he is the living God, God does for them something very similar to what he had done for the previous generation. Moses and the people had crossed the Red Sea on dry ground. Now Joshua and the people will cross the Jordan on dry ground.

The hand of God is not shortened. He can do for us what he has done for people in the past. He may not act in such obviously miraculous ways as he did in the days of the Bible when he had not yet so fully revealed himself through his Son, but he is the living God who loves us and will do even greater things for us as we put our lives in his hands. And what he does for us we must tell our children (4:22).

Prayer   *Father, increase our faith, knowing that the great God of the Bible is the living God today. Through Christ. Amen.*

Day 66   Read Joshua 5–7

VICTORY AND DEFEAT

Here we have an illustration of the principle of Deuteronomy: obedience brings blessing; disobedience brings sorrow. Having crossed the Jordan, Israel must now conquer a key city, Jericho. God has a plan. This plan gives the Israelites a responsibility. They must march around the city and blow the trumpets precisely as God commands. They do this and God causes the walls to fall down; he produces the victory. So also with us. We are saved by grace alone; to God be the glory, but we must do what he tells us to do.

Having conquered powerful Jericho, the Israelites are faced with the little town of Ai. They send up a small force for this purpose and are shocked by being soundly defeated. Joshua does what he needs to do. He turns to God. He cried out as we often cry out, "Why?" The answer is, "Israel has sinned." One man had sinned and it had affected the whole nation. The Bible constantly emphasizes corporate responsibility over against unhealthy individualism.

Could it be that unconfessed sin in a congregation today hinders the blessing of God from being received? Has someone secretly committed adultery? Is there some businessman, perhaps a leader in the church, who is involved in dishonest practices? Is that why the church is not succeeding in its great mission? Let there be repentance!

Prayer   *Father, cleanse us that we may be effective in your service. For Jesus' sake. Amen.*

Day 67   Read Joshua 8–10

GOD'S METHODS

Someone has said, "The Seven Last Words of the church are, 'We have always done it this way.'" We have a tendency to get in a rut, to fail to deal with opportunities creatively. Change is not to be inaugurated for the sake of change, but neither are we to keep doing something a certain way merely for the sake of tradition.

In this section of Scripture, we see that God uses a variety of methods to accomplish his purposes. In the case of Jericho, he causes the walls to fall down miraculously. Now in the second attack on Ai, he leads Joshua to use clever military strategy. Then in the attack on the Amorites, he uses the ordinary fighting of the Israelite soldiers but augments their efforts by sending hailstones and causing the sun to stand still. Following this, he uses ordinary military activities to defeat the rest of the inhabitants in the Promised Land.

God uses a variety of methods and so should we. The essential message of the church must not change, but we need to adapt our ways of presenting the gospel to a particular culture.

The miracle of the sun appearing to stand still is a greater miracle than it seems at first, because it really means the earth stood still and at the same time God kept everything on earth from shifting. We are not sure how to explain this miracle, but we believe God can do whatever he chooses.

Prayer   *Father, use us in your service. In Jesus' name. Amen.*

Day 68   Read Joshua 11-13

IT IS FINISHED BUT

Having conquered the southern part of the Promised Land, Joshua now gives his attention to the north. Here he is faced with an army much larger than his, one equipped with horses and chariots, with the kind of military power he did not possess. But God said, "Do not be afraid" (11:6). As someone has said, "One plus God is a majority." "If God be for us, who can be against us" (Rom. 8:31 KJV).

Then we read, "Joshua took the whole land" (11:23). Yet at 13:1 we read, "There remains yet very much land to be possessed." This is not contradictory. When Christ died on the cross, he said, "It is finished." The perfect sacrifice was complete, but yet much needed to be done by the people of God in spreading the gospel. In similar fashion, on the one hand God had given the entire Promised Land into the hands of Joshua and his people, but there were still pockets of resistance in various parts of the land.

So in our lives. We are redeemed, but there is a great deal of mopping up to do. We are justified, but we are only partly sanctified. There are areas of our lives which need work. Are we neglecting them?

There is in our lives the "already" and the "not yet." We are already God's children, but we do not realize how many more wonderful blessings are yet to come.

Prayer   *Father, I am thankful that I am no longer what I used to be. I look forward to what I shall be. In Christ. Amen.*

Day 69 — Read Joshua 14-17

ACCEPTING A CHALLENGE

Having conquered the land , Joshua now divides it so that each tribe may have a territory. In the midst of the (to us) rather boring description of this process of dividing, we come across the story of Caleb. Forty-five years earlier he had been one of the spies sent by Moses to see what the Promised Land was like. Ten had come back saying the task of conquering the land was hopeless. But Caleb and Joshua had come back saying that with God's help the job could be done.

Now Caleb is 85, but he doesn't sit on his rocking chair. He asked for a difficult assignment, conquering the giants that live in the hill country. Notice that he is described as a man who "wholly followed the LORD" (14:8). God is still looking for people like that, people who will be completely dedicated to him, people who will be willing to accept a challenge. Will you be one of those people, no matter what your age? How would people describe you? Would those who know you best say that you "wholly follow the Lord"?

Caleb volunteers for a challenge, but others need to be urged to accept one. In the last part of chapter 17, the Josephites (the tribe of Ephraim and the half tribe of Manasseh) complain that they have not been allotted a large enough territory. Joshua challenges them to clear out a territory which is now being held by the enemy.

Prayer   *Father, help us to be wholly devoted to you and therefore ready to accept a challenge. In Jesus' name. Amen.*

Day 70 Read Joshua 18-20

RECEIVING OUR INHERITANCE

Since two and a half tribes had received their inheritance on the east side of Jordan, nine and a half tribes received theirs on the west side. Of those nine and a half, the dominant tribes—Judah, Ephraim, and the half tribe of Manasseh—already had territory allotted to them and were aggressively occupying it. Their later history was to be marred by intertribal rivalry. After the days of Solomon, it led to the nation's split into northern and southern kingdoms. So often our strengths are our weaknesses. We too need to be aggressive in the work of Christ, but we must be careful that this does not lead to rivalry.

Now the remaining seven tribes needed to receive their inheritance. They had not been aggressive enough. God had provided the land, but they had not gone up to possess it. God has great good in store for us, but we can miss it through spiritual laziness.

The thought that there were those who had not yet received their inheritance reminds me of the idea that God has an inheritance for many people throughout the world which they have not received because they do not realize they are heirs. This should provide us with missionary zeal. How wrong it would be if two brothers had an inheritance, but only one knew about it and did not make great efforts to find his brother and inform him of what he could receive. Let us be zealous in telling others that they can be heirs of God.

Prayer — *Father, help us to possess the riches you have in store for us and tell others what they also can have. Amen.*

Day 71   Read Joshua 21–22

MISUNDERSTANDINGS

Remember that two and a half tribes wanted territory on the east of Jordan. Moses had approved this on the condition that their fighting men help the other tribes possess the land on the west side. This had now been accomplished and they were headed back home.

When they came to the Jordan, they set up a large altar. This was taken as a sign of rebellion, in that they built their own altar instead of recognizing that the one altar should be at the tabernacle. The nine and a half tribes felt they had to quell the rebellion.

Fortunately they had a discussion about the matter before they attacked. The two and a half tribes explained that this was not meant to be an expression of rebellion at all. They were concerned that in years to come the nine and a half tribes might deny them their part in the altar at the tabernacle. This altar, built on the same design, would prove they should have a part in the worship at the tabernacle.

How often when we see someone do something, we assume they are doing it for certain motives, perhaps the motives we ourselves would have under such circumstances. The result is a misunderstanding. How important to keep lines of communication open to others, especially those in our own family. God wants us to live in peace and harmony with others and that only comes when we communicate openly.

Prayer   *Father, forgive us where we fail to be open. Help us to be honest speakers and good listeners. In Christ. Amen.*

Day 72 — Read Joshua 23–24

CHOOSE WHOM YOU WILL SERVE

As old Moses had gathered the people together to urge them to serve God, so Joshua does the same thing. He recounted the history of God's gracious dealings with them. He pleaded with them, "Now therefore fear the LORD, and serve him in sincerity and in faithfulness" (24:14). Then he told them that they must make a choice. Will they serve false gods or the one true God? He makes it clear where he stands: "As for me and my house, we will serve the LORD" (v. 15). He points out to them that the decision to serve the one true God must not be a glib one, because it will not be easy; there will be many temptations. He reminds them that serving the true God means ridding one's life of things which are not consistent with such service. We see that Joshua's influence lasted for a generation, but regrettably no longer than that.

What lessons are here for us! Let us consider the history of God's gracious dealings with our spiritual forefathers and with us. Let us be moved by the plea to serve God sincerely and faithfully. Let us realize that for us too the choice entails a lifestyle contrary to the common way of life all around us, a life which we are so easily tempted to live.

No matter what other people do, let us commit ourselves wholeheartedly to serving God and training our family to do the same.

Prayer   *Father, give us grace to be faithful to our commitment to you who are so faithful to us. In Christ's name. Amen.*

Day 73   Read Judges 1–3

SIN AND GRACE

There is a pattern which continually repeats itself in the book of Judges. The people of Israel sin by serving the gods of neighbors whom they had neglected to drive out of the land. After a time of such sin, God allowed them to fall under the power of some nearby country. They lived in subjection for some time. Then they cried out to God for help. God graciously helped them by raising up a judge (a military leader) and through the judge ridding them of their oppressors. But after the judge died, they returned to their old sinful ways. This happened over and over again. How patient and gracious is God!

The first judge was Othniel. He was the nephew of Caleb. Some families seem to produce leadership ability. But much more important, we read that "the Spirit of the LORD came upon him" (3:10). God usually works through human beings. They are his instruments. They must act responsibly. But only by the Spirit of God can God's people be delivered. Then the Spirit came temporarily on individuals, but since Pentecost the Spirit dwells continually in the hearts of all of God's people. The purpose of such indwelling is that we might be instruments empowered to carry out God's redemptive plan.

The judges were different from each other, but this they had in common: God used them.

Prayer   *Father, fill us with your Holy Spirit and use us as your instruments of deliverance in our day. Through Christ. Amen.*

Day 74   Read Judges 4–5

THE TALE OF THREE WOMEN

One must admit that in many ways the Old Testament is primarily a story about God and men. There are exceptions, however, and this is one of them.

The first woman in the passage is Deborah. She is a prophetess, a woman who shares the message of God with God's people. In this time of oppression by the Canaanites, she calls Barak to lead the armies of Israel against the enemy. He is very reluctant; in fact, he refuses to go unless Deborah goes with him.

The second woman is Jael. Having been defeated by the intervention of God, Sisera, the enemy general flees on foot and seeks refuge in the tent of Jael. She lures him into false security and when he is asleep drives a tent peg through his head. It is not a pretty picture, but war never is.

The third woman is the mother of Sisera. She is anxiously waiting for her son to return home from the battle, bringing the spoils of war with him. But she waits in vain, for he does not return. How many mothers and wives have had similar experiences? Oh, the tragedy of war!

Today God still wants to use men and women in the battle against unrighteousness, which we are to wage not with military weapons, but through prayer and faithful witness by word and deed. Whether you are a man or a woman, God has a ministry for you.

Prayer   *Here am I, Lord. Use me! In Jesus' name. Amen.*

Day 75   Read Judges 6–8

GOD USES IMPERFECT PEOPLE

Throughout the Bible, God uses people, imperfect people, because no other kind are available. But the imperfections are a hindrance. Gideon had his faults. He was very reluctant to be God's instrument. As we have opportunity to serve the Lord, let us not hold back. Later Gideon made a golden ephod. We cannot be sure what the ephod was, but in any case, it became an object of false worship.

Yet Gideon also had good points. He was reluctant to serve, but he did serve. He was courageous, breaking down the image of the false god Baal. He was obedient, getting rid of the large army and ending with only 300 men, so that God could show that the victory was not by human might but by God's grace and power. And he refused to become king, realizing that this would be seeking to bring glory to himself instead of to God.

There are important lessons in the fact that God uses imperfect people like Gideon. It should make us less critical of pastors and lay leaders in the church. It should make us realize that God can use us whatever our failures. But, on the other hand, this must never make us complacent about our weaknesses. God may use us in spite of our faults, but we would be more useful if we, with God's help, got rid of them. The Spirit of God came upon Gideon. That same Holy Spirit lives in us to make us more holy.

Prayer *Father, we praise you for graciously using imperfect people. Take away faults that hinder our usefulness to you and your kingdom. In Christ. Amen.*

Day 76   Read Judges 9–11

FOOLISH PEOPLE

What a foolish man Abimelech was! He did not follow the wise decision of his father not to become king; instead he became king at the price of shedding much innocent blood. And how did he end? He was killed when a woman dropped a heavy stone on his head.

And how foolish were the people of Shechem to choose such a man as their ruler! It is not surprising that there was a falling out between them and Abimelech, leading to the destruction of the city.

And how foolish was Jephthah! He was a rough character, but yet he was chosen to lead Israel against the enemy. He was foolish to promise to sacrifice whatever first came out of his home when he returned victoriously. How sad he was when what emerged to greet him was his own beloved daughter! There are those who try to make the story less repulsive by saying he required her to be a virgin all her life. No, the evidence is that he kept his vow, and sacrificed her. Those were crude and cruel days, and it does us no good to try to think otherwise. The Bible makes this clear.

It is wise to do what is right and good. It is foolish to live sinfully, ignoring the wise instructions of God. What tragic results of all kinds, in the lives of so many people who want their own way instead of the lordship of Jesus Christ!

Prayer   *Father, work powerfully by your Spirit so many may turn to your Son and experience the good life of knowing him. Amen.*

Day 77   Read Judges 12-14

THE BOY WITH POTENTIAL

What great possibilities there were for Samson. From his birth, he was called to be a Nazirite, that is, a person dedicated in a special way to the service of God. He had wonderful parents. When they knew they were to have a son, their prayer was that God would show them how to care for this child. They worshiped the true God with great awe. And best of all, the Lord blessed him by sending his Holy Spirit upon him. What great things can be done by one in whom God himself is at work.

But this strong man was weak. Because of this he never reached his full potential. He did some great things, but he could have done so much more for the kingdom of God. His weakness was that he was not wise in dealing with people of the opposite sex. How true this is of so many today. Instead of choosing a woman who loved and served the true God for a life partner, he was foolishly attracted by the outer beauty of a woman who served false gods.

Samson was also a gambler, betting that the guests at the wedding could not solve his riddle. As he would do again later to his downfall, he allowed a woman to tease him into telling his secret. And she was untrue to him. The result was anger and bloodshed. "Do not be unequally yoked with unbelievers," says Paul (2 Cor. 6:14). Yet today many will not listen.

Prayer   *Father, keep us from making foolish mistakes which will rob us of our potential for service. In Jesus' name. Amen.*

Day 78 Read Judges 15–16

STRONGER THAN ANY MAN, BUT . . .

Samson was physically stronger than any man, but he was putty in the hands of any woman. When he went to get his wife back, he ran into all kinds of trouble. When he slept with a prostitute, it almost cost him his life. And when he surrendered to another pagan woman, Delilah, in the end it did.

How foolish Samson was! Couldn't he see what was going on? Every time he told Delilah a lie concerning how he could be defeated, the Philistines attacked. The secret of his strength lay in his uncut hair, symbol of keeping his vow as a Nazirite, one especially dedicated to God. It is significant that the time before he told her the truth, he began making up a lie regarding his hair. He was like a moth which cannot resist the light which can burn it to death. He wasn't quite there when he said his hair should be tied, but he was getting close.

Delilah says he doesn't love her because he will not tell her the secret. Couldn't he see that it was she who did not love him, since she kept calling in his enemy? Some say love is blind, but it is really lust that is blind.

Finally he tells her the truth, his hair is cut, and he becomes as weak as other men. When the Philistines come, Samson "did not know that the LORD had left him" (16:20). But he should have known! No one can disobey God and get away with it.

Prayer *Father, open our eyes that we might see how we may be playing with some sin which can hurt us. In Christ. Amen.*

Day 79   Read Judges 17–18

RELATIVISTIC ETHICS THEN AND NOW

Today some tell us that the absolute moral standards of the Bible are no longer meaningful for our society. Instead we should decide each situation in a way which seems best to human wisdom. One would think that this passage was written specifically for our day.

This is one of two appendixes attached to the book of Judges to illustrate the immorality which results when "every man did what was right in his own eyes" (17:6). We see here the tragic results of mixing true and false religion, of having superstitious ideas.

Micah steals from his own mother. She then uses the silver he returns to make an idol, saying it is consecrated to the Lord. He hires a Levite to tend the idol, thinking this will cause the Lord to prosper him. A group of Danites takes the idol and the Levite from him, threatening to harm him if he protests. The Levite is happy to be a priest for a whole tribe rather than of one family. The Danites go on to destroy "a people quiet and unsuspecting" (18:27) and to worship the stolen idol instead of going to the right place to worship, the tabernacle of Shiloh. Such are the things that happen when every man does what is right in his own eyes.

And in our own day, what moral chaos results when the nations abandon the Ten Commandments.

 *Father, work in our world, turning people back to you and to biblical morality. In Jesus' name. Amen.*

Day 80   Read Judges 19-21

MORAL CHAOS

If you have never read the Bible through, this may be the first time you have come across this story. It is certainly not one taught in Sunday school. But it is in the Bible, the second of the two appendixes which show what happened when again "every man did what was right in his own eyes" (21:25).

A man and his concubine are given hospitality by an old man in Gibeah of the tribe of Benjamin. Men come to the door insisting that they be allowed to have homosexual relations with the guest. To prevent this, the man throws out his virgin daughter and the guest's concubine to the men. They abuse the concubine all night and leave her lying dead on the doorstep.

The man returned to his home and then cuts her body in pieces and sends each piece with a message to the various tribes, protesting what the Benjaminites have done. The result is bloody conflict between Benjamin and the rest of Israel. Finally there are only 600 men and no women left in Benjamin. The other tribes vowed not to give wives to the Benjaminites. But then they realize this will cause one tribe to cease to exist. So they suggest to the Benjaminites that they slaughter a community and only leave 400 virgins for themselves. Since this still leaves 200 men without wives, they suggested that the Benjaminites kidnap young women attending a dance. Everyone does what he thinks is right. When God's wisdom and moral boundaries are despised, such chaos and death often result.

Prayer   *Father, open the eyes of the blind that they may see the tragic results of sin and flee to Christ. Amen.*

Day 81 — Read Ruth 1–4

GOD IN THE MIDST OF EVIL

The story of Ruth takes place during the period of the judges. It was a time of immorality, but in the midst of such a setting we see that family life can yet be noble and beautiful. So also in our day. Our headlines are full of crime and violence. Yet it is possible for a family centered in Christ to express the same kind of love and loyalty we find in the book of Ruth.

This is not a picture of perfection. It is not wise for this family to leave the environment of God's covenant people and go to a pagan land for the sake of food. There the two sons marry pagan wives, yet God overrules and brings good out of the situation.

Both daughters-in-law are good to Naomi, but because Ruth is especially loyal, with time good things happen in her life by the kind providence of God.

Ruth works hard caring for her mother-in-law and this does not go unnoticed either by God or by Boaz. We see here some strange customs that we do not fully understand, but the bottom line is that the good and rich Boaz marries Ruth. David becomes one of their descendants and therefore ultimately Jesus springs from their line.

No matter how much evil is around us, let us express love and loyalty to our family members and trust God will bless us as seems best to him in his time.

Prayer *Father, give us the grace to treat our family members lovingly and may this provide a good witness to others. In Jesus' name. Amen.*

Day 82 — Read 1 Samuel 1–3

AN ANSWER TO PRAYER

The book of 1 Samuel carries the story of God's people forward from the birth of Samuel to the death of King Saul. It tells us the story of a godly leader in Israel named Samuel.

In the days of the Old Testament, God permitted people to live below the standard he had set for marriage by design, which is one man and one woman for a lifetime. He allowed polygamy among his people. But how much pain resulted from living below God's standard! How painful it was for Hannah who had no children while her husband's other wife did and didn't let her forget it. In her grief, she cried out to the Lord in prayer, and although Eli, the spiritual leader at Shiloh, misunderstood her, God did not. He answered her prayer, and therefore she named her son *Samuel*, which means "I have asked him of the Lord" (1:20). We need to be more sensitive to the pain of people who would like to have children but cannot conceive.

The prayer of thankfulness prayed by Hannah is reflected in that of the Virgin Mary many centuries later. Both recognize that the God of grace raises up the lowly and brings the proud down to defeat.

Keeping her promise, Hannah gives her son to God's service. There, at a young age, he heard the call of God and said willingly, "Speak, Lord, for thy servant hears" (3:10). May God raise up godly leaders to lead his church today who hear and obey him.

Prayer — *Father, answer our prayers in ways beyond our imagination for your glory. For Christ's sake. Amen.*

Day 83 — Read 1 Samuel 4–7

AWAY WITH SUPERSTITION

One of the tragedies of our day is that people are turning from serving the God of the Bible to horoscopes and other forms of superstition. Such superstition is almost as old as the human race. Here the elders of Israel thought that having the physical presence of the ark of the covenant in battle would bring magical results and victory. They were wrong. They lost the battle and they lost the ark.

The Philistines also trusted in magic. They thought their defeat of Israel was a sign of the defeat of Israel's God. They also were wrong. Placing the ark in the temple of Dagon as though it were a trophy led in the end to the idol Dagon lying face down, decapitated and dismembered. And the presence of the ark among the Philistines resulted in God sending a painful plague upon them. They had not defeated Israel's God after all.

The Philistines sent the ark back to Israel on an ox cart. There, when the people failed to consider the holiness of God, there were further difficulties. But Samuel called the people to repentance. And repentance, not the physical presence of the ark, brought the victory so that Samuel could say, "Till now the LORD has helped us" (7:12 ESV). God in his mercy has brought us this far. Surely he will help us in the future as we trust and obey. So have nothing to do with horoscopes or any other superstitions. Trust in God alone!

Prayer *Father, deliver many people who are trapped in superstition and turn them to Christ. In his name. Amen.*

Day 84   Read 1 Samuel 8–11

WANTING TO BE LIKE UNBELIEVERS

The apostle Paul said that we are not to be conformed to this world, but that temptation is very powerful. Here the Israelites wanted to be like the pagan nations around them, each one of which had a king. God's plan for them was that he should be their king, ruling through godly men like Samuel.

The people rightly feared the rule of Samuel's sons. Apparently Samuel had been so busy ministering to other people as he made his circuit that he had neglected his own sons, and they had become ungodly. Let us be sure that we are not too busy to give our families the time they need.

As he so often does, God allowed his people to have their own way, even though that was not best for them. They wanted a king, so God let them have one, even though that was not his will. Though they insisted on their own way, he did not abandon them. He still loved them and cared for them. That is how God treats us and how we ought to treat others.

Saul was anointed king. Oil was poured over his head symbolizing that he was set aside and qualified for his task. This practice gives us the image of "the anointed one," which is what the Hebrew term *Messiah* and its Greek equivalent *Christ* mean. Jesus later became the perfect prophet, priest and king. With the Spirit of God mightily upon him, Saul defeated the enemy. May that same Spirit fill us, empowering and giving us spiritual victories.

Prayer   *Father, help us to take as our model not the sinful world around us but Christ. In his name. Amen.*

Day 85   Read 1 Samuel 12-14

COSTLY MISTAKES

Before he was king, Saul had been a very humble person. But now power it seems had gone to his head and he used his power foolishly. Lord Acton once said, "Power tends to corrupt, and absolute power corrupts absolutely." That is why the Constitution of the United States wisely provides for a balance of power. Those who have any power in the church or in business or in government should heed this lesson.

The first mistake Saul made was to act impatiently. Refusing to wait for Samuel, he took to himself power which was not rightly his; he offered sacrifices which ought only to be offered by a priest or by a representative of God like Samuel. Samuel warned Saul that this would cause him to be replaced.

The second mistake Saul made was to issue the foolish order that the soldiers should not pause to eat, and that anyone violating this order was to be killed. This led to two tragic results. One was this: the soldiers became so hungry that they ate meat not prepared according to the law of Moses. Also, Jonathan, Saul's son, unwittingly disobeyed the order and would have been executed if the people had not intervened. It is the part of wisdom to carefully think through all of the implications and potential consequences before we make important or severe decisions.

God used Saul, in spite of his mistakes, to accomplish his purpose of delivering Israel from the nations.

Prayer — *Father, in all of our decisions, help us to be wise and patient. Use us in spite of our faults. In Christ. Amen.*

Day 86   Read 1 Samuel 15-17

THE RISE OF DAVID

Saul makes yet another mistake. When told to destroy the enemy's cattle, he saves some to use for a sacrifice. Samuel expressed a biblical principle: "To obey is better than sacrifice" (15:22). Today also, God is far more concerned with obedient living than with impressive liturgy.

God sends Samuel out to look for a replacement for Saul. He is sent to choose from among the sons of Jesse. Even though handsome Saul had been a failure, he is impressed with the first good-looking son of Jesse. But God reminded him, "Man looks on the outward appearance, but the LORD looks on the heart" (16:7).

After being anointed, David continues in a servant role, playing music to soothe the distraught heart of Saul. Then the battle lines form between the Philistines and the Israelites. The giant Goliath issues a challenge and defies God of the armies of Israel. David is sent to bring food to his brothers in the army. Seeing Goliath and hearing his defiance, he offers to fight him.

David's faith becomes evident when he said, "The LORD who delivered me from the paw of the lion and . . . bear, will deliver me from the hand of this Philistine" (17:37), and when he said, "You come to me with a sword and . . . spear and . . . javelin; but I come to you in the name of the LORD of hosts" (v. 45). May God increase our faith so that we will not be afraid as we face challenges.

Prayer   *Father, help us to see the opportunities for service which lie before us and face them with assurance. Amen.*

Day 87   Read 1 Samuel 18–20

UNSELFISH JONATHAN

As David grew in popularity, Saul became more and more jealous of him. Twice, in a rage, he tried to pin David to the wall with his javelin, but failed. Then he tries to lure David into unwise risks in fighting the Philistines, hoping they will kill David for him. He offers to give his own daughter to David as his wife if he kills 100 Philistines. David kills twice that many and comes back safely. Then Saul instructed his son Jonathan and his servants to kill David.

Jonathan has everything to gain if David is killed. If so, at the death of Saul, Jonathan would become king. If David lives, Jonathan knows that David will become king instead. But he had become David's best friend. He protects David, even though he knows that will result in him not becoming king. In fact, he risks losing his own life at the hands of his father to protect David. David is forced to flee, losing his high position in the army, and yet Jonathan is still loyal to him.

What a lesson for us! Let us do what is right even though it may cost us advancement. Let us be loyal to our friends even though it may seem to be to our own disadvantage, especially when allegiance to God is at stake. God is a God of faithfulness, and he highly prizes our faithfulness to him and to our fellow human beings. Let us especially be loyal to our husbands or our wives, even when not doing so looks attractive.

Prayer   *Father, in a day when so many throw aside loyalties for selfish gain, help us to be faithful. In Jesus' name. Amen.*

Day 88   Read 1 Samuel 21-23

DAVID THE FUGITIVE

Realizing his life is in jeopardy, David flees from Saul. First he goes to the priest Ahimelech at Nob. He and the men with him are desperately hungry and eat the bread which was kept in the holy place of the tabernacle. Jesus later used this as an argument in favor of his disciples eating heads of grain they picked on the Sabbath day. The point is that human need in such situations takes precedence over legalistic requirements.

David flees to Achish, king of Gath, and when he hears that Achish is ready to kill him, he makes believe that he is insane and thus escapes. He then goes to the cave of Adullam where he gathers a band of malcontents into a small army.

When David hears that the Philistines are attacking the town of Keilah, he seeks to know if it is God's will that he should fight against them. He rescues the people of Keilah but again inquires of the Lord and finds out that they would betray him into the hands of Saul. He inquires of the Lord this time through the priest Abiathar who is now with him. The priest had a breastplate with a pocket containing the Urim and Thummin, a device for finding out what answer God would give. So David flees into the wilderness.

This was a difficult time in the life of David. He had previously held a high place in Saul's household. Later he would be king, but now as a fugitive the going is rough.

Prayer   *Father, when difficult times come in our lives, give us special grace to deal with them. For Jesus' sake. Amen.*

Day 89   Read 1 Samuel 24-25

DEALING WITH PEOPLE

As Saul is trying to track him down in the wilderness, David at one point has an opportunity to kill him. He refuses because Saul is "the LORD's anointed" (24:10). He does use this opportunity to show Saul that he has no evil intent against him. The king admits that David is more righteous than he, realizes that David will become king, and stops pursuing him. Our society would be strengthened today if there were more respect for office holders in church and state. Such people have been placed in these positions of responsibility by God. Officeholders in turn must constantly realize that they are responsible to God.

David's band of men became protectors of people who had businesses in the wilderness. David therefore felt such people should provide him and his men with food. One of these businessmen, Nabal, responded with contempt. David was tempted to teach him a lesson. However, Nabal's wife Abigail interceded. David is pleased with her, and when Nabal dies, he takes her to be his wife. In the meantime, his wife Michal was given by her father Saul to another man.

Nabal did not know how to deal with people. Abilgail did. It takes wisdom to do just the right thing in our many complex relationships. May God give us that wisdom as we ask him for it so we may be peacemakers in a world full of tensions.

Prayer   *Father, give me the sensitivity to understand people so that I may deal with them helpfully. In Jesus' name. Amen.*

Day 90 Read 1 Samuel 26–28

SAUL BECOMES DESPERATE

Sinners have short memories. A little time before this, Saul realized he had been wrong in pursuing David and had stopped doing so. But now he is back at it again. And again David has the opportunity to kill him and refrains because Saul is "the Lord's anointed" (26:11). When Saul learns of David's mercy, he again acknowledges he is wrong and goes back home. We are all quick to forget the lessons we learn.

Saul had started out well when he was first king. One thing he had done was to remove the mediums and necromancers from the land. But now he feels abandoned because Samuel is dead and God refuses to communicate with him. He looks for a medium who he thinks may be able to contact Samuel for him. He finally finds such a witch at Endor. When she seeks to call Samuel up from the dead, she is evidently surprised herself when Samuel appears. On other occasions, she had probably deceived those who came to her to serve as a medium, but now God apparently lets Samuel return to confront Saul. But Saul finds no consolation from Samuel who predicts tragic death for him and his sons.

We all need a source of supernatural guidance. Sad to say many today seek such guidance from horoscopes and fortunetellers. Let us study the Scriptures diligently that we might obey what God commands and ask mature Christians for help and wisdom in those areas not covered by divine command.

Prayer   *Father, help us to make the right decisions based on the commands and principles found in your Word. For Jesus' sake. Amen.*

Day 91   Read 1 Samuel 29-31

A VICTORY AND A DEFEAT

When David's little army returned to their home base of Ziklag, they found the Amalekites had burned it to the ground and taken all they had, including their wives and children. David and the men with him were deeply troubled, but we read that he "strengthened himself in the LORD his God" (30:6). What an example to us! When difficulties come, let us find our strength to cope with them in God. Let us nurture our relationship with him now, so that when the time of trouble comes God will not seem to be a stranger.

Again, David consults God through the priest to find out what he should do. Receiving guidance, he pursues the enemy and regains all that had been lost. Trusting in God, David goes from victory to victory.

Not so with Saul. He and his army meet the Philistines at Mount Gilboa and are badly defeated. Seriously wounded, Saul commits suicide. His sons, including Jonathan, are killed by the Philistines. Having rebelled against God, Saul goes from one defeat to another.

We are confronted with the choice of being like David or like Saul. We are constantly tempted to be like Saul, trying to run our own lives for our own glory. This is the road to defeat. God calls us to be like David, a frail human sinner, but constantly seeking God's will and constantly seeking God's help in doing his will. This is the road to victory.

Prayer   *Father, help us to surrender to your will completely and to receive your guidance. In Jesus' name. Amen.*

Day 92   Read 2 Samuel 1–3

KING OF JUDAH

The book of 2 Samuel tells us of the rule of David as king. When David hears of the death of Saul and Jonathan, he is filled with sincere grief. He writes a lament with the theme "How are the mighty fallen!" We should all grieve rather than gloat when we hear of the fall of a religious leader or the decline of a once prominent church. How truly sad when such things happen. How we must be on our guard lest we also fall.

David is now made king of Judah while Ish-bosheth, a son of Saul, is made king of the northern tribes. We see here a division which will reappear after the death of Solomon. It is God's will that his people should be united. In John 17, Jesus prayed that all true Christians "may be one." In the tension between the unity and the purity of the church, we must hold both in high regard. Christians are far too ready to split from their fellow Christians. The doctrine of the unity of the church is a fundamental biblical doctrine.

This transition in Israel's leadership is also a time of intrigue and murder. Abner is the power behind the throne of Ish-bosheth, and Joab, the general of David's forces, murders him. Joab was a very capable person, but he was also to be a thorn in David's side throughout his reign. Most of us have difficult people to work with. May God give us wisdom to deal with them judiciously and whenever possible constructively.

Father, may there be peace and purity in the church for which your Son gave his precious blood. May we be instruments to help produce such spiritual health. In Jesus' name. Amen.

Day 93 — Read 2 Samuel 4–7

BUILDING A HOUSE

With the death of Ish-bosheth, David becomes king of all Israel. He has a palace built for him. He takes more wives and has more children. The Philistines see him as a threat and come to attack him. As is his custom, he seeks God's guidance regarding how to deal with this threat. With God's help, he defeats the Philistines.

We must never sit back and think we are secure. New threats to our spiritual life constantly arise, and it is important that we seek to know God's will. That will in terms of what we ought to do in life is first of all revealed in Scripture, yet the advice of people who love the Lord and love us is also valuable.

Having his own house built, David's thoughts turn to a house for God. He decides to move the ark of the covenant to Jerusalem. But while the law of Moses specified exactly how it was to be moved, he uses another method, with sad consequences. He does not allow this to deter him, however, but tries again. This time he uses the biblically prescribed method.

Now that the ark is in Jerusalem, David thinks it would be a good idea to build a temple in which to place the ark. God, however, makes it clear that David is not to build a house for God but that God will build a house for him: God will cause his *household* to reign forever, a promise fulfilled in Christ, who in the Gospels is called "the Son of David."

Prayer   *Father, we realize that what is most important is not what we do for you, but what you do for us. In Christ. Amen.*

Day 94   Read 2 Samuel 8-11

A GREAT MAN COMMITS A GREAT SIN

David soundly defeats his enemies on all sides. He is riding high. But the time of success can be a time of special spiritual danger. David no longer goes forth to battle himself; he sends others. He is in control of everything—except himself! Bathsheba was also at fault. Should she not have been more careful to be modest? In a day of great immodesty, Christian women should dare to be different, difficult as this may be. The Bible specifically says to dress modestly (see 1 Tim. 2:9-10).

But David was fully responsible for his action. He should have put the sight of Bathsheba out of his mind. But he chose to dwell on it. Wrong thinking led to wrong action.

David committed adultery. How could this man after God's own heart do such a thing! No matter how common adultery is today, it is abominable in the sight of God. David got the woman pregnant. He tried to cover it up by calling her soldier husband home from battle. When that didn't work, he arranged to have her husband killed. Once caught in the web of sin, we are tempted to try to cover up one sin through another. It may succeed temporarily, but not in the long run, because God will reign in righteousness.

Prayer   *Father, give us the wisdom to avoid temptation and the strength to say no when it comes. In Jesus' name. Amen*

Day 95   Read 2 Samuel 12–13

CONSEQUENCES OF SIN

The Lord sends his prophet Nathan to David, and Nathan tells him a story which fills David with righteous indignation. Then Nathan whirls around and, pointing his finger in David's face, says, "You are the man!" (12:7). David can see a lesser sin in the life of another, but is blind to his own sin. As Jesus said, "Take the log out of your own eye, and then you will see clearly to take the speck out of your brother's eye" (Matt. 7:5). We are prone to be critical of others while we excuse ourselves.

But now, confronted with the truth, David repents in sincerity and God forgives him completely. How good to know that whatever our sin, it is completely washed away in the blood of Christ if we repent and accept God's forgiveness. But forgiveness does not mean that there will be no consequences resulting from our sins. There will be.

In David's case, the prophet tells him that the consequences will be trouble in his household. Amnon is infatuated with his half-sister Tamar, so under pretense of illness he lures her into his bedroom and rapes her. Having done so he loathes her. Absalom, her full brother, plans revenge. He has Amnon murdered, and as a result, flees into exile.

Sexual sins are devastating to family life. Amnon's "love" for Tamar was nothing but licentious lust. Likewise, what the world calls "an affair," God calls adultery. Sin still produces tragic results.

Prayer   *Father, help us to teach purity of life by word but especially by example. For Jesus' sake. Amen.*

Day 96   Read 2 Samuel 14-16

REBELLIOUS SON

Joab was always causing trouble for David. Instead of leaving Absalom in exile, he persuaded David to bring him back home to Jerusalem. Then, having set Joab's field on fire to get the king's attention, Absalom had Joab persuade David to receive Absalom back into the king's presence.

Back in good standing, Absalom begins to court the favor of the people. When he gets enough support, he gathers a large army and marches on Jerusalem. When David hears of this, he flees from Jerusalem, barefoot, with his head covered as a sign of this sorrow.

David's counselor Ahithophel joins the conspiracy. David does two things about this. He prayed to the Lord that Ahithophel may be foolish instead of wise and he asked Hushai to defeat Ahithophel's counsel by joining the conspiracy as a spy for David.

In the midst of the story, a number of the characters sin against others. Ziba, Mephibosheth's servant, lied and told David that Mephibosheth had joined the conspiracy. Hushai claimed to be loyal to Absalom. Shimei, of the house of Saul, cursed and threw stones at David. Ahithophel counseled Absalom to go in to his father's concubines in public. But does all this sin belong just to ancient history? Don't the soap operas and sitcoms today, reflective of our culture's immorality, tell similar stories? Such is the moral chaos when people go their own way instead of surrendering to the Lord.

Prayer   *Father, in the midst of a corrupt generation, help us to live Christ's way. In his name. Amen.*

Day 97   Read 2 Samuel 17-18

O MY SON ABSALOM

Ahithophel urged Absalom to send a force against David at once while Hushai advised him to wait to gather a large army. He heeded the advice of Hushai. The Bible gives this explanation: "For the LORD had ordained to defeat the good counsel of Ahithophel, so that the LORD might bring evil upon Absalom" (17:14). On the one hand, the Bible teaches that we are responsible for our decisions; on the other hand, that the sovereign God controls them. This is a paradox we cannot understand, but we must hold to both sides of the paradox.

David's men defeat Absalom's. The beautiful long hair that had been Absalom's glory becomes his downfall as his head is caught in a tree letting him hang as his mule runs on. Others dare not kill him, but Joab thrusts javelins into his heart. When the messengers tell David of the victory, his concern is for the fate of Absalom, and hearing that he has been killed, he cried out, "O my son Absalom . . . Would I had died instead of you" (18:33).

What tragic events result from David's terrible sin and the sins of Joab, Absalom, and others! The Bible is full of examples to warn us of the consequences of sin, but only those who know the contents of the Bible will benefit from such warnings.

Prayer   *Father, give us wisdom to be creative in plans to overcome the biblical illiteracy of our day. In Christ. Amen.*

Day 98   Read 2 Samuel 19–20

A DAY OF REJOICING, BUT

Having defeated Absalom, David is now to be brought back to Jerusalem. Shimei, who has thrown stones at him, begs for mercy. Ziba, who has tricked his master Mephibosheth, and Mephibosheth himself make counterclaims concerning what happened. The well-respected Barzillai comes to escort David across the Jordan. It is a time for honoring the king.

But there are some sour notes. The men of Judah and those of Israel argue fiercely as to who should have the preeminence in reinstalling David as king. The result is that an Israelite, Sheba, tries to take advantage of the situation and lead the northern tribes in rebellion. Joab takes the opportunity to murder his rival, Amasa, and then goes on to quell the rebellion.

Someday the King of kings will return. He will render perfect judgment. All those who have rebelled against him throughout history will be punished as they deserve. Those who love him will not argue but rejoice together in the return of the glorious King of kings.

This was not the first trouble between Judah and Israel, nor would it be the last. It anticipated a split which would come to pass after the death of Solomon, when the kingdom would be tragically divided.

Prayer   *Father, we rejoice that the day will come when we can welcome Christ back to earth. In his name. Amen.*

Day 99 — Read 2 Samuel 21–22

PRAISE FOR DELIVERANCE

These chapters are apparently appendixes describing long-past events.

The ideas of justice here are hard for us to understand. One help is to realize the concept of "the corporate" in the Bible. Today we emphasize individualism. But the Bible teaches that we are part of a people, and that the sins of one have a tragic effect on others in the group. This is still true today. The lives and actions of the fathers affect the children for generations. When we sin we not only hurt ourselves; we hurt others.

Having won a victory over enemies early in his reign, David wrote this psalm in this passage. In it he praises the Lord. He sees the Lord as the One who has delivered him. He does not take the credit to himself but recognizes that the Lord has helped him in his times of desperation. He uses vivid poetic language to help us understand how great God is. Among the many praises he offered to God, he said, "This God—his way is perfect; the promise of the Lord proves true" (22:31). May God give us this same outlook. May we recognize how great he is and how good he has been to us, and as a result we praise him from the heart and with our mouths. The scope of David's psalm reminds us that through missionary work God not only saves the lost, but also prompts us to praise him: "For this I will extol thee, O Lord, among the nations" (22:50).

Prayer *Father, enable us to see the truth, that all our blessings come from you. For Jesus' sake. Amen.*

Day 100   Read 2 Samuel 23-24

THE HELP OF GOD AND THE HELP OF MAN

Once again, in a psalm, David recognizes the help of God. God spoke through him. God blessed him for ruling justly. God made a covenant with him. There is also a list of the many people who had helped David by serving him faithfully as king.

The help of God is foremost. But we also need people to help us. God uses people. There was Shammah who took his stand against the Philistines. There was Benaiah who killed a lion in a pit on a snowy day. The pit and the snow were factors which made his task difficult, but he did not flinch. Many today are more interested in their ease and comfort than in fighting the Lord's battles with the sword of the Spirit, which is the Word of God.

Again David sins. In his pride, he wants to number his fighting men to show how great he is. This time Joab gives good advice, but David does not heed it. Then he recognizes his sin. But the deed is done and consequences follow. When allowed to choose what his punishment will be, he chooses the plague over famine or foes, realizing God will be more merciful to him than his enemies would. Obedient to God's prophet, David builds an altar at the cost of personal sacrifice. The final word of the book is "The LORD heeded supplications."

Prayer   *Father, we need you and we need to learn to work with others. Forgive us. For Jesus' sake. Amen.*

Day 101   Read 1 Kings 1-2

SOLOMON BECOMES KING

The book of 1 Kings tells the story of God's Old Testament people from the beginning of the reign of Solomon through some of the kings of the divided kingdom. Books like 1 and 2 Samuel and 1 and 2 Kings were probably divided as such simply due to the size of the scrolls required.

The Bible is very honest in describing some of the strange practices of God's ancient people. Now that David is about to die, one of his sons, Adonijah, tries to make himself king. First Kings 1:5 says that "he exalted himself." Again and again the Bible teaches that when someone exalts himself, God will bring him low. But if one humbles himself, God will exalt him. The passage also makes it clear that Adonijah's foolish behavior was partly caused by the fact that his father, David, had never disciplined him.

The prophet Nathan warned Bathsheba of what was happening. They go to David to intercede for Bathsheba's son, Solomon, to whom David had promised the kingdom. Upon David's instructions, Solomon is proclaimed king. David advised Solomon to obey God's commandments, but he also gave him instructions on how to settle the score with certain enemies of his who were still alive, so that they will not be in a position to undermine his authority. Later in New Testament times, God through Jesus taught his people to deal with their enemies in better ways.

Prayer   *Father, give us the grace to humble ourselves before you, knowing then that you will give us success. In Christ. Amen.*

Day 102 — Read 1 Kings 3–5

THE WISDOM OF SOLOMON

God said to Solomon, "Ask what I shall give you" (3:5). Likewise, Jesus invited his disciples, and by extension us as well, to ask in his name for whatever we wish (John 14:13-14). Solomon asked for wisdom, and in James we are told that if we ask for wisdom, God will surely give it to us if we ask in faith (James 1:5-6).

God seemed pleased with what Solomon does not ask for: riches and honor. It is a striking thought that God is often pleased with what we do not pray for! Because Solomon asked for wisdom, God not only gave him that but also riches and honor. Jesus teaches us in similar fashion: "Seek first the kingdom of God and his righteousness, and all these things [that is, material things we need] will be added to you" (Matt. 6:33 ESV).

Following the opening chapters of 1 Kings is an outstanding illustration of Solomon's wisdom. Like the true mother, when we really love someone, we are willing to sacrifice our desires for his or her sake. Solomon was wiser than those who had a reputation for their great wisdom. In his wisdom, he wrote proverbs and songs telling how to live. First Kings 4:20 tells us that with such a wise king, the people of Judah and Israel were happy. Those who are in responsible places of government today should realize that they have been placed in such positions not for their own gain but for the sake of others. We should each use whatever power and abilities such as we have to serve others.

Prayer *Father, raise up government leaders in our day who will seek the welfare of the people. In Jesus' name. Amen.*

Day 103   Read 1 Kings 6–7

BUILDING THE TEMPLE

In the days when Israel traveled through the wilderness, the center of worship was the tabernacle, which and had been built according to God's instructions and was also portable. It had been David's desire to build a more permanent temple, but God said that Solomon should build it instead. The temple was now built in the same form as the tabernacle, only with all the dimensions twice as great.

A cubit is about 18 inches long, the approximate length from a man's elbow to his fingertips. The inner sanctuary, the Holy of Holies, was shaped in the form of a cube, the height, length and width being equal. Although there was a huge labor force of drafted Israelites and of the men of the king of Tyre, it took 7 years to complete the temple. Interestingly, it took 13 years to finish Solomon's palace.

The Bible makes it clear that worship in the temple was a temporary arrangement. In John 4, Jesus said to the Samaritan woman that true worship would take place neither at the Samaritan temple nor at the temple in Jerusalem but that true worship is in spirit and in truth. The Bible also teaches that the church (not the building but the people) is God's temple and that each of our bodies is a temple of the Holy Spirit. Therefore, we should treat our bodies accordingly.

Prayer   *Father, help us to worship you from the heart, not only when we are in the church sanctuary but everywhere, and to treat our bodies as the temple of the Holy Spirit. In Jesus' name. Amen.*

Day 104 — Read 1 Kings 8

HEARTFELT PRAYER

Having completed the temple, Solomon installed the ark of the covenant in the Holy of Holies and gathered the people for a service of dedication, the central feature of which was a beautiful prayer. Both in the prayer and in his remarks, Solomon dwells on the fact that God keeps his promises. The Bible is full of promises that God has made to us, and he is a covenant-keeping God. Solomon is aware of the fact that many of the promises are conditional, that is, their fulfillment depends on our obedience. When God does not seem to be keeping one of his promises, the first thing to do is to examine our lives to see if we are meeting the conditions God has set forth.

Solomon is aware that God is omnipresent, and therefore cannot be contained in a building. The main thrust of his prayer is a plea that God will answer the prayers of those who pray toward the temple. It represents God's presence among his people. Solomon sets forth a number of cases: if Israel is defeated but repents and prays, or if there is no rain because of sin but they repent and pray, and the like, then may God hear that prayer and deliver his people from the problems which they have brought upon themselves. We, too, must pray from the heart with a repentant spirit.

Prayer   *Father, we thank you for the promises of Scripture that you will hear our prayers. For Jesus' sake. Amen.*

Day 105   Read 1 Kings 9–11

RISE AND FALL OF THE KINGDOM

After the dedication of the temple, the Lord again appeared to Solomon and promised to bless him *if* he remained faithful but to punish him if he did not. There follows a description of the greatness of Solomon and of how he impressed the queen of Sheba.

Solomon's downfall came because he married unbelieving wives. They led him to worship idols. He did not cease to worship the Lord, but he "was not wholly true" to him and he did not "wholly follow the LORD" (11:4, 6). God is not satisfied if we divide our allegiance between him and anything else.

God was angry with Solomon. The Bible speaks not only of the love of God but also of his wrath. God raised up enemies which made life difficult for Solomon. One especially dangerous enemy was the head of his forced labor battalion, Jeroboam. The prophet of God came to Jeroboam and promised to give him 10 of the tribes. However, God would allow Solomon's descendants to keep the tribe of Judah.

What a blessing to have godly ancestors! Let us be sure that we so live that our godliness will be beneficial to our children and grandchildren. Again, God promised to bless Jeroboam *if* he was obedient to God. Subsequent history shows that he was not obedient and therefore lost the blessing.

Prayer   *Father, help us to be wholly true to you so that we and our children may be blessed. For Jesus' sake. Amen.*

Day 106   Read 1 Kings 12-13

DIVISION OF THE KINGDOM

It is God's will that his people should be united, but sin causes division. Solomon is dead. Now, as God had warned, the kingdom is divided. Rehoboam, the son of Solomon, seeks advice as to what his policy should be in response to the request of the people. They want him to remove the heavy yoke of taxation Solomon had laid upon them. The old men tell Rehoboam to "be a servant to this people" (12:7). It is God's will that leaders should assume the servant role. But the young men urge Rehoboam to assume a hard stance. When he does the latter, the 10 northern tribes rebel and make Jeroboam their king, leaving Rehoboam with only Judah and Benjamin.

But Jeroboam also acts unwisely. He realizes if his people travel to Jerusalem to worship they might again fall under the influence of Rehoboam. So he establishes two alternate places of worship, one conveniently located in the southern part of his territory and the other in the north. There he places golden calves, claiming they are the gods who had brought the people out of Egypt. Sad to say, the people accept the plan. A man of God, who himself perishes as a result of disobedience, warns Jeroboam of the tragic consequences of his policy. But Jeroboam persists and suffers the consequences.

Prayer   *Father, help us to learn from the examples of disobedience that you have placed in the Bible. In Christ. Amen.*

Day 107   Read 1 Kings 14–16

IN THE SIGHT OF THE LORD

The rest of 1 Kings and the subsequent book of 2 Kings alternates between describing the kings of Israel and the kings of Judah. The Bible provides reliable historical accounts, yet it is not interested simply in facts. It describes how God deals with people in history depending on their response to him.

Rehoboam did what was evil in the sight of the Lord and was punished by losing much of his wealth to the king of Egypt. His son Abijam was king of Judah and "walked in all the sins which his father did" (15:3). Asa his son, however, did what was "right in the eyes of the LORD" and was commended for it (v. 11).

In the northern kingdom, all the kings did what was evil in God's sight. They continued committing the sin of Jeroboam. They maintained the idol temples in Dan and Bethel. Nadab, the son of Jeroboam, was killed by Baasha who reigned in his place. Elah, the son of Baasha, was killed by his general Zimri while Elah was drunk. When Zimri began to reign, Omri, another general, proclaimed himself king and prevailed. Omri "did more evil" than any king of Israel before him (16:25). His son Ahab did even greater evil. Part of Ahab's sin was marrying the pagan Jezebel and through her introduced Baal worship. Are you doing good or evil in the sight of the Lord?

Prayer   *Father, help us to ever keep in mind that it is what we do in your sight that counts. In Jesus' name. Amen.*

Day 108   Read 1 Kings 17–18

VICTORY FOR TRUTH

During the reign of wicked Ahab, king of Israel, God raised up a true prophet, Elijah. He told Ahab there would be no rain, and there was none for three years. During the famine God provided for Elijah, first through ravens and then through a widow. To the widow he spoke those words so often repeated in the Bible: "Fear not." This is God's message to us also, to not be afraid, whatever the problem, for God will help us. Elijah performed a great miracle. He brought the widow's son to life again.

Then Elijah is commanded to confront Ahab, who calls him "you troubler of Israel." Elijah points out that it is Ahab who is the source of the trouble because of his sin. Elijah then challenges the 450 prophets of Baal. The prophets of Baal cry out to their false god in vain. But when Elijah builds a water-drenched altar and prays, fire from heaven consumes his sacrifice. The people realize who is on the side of truth and execute the false prophets.

In every generation, there is a constant struggle between truth and falsehood. Sometimes God allows evil to be victorious for a considerable period of time, but "though the wrong is oft so strong, God is the ruler yet." In his good time, the Lord causes truth to be victorious. In the meantime, like Elijah, we are called to be faithful whatever the cost.

Prayer   *Father, cause truth to be victorious in our day to your glory and the benefit of needy people. In Christ. Amen.*

Day 109   Read 1 Kings 19-20

THE PROPHET AND THE KING

Elijah the prophet was "a man of like nature with ourselves" says James (5:17). At this point he experiences the phenomenon of "burnout" so common today. He had been so brave, but now the threat of Jezebel sends him running. The story shows that God knew he needed rest and food. We must put the spiritual first, yet always realize that we are human beings who have physical limitations and needs. Most people do not work hard enough for the Lord, but some forget that they need a balance between work and play.

Elijah, at this point, is also suffering from self-pity. He thinks he is the only one who is faithful, but God reveals that there are 7,000 beside him.

Ahab the king is attacked by Syria. He is a foolish man, but he shows real wisdom when he said to his opponent, "Let not him that girds on his armor boast himself as he that puts it off" (20:11). No matter how mature we become as Christians, we must not forget that pride goes before a fall. Peter boasted vehemently that he would not deny his Lord, but he did.

When Ahab asked the Lord, "Who shall begin the battle?" he got the answer, "You" (20:14). Whenever you think of something that needs to be done for the Lord, begin by asking yourself if you are the one God wants to use to get it done.

Prayer   *Father, give us vision and give us the wisdom to carry out that vision. Through Jesus Christ. Amen.*

Day 110   Read 1 Kings 21-22

THE TRAGIC RESULTS OF SIN

We see the smallness of Ahab's character in his sulking because he cannot enlarge his property. We see the courage of Naboth in standing against the king rather than give up the inheritance of his forefathers. We see the evil heart of Jezebel in her heinous plotting of Naboth's murder. We see the interest of God in the affairs of human beings by telling his prophet to bring his message condemning the evil which has been done. We see the prophetic stance of Elijah when he said, "Thus says the Lord."

Here is another case of poetic justice. Later in another part of the larger biblical story, Haman is hanged on the gallows he prepares for Mordecai. Here Ahab's blood will be shed in the same spot as where the blood of his victim was spilt.

Ahab called Elijah his enemy, but Ahab's real enemy was himself. The same is true of us if we are not careful. Once again the point is made that what counts is whether one does good or evil in the sight of God. One may get his way, as Ahab did in the case of the vineyard, but in the end what counts is what God thinks and does in his righteousness.

Ahab will not listen to the prophet Elijah, neither will he listen to the prophet Micaiah. He prefers false prophets. Today the danger is that some prefer to hear preachers who do not preach against sin.

Prayer   *Father, help us to realize that all that counts is that we trust in Christ and do right in your sight. In Jesus' name. Amen.*

Day 111   Read 2 Kings 1–3

A NEW PROPHET

The book of 2 Kings continues the story from the death of Ahab, king of Israel, to the destruction of Jerusalem, the capital of Judah. When Ahaziah, son of Ahab, sends soldiers to capture Elijah, the prophet calls down fire from heaven to consume the soldiers. When Jesus' disciples want to do something similar, Jesus rebukes them, reminding us that we of the new covenant are to fight the battle of the Lord with different kinds of weapons.

When the time of Elijah's departure arrives, he ascends to heaven in a fiery chariot, and Elisha takes his place. Elijah had struck the water with his mantle and it had parted. Now Elisha strikes the water with Elijah's mantle and it again parts, evidence that Elisha has inherited the spiritual power of Elijah. Elisha was to be a different kind of person than Elijah, but the important thing is that God had given him the same power. Today, one pastor replaces another in the church. Church members must realize that they cannot expect the new pastor to be like the old one. The important thing is that pastors, new and old, be filled with the Spirit, who alone can give them the power to have an effective ministry.

Most of Elisha's miracles were positive, such as changing foul water into purified life-giving water. In this, his miracles foreshadow those of Christ. But there is also the incident with the disrespectful youths!

Prayer *Father, fill the pastors of your church with the power of the Holy Spirit. In Jesus' name. Amen.*

Day 112   Read 2 Kings 4-5

ONE GREATER THAN ELISHA

Like Jesus, Elisha goes from place to place meeting the needs of people. He does miracles, similar to those of Jesus, but not as great. He provides for a poor widow by causing her vessels to be filled with oil through the power of God. The implication is that if the woman had the faith to gather vessels with twice as much capacity as she did, she would have had them all filled. So often we receive little from God because we expect little. William Carey, the pioneer missionary, said, "Expect great things from God; attempt great things for God."

Elisha raises a person from the dead. It is recorded that Jesus raised three people from the dead. Elisha feeds one hundred men with twelve loaves of barley and some fresh ears of grain. Jesus feeds many more people with only a few loaves of bread and a few fish.

At first Naaman is too proud to use the means he is instructed to use, but he humbles himself and is cured. Elisha had been Elijah's servant and took his place as a prophet. Perhaps Elisha's servant would have, in turn, taken his place were it not for his foolish greed. The blessing of God comes upon those humble enough to obey him and depend upon him.

Prayer   *Father, we praise you that One far greater than the great men of the Old Testament has come to rescue us. In Jesus' name. Amen.*

Day 113 — Read 2 Kings 6-8

OPEN OUR EYES

God gives Elisha supernatural power and he is able to tell the king of Israel the military plans of the king of Syria. The king of Syria foolishly thinks that he can capture Elisha. He sends troops to do this, and when the servant of Elisha sees these troops surrounding the city, he is filled with fear. But Elisha said, "Fear not, for those who are with us are more than those who are with them" (6:16). Again and again, God tells his people in the Bible not to be afraid. That is his message to us today. Some time ago, I had open-heart surgery. All through the first agonizing night, I kept repeating God's promise to me, "Fear not, for I am with you," and that got me through the night.

We need not be afraid because we serve a sovereign God. Elisha prayed that the eyes of the servant may be opened so that he would see the powerful forces of God surrounding them to protect them. May God open our eyes so that we may see, with the vision of faith, unseen spiritual realities.

Elisha prayed that Ben-hadad's army would be smitten with blindness. He then lead them into captivity and prayed that their eyes may again be opened so they may see the dangerous situation they are now in. May the eyes of those who are not God's people in our day be opened to see their spiritual danger and flee to Christ.

Prayer — *Father, open our eyes to see your great power so that we may not fear. In Jesus' name. Amen.*

Day 114   Read 2 Kings 9–10

THE DAY OF RECKONING

Ahab was the most wicked of the kings of Israel. He was stirred up to great wickedness by his wife Jezebel. She had introduced Baal worship into Israel. Baal worship included many disgusting practices that were abominations in the sight of God, who predicted through his prophet that the house of Ahab would be severely punished.

Now the time for this punishment had come. Jehu, a wild chariot driver, was the one through whom this punishment would be administered. He was ruthless in carrying out his assignment.

But, while Jehu wiped out Baalism throughout the land, he still clung to the idolatry which Jeroboam, the first king of Israel, had introduced in the form of golden calves at Dan and Bethel. He was "not careful to walk in the law of the LORD" (10:31). Therefore, enemy nations began to chip away at Israel's territory.

God often permits evil to continue far longer than we think it should. Evil people seem to be "getting away with murder." But be sure of this: God will punish sin, either in this life or in the life to come. He is a God of justice, and the Bible makes it clear that in the long run people will be punished for their sin. The only hope for any of us is to look with sincere faith to Jesus Christ for forgiveness.

Prayer   *Father, your Word reveals that you are not only a God of love, but also of justice. Forgive us for Jesus' sake. Amen.*

Day 115   Read 2 Kings 11–13

TIME OF RENEWAL

After Jehu had killed Ahaziah, king of Judah, Ahaziah's mother, Athaliah, daughter of Jezebel, ruled. She murdered everyone in the royal family except Joash, who was hidden from her. Jehoida the priest later set young Joash on the throne. Under Jehoida's influence, Joash did what was right in the eyes of God.

He also repaired the temple, which had been neglected for many years. This was a spiritual renewal. Like Israel, the church today, because its members are sinful human beings, is always tending to decline. From time to time it needs spiritual renewal, the revival of fervent faith. As in the days of Judah's kings, so today, God uses people. May he raise up leaders in his church who will be instruments of renewal!

In the meantime, the northern kingdom Israel had another wicked king, Jehoahaz, son of Jehu. Because his wickedness angered God, the Syrians were able to oppress Israel. The constant theme of the Old Testament is that sin leads to trouble. It still does today!

Jehoahaz's son Jehoash was also wicked, yet he had great respect for Elisha and visited him on his deathbed. When commanded by Elisha to strike the ground with his arrows, he struck only three times. Therefore, Elisha said that he would have victory over the Syrians in only three battles instead of defeating them completely.

Prayer   *Father, we pray that there may be renewal in the church today. Use us, Lord. In Jesus' name. Amen.*

Day 116 — Read 2 Kings 14–16

THE PERSISTENCE OF EVIL

Israel had one wicked king after another. The problem was that they continued the evil practices started by Jeroboam, the first king of Israel, who set up golden calves at Bethel and Dan. Once evil practices have taken root, they are difficult to eradicate. Today, also, there is wickedness which has been practiced for so long that it is taken to be acceptable. We must measure all actions, our own and those of people in our society, by the standard of the Word of God and work for changes to conform life to his will.

Even in the case of the good kings of Judah, we read that while they did what was right in the eyes of the Lord, "Nevertheless, the high places were not removed; the people still sacrificed and burned incense on the high places" (15:4). Worship was to be centered in the temple where orthodox views could be promoted, but the people worshiped in other places where there was the danger of combining the worship of the Lord with that of idols. Again, the evil persisted and even the good kings were unable to eradicate it.

Not all of the kings of Judah were good. Ahaz went so far as to build a replica of the pagan altar he had seen in Damascus. Furthermore, he tore down the altar dedicated to the Lord at the temple as well as the laver where the priests washed themselves.

Prayer   *Father, help us to see what is evil and to fight against it with all diligence. In Jesus' name. Amen.*

Day 117   Read 2 Kings 17

INTERPRETING HISTORY

From Genesis to Esther, the books of the Bible are historical. But the writers are not interested in simply stating facts. They are inspired by God's Spirit to interpret the meaning of the facts. These things happened because God responded to the actions of people. The Israelites sinned constantly (v. 7). They walked according to the customs of the pagan nations around them (v. 8). They did things in secret that were wrong (v. 9). The Lord sent prophets, but Israel would not listen to them (v. 13). They were stubborn (v. 14). They failed to believe in the Lord. They even offered their children as burnt offerings (v. 17). Therefore, the Lord punished them by causing them to be taken captive by Assyria.

God is not mocked; whatever we sow, the same shall we also reap. The God of 1 and 2 Kings is the God who rules supreme today. He has not changed. He will call all nations and all individuals to account for their deeds in the time of judgment. Christ is our one hope.

The Assyrians replaced the Israelites with people of other nations whom they had captured. When these transplanted people suffered from disobeying the Lord, the king of Assyria sent back a priest to teach them about the Lord. They then mixed true religion with false. Today, also, many people try to mix worship of the true God with that of their own gods, perhaps of pleasure or other false paths.

Prayer   *Father, help us to understand what is happening in the world in light of your judgments. In Christ. Amen.*

Day 118   Read 2 Kings 18-20

A VERY GOOD MAN

Hezekiah now became king of Judah. He did what was right in the sight of God. He broke down the altars throughout the land where the people did not worship as they should. He trusted the Lord. He was better than any of the kings before him or after him. He kept the commandments God had given to Moses.

What are your goals? Are they to become rich, to be highly regarded by man, to enjoy as much pleasure as you can? Those are the wrong goals. Instead, seek to be godly, to be good as God measures goodness.

The result of Hezekiah's godliness was that the Lord was with him and he prospered. Jesus taught a similar principle: "Seek first the kingdom of God and his righteousness, and all these things will be added to you" (Matt. 6:33 ESV).

Godliness does not guarantee that we will have no trouble. The king of Assyria, who had captured Israel, now came to attack Judah. He boasted that since the gods of other nations could not protect them, neither would the Lord be able to protect Judah against him. But Hezekiah knew where to turn in the midst of his problems. He took the threatening letter and laid it before the Lord. He prayed for deliverance and God, through the prophet Isaiah, assured him of that deliverance.

Prayer   *Father, give us the grace to live godly lives knowing you will be with us in our need. In Christ. Amen.*

Day 119 — Read 2 Kings 21–23

PARENTS AND CHILDREN

Why do some godly people have children who are ungodly? We do not understand. All we can do is seek to be faithful in raising our children in the ways of the Lord. Hezekiah, who had been such a good man, had a son, Manasseh, who was one of the worst kings of Judah. Amon, son of Manasseh, was also evil.

But Amon's son Josiah was a very good man, carrying out a most extensive reformation. He repaired the temple. During the process, some portion of the law of Moses was discovered. When it was read to the king, he was appalled because he realized that the evil which had been done would bring God's punishment. The prophetess Huldah assured him, however, that because of his penitence the punishment that must come would not take place in his day. Again and again the Bible teaches that a penitent spirit can forestall the wrath of God for a season.

Josiah gathers together the people and has the book read to them, which had been found. He then does a thorough job of ridding the land of altars and other objects used for idolatrous worship. He gets rid of all objects used for fortune-telling, of which there are plenty in our land today. On the positive side, he reinstates the Passover. But when he is killed by the king of Egypt, even after all his reforms, the son who takes his place is evil.

Prayer *Father, work in the hearts of our children that they may walk in your ways. For Jesus' sake. Amen.*

Day 120   Read 2 Kings 24-25

THE END COMES

Nebuchadnezzar, king of Babylon, now crushes Judah. This Scripture says he did it at God's command because of Manasseh's sins. It says further that God would not pardon. Why? Because God only pardons those who repent and put their trust in his promises (24:3-4). The leaders and those with technological skills are taken into exile in Babylon. Only the poor who had no means of resistance remain.

Babylon places Zedekiah on the throne of Judah, and when he rebels his sons are killed in front of him and then he is blinded. Enemies burn the temple and break down the walls of Jerusalem. They carry booty including the temple vessels back to Babylon. How tragic the results of continual rebellion against God!

Gedaliah is made governor of Judah, but he is assassinated. The remnant of the people flee to Egypt. The end has come. But this is not the end of the story; there are further chapters. A gracious God will bring a remnant back from Babylon to rebuild the temple. For now, however, the end has come for Judah.

The Bible tells us that someday the whole world will come to an end. In the judgment, God will destroy with fire the present heavens and earth, which we have polluted with our sins and in other ways. But God in his grace, after purging this world through its fiery dissolution from evil, will bring new heavens and a new earth where there will always be righteousness and peace (2 Peter 3).

 *Father, we praise you for your grace in making all things new out of what has been ruined by sin. In Christ. Amen.*

Day 121   Read 1 Chronicles 1-3

FROM GENERATION TO GENERATION

If you only skimmed through these chapters, I do not blame you. This probably is the best way to handle the material before us. Until now the narrative from Genesis to 2 Kings has been pretty much in chronological order. Here, however, another author covers basically the same material as 2 Samuel, the reign of David. Tradition has it that the author was Ezra, who continues the story through his own time.

These genealogies often seem boring, but they originally served an important purpose, establishing who should inherit the land at the return from exile.

The author begins by listing the generations from Adam to Noah. He then lists the three sons of Noah, and then the descendants of the three sons of Noah. It was with the line of Shem that God dealt especially. When we come to Abraham, God focuses especially upon him and his descendants. Our author lists the descendants of Abraham's son Ishmael. He then lists the descendants of Isaac's son Esau who was the forefather of the Edomites. He then considers the descendants of Israel (Jacob) who constitute the people with whom God had made his covenant. What are we to learn from this? God works through families. We influence our children and our children's children. We need to think long-term and do today what will develop and strengthen the spiritual inheritance for tomorrow's generations.

Prayer   *Father, in a day when family life is breaking down, strengthen our family and make it a good influence. In the name of Christ. Amen.*

Day 122   Read 1 Chronicles 4–6

PRAYER AND SERVICE

Here and there in the genealogical records we have a note about an individual. Jabez is called "more honorable than his brothers" (4:9). He was a man of prayer who desired God's blessing and his protection and "God granted what he asked" (v. 10). Mention is made of expert soldiers "ready for service" (5:18). While they were carrying out their responsibilities, they were also praying and God "granted their entreaty because they trusted in him" (v. 20).

We must pray and we must be honorable. We cannot expect God to hear our prayer if we are dishonest in any way. And we must pray and carry out our responsibilities. Prayer is not a substitute for hard work, but the hardest work will be in vain if we do not look to God for help. And our prayer must be accompanied by faith. We expect God to answer our prayer in wonderful ways because we put our trust in him.

There were also those who were "in charge of the service of song" (6:31). Faith in the true God is a singing faith. We have reason to sing. Those who provide the musical ministries of the church carry out a worthy form of service. The musical ministry of the church has been called the "war department," but it need not be so if congregations and musicians unite in the desire to glorify God above all.

Prayer   *Father, answer our prayers to your glory and use our service for your glory. For the sake of Christ. Amen.*

Day 123 — Read 1 Chronicles 7–9

SORROWING AND SERVING

Mention is made in the midst of the genealogies that Ephraim lost two sons and people came to comfort him. We are reminded that, although we have here a long list of names, all of them were human beings with the same kinds of joys and sorrows that we have. The world today is full of billions of people who are having similar experiences. We become so absorbed in our own concerns and those of a small group of people around us that we forget that. We need to become less self-centered. We need to have compassion for sorrowing people. There are so many human needs. We cannot do everything but we can help a few people. If everyone who claims to be a Christian would do that, what a different world this would be!

The genealogies come to an end with a focus on the priests and Levites. Each had his task. Some seem rather menial, for they had to make the bread to be placed in the Holy place of the tabernacle. But is any task really menial if it is done for the Lord? A monk in the Middle Ages, Brother Lawrence, wrote that he felt as close to God when washing pots and pans in the monastery kitchen as when he partook of the sacrament. May we be glad to perform any small service in the work of Christ's church!

Prayer — *Father, give me joy in doing whatever I can do in sharing in the work of the ministry of Christ. Amen.*

Day 124 — Read 1 Chronicles 10–12

NOT BY OURSELVES

The writer of 1 Chronicles now tells us the same story we studied in 2 Samuel, adding some details and omitting others. Here he tells us about all the people who helped David. Even David could not do what needed to be done by himself. So also we need to work as a team with others in the church of Jesus Christ. The New Testament makes it clear that all Christians are part of the body of Christ, with different gifts of the Spirit all to be used for God's kingdom.

Two men helped David by each slaying 300 of the enemy at one time. Another helped by taking his stand in the middle of a field and defending it. Yet another killed an Egyptian seven and one half feet tall. Others gave help of a more intellectual nature, such as the men of Issachar who "had understanding of the times" (12:32). Today, we do battle against unrighteousness, not with spears and swords, but with understanding gained from studying the Word of God.

Yet David received help most of all from God. We are told that "David became greater and greater, for the LORD of hosts was with him" (11:9). Amasai is led by the Spirit to say of David, "For your God helps you" (12:18). We need the help of other people, but far more important is the help that God will give us as we look to him in faith.

Prayer — *Father, help us to work in the church as a team always relying on you. For Jesus' sake. Amen.*

Day 125   Read 1 Chronicles 13–16

SUCCESSFUL ON THE SECOND TRY

David now turns to concerns about the ark of the covenant. He provides a tent in which to house the ark. Then he has the ark moved to Jerusalem. But it doesn't make it. The ark is being moved contrary to the clear instructions in the Word of God. Uzzah reaches out to keep it from tipping when the oxen stumbled and he is struck down dead.

Having secured his borders by decisively defeating the Philistines, David again turns to the matter of moving the ark to the tent he had erected in Jerusalem. In the meantime, he or someone else must have been studying the Scriptures, for now he uses the means clearly specified in the Word and succeeds in bringing the ark into the place he had prepared for it. We need to know what the Bible says. We need to do what the Bible says.

As a pastor, I often had men say to me, "I know that God wants me to get divorced so I can marry this other woman who will make me happy." They did not want to hear it but I had to say, "I know God does not want you to get divorced because the Bible says you should remain faithful to your wife." If we want to be truly successful in life, we must not follow our whims but God's Word. Having moved the ark into place, David had a choir sing a psalm of praise to God.

Prayer   *Father, help us do what you tell us in your Word that we might avoid the price of disobedience. In Jesus' name. Amen.*

Day 126   Read 1 Chronicles 17–20

VICTORY WITH GOD'S HELP

David wants to build a house for God, a temple in which to place the ark. But God says that instead he will build a house for David. God will establish the household of David forever. This is ultimately fulfilled in Christ, for David's descendants no longer occupy a throne in the land of Israel, but Christ whom the Gospels call the son of David will be king forever. We must focus on what God does for us before we consider what we can do for God. Salvation is by pure grace, completely the work of God. We now are to serve him in gratitude for such a great salvation. And we must look to God for help as we serve him. This, also, is of grace. Let the focus be on what God does for us and let this motivate us to serve him faithfully.

God's wonderful promises evoke a beautiful prayer from the heart of David. In it he humbles himself. He also exalts God. He says that what God has revealed gives him courage to pray. So it should be with us as we pray.

After we read of the promises God made to David, we read of David's victories, one after another, against those who had been a threat to God's people. God was already beginning to fulfill his promise to build the household of David. May we too experience victories over the evils which still hold us in their grip.

Prayer   *Father, we praise you for what you have done for us. Enable us to serve you faithfully. In Jesus' name. Amen.*

Day 127   Read 1 Chronicles 21–24

PREPARING OUR CHILDREN TO BUILD

We must use our lives in service to the Lord. But there is something else we can do. We can prepare our children to play their role in the advance of God's kingdom in the world. David was not to build the temple, but he could make as many preparations as possible so that his son Solomon could build it. We must first of all introduce our children to Jesus Christ. Only then can they truly be of service to him. Beyond that, we can give them the best possible education to equip them for service.

David prepared by purchasing the land for the temple. This happened in an unexpected way. The land was a place to offer sacrifices of thanksgiving. God had stayed the plague caused by David's sin of pride in numbering the people.

David also prepared materials for building the temple. More importantly, he prepared Solomon by giving him advice. He told him that he would only prosper if he was careful to obey God's law. Let us give this advice to our children also. We are saved by grace alone, but being saved we are called to a life of obedience coupled with the promise that God will bless such obedience.

David also prepared Solomon by encouraging him not to be afraid. Faith brings courage to obey.

Prayer   *Father, help us to be very wise in preparing our children to serve you. For Jesus' sake. Amen.*

Day 128   Read 1 Chronicles 25–27

SET APART FOR SERVICE

A few days ago we considered the services rendered by musicians and gatekeepers. Here these are mentioned and several other types of service as well. The New Testament says that the church is made up of members, each of whom has some spiritual gift to be used in service. The church is to be a team, with each member playing his or her part in the Lord's work.

Some of the Levites were in charge of the treasuries. Today the deacons have a very important job keeping account of the offerings of God's people and distributing them to do God's work. Other Levites were to be officers and judges out in the field (26:29). Elders have the important responsibilities of administration and discipline.

Individuals in these chapters are mentioned as counselors and men of understanding. Elders are to serve by giving good advice both to the pastors and members of the congregation. Great wisdom is needed to do God's work well, and he promises such wisdom to those who pray for it in faith.

Hushai the Archite is mentioned as the king's friend (27:33). Perhaps this is the best service of all. Everyone needs a true friend, one with whom we can share our anxieties, one who will give us good advice because he or she loves us enough to tell us the truth.

Prayer   *Father, help us to work together in the church as a team and especially to be a friend. In Jesus' name. Amen.*

Day 129　　　　　　　　　　Read 1 Chronicles 28–29

GIVING FOR BUILDING

It is fitting that we should give generously to build church buildings in which God may be worshiped and his Word may be taught. But we should always keep in mind that the New Testament says that the church is people, that we together are to be a holy temple. Again and again Paul speaks of doing that which edifies, that is, that which builds up the church of Jesus Christ.

Therefore, let us give generously so that the church may have the resources to teach its people the Word and especially that the church may send forth the Word of God to others that they, too, may be built up in the faith.

Notice how David himself gives: "Because of my devotion to the house of my God I give it to the house of my God" (29:3). In response to the grace of God by which he has redeemed us through Christ we should have a great devotion to the church, the "building" of his people built on the one foundation, Jesus Christ. That devotion ought to motivate us to give generously. The Bible sets a tithe as a guideline for giving, but in light of the great opportunity to build God's "temple" by spreading the gospel today, and in the light of the great resources God has placed in the hands of many Christians, these should give more than a tithe, however much they have made up in their mind to give (2 Cor. 9:7).

Prayer　　*Father, give us grace to build the church by generous giving and according to your plan. In Christ. Amen.*

Day 130   Read 2 Chronicles 1–4

WHAT NOT TO PRAY FOR

The book of 2 Chronicles takes the story of God's dealings with his people from the beginning of the reign of Solomon to the return from the exile. It begins with God inviting Solomon to pray for whatever he wants. We are also invited to pray in Jesus' name for whatever we wish (John 14:13-14).

God is pleased because Solomon does not pray for riches, honor, revenge, or long life. God is pleased that Solomon has his priorities straight. His one desire is for wisdom so he may carry out his calling as king in such a way as to be a blessing to the people. Jesus teaches us not to be anxious about material possessions, something which we really need to hear in a world and culture whose materialism is influencing us more than we realize. But Jesus does teach, "Seek first the kingdom of God and his righteousness, and all these thing will be added to you" (Matt. 6:33 ESV). When we ask for the right things because we have the right priorities, God gives us what we ask for and much more besides.

In his wisdom, Solomon now begins to plan for the building of the temple. His logic is this: since God is far greater than all gods (in actuality they do not even exist), his temple ought to be greater than theirs. So he builds a temple after the pattern of the tabernacle, only with all dimensions doubled, and he uses a great deal of gold. We should surely give God our best, not the leftovers.

Prayer   *Father, we do not ask for riches or honor, but give us wisdom to carry out our calling. In Christ. Amen.*

Day 131 Read 2 Chronicles 5–7

GREAT THEMES

There are some great themes which run through the Bible. This passage includes some of the greatest. One theme is that of the covenant. God has made promises to his people, and he will surely fulfill them, for he is a God of steadfast love. The Hebrew word translated "steadfast love" is a beautiful word that expresses God's covenant faithfulness. His love is not fickle; it is utterly dependable. He shows his love by keeping his promises. Marriage is a covenant between a man and a woman, so let there be steadfast love, a love which faithfully keeps the promises made.

Another theme is the seriousness of sin and the possibility of forgiveness. This is the main emphasis of Solomon's great prayer. All sin is most serious because it is sin against a faithful God. Therefore, there must be heartfelt repentance and faith.

Yet another theme centers around the word "if," which is found several times in this passage. God will bless wonderfully, but only *if* his people will walk in his ways and keep his commandments. If they turn away from obedience, the wonderful promises will not be fulfilled. We live in a day when there is danger of "cheap grace," when people think God will bless them regardless of how they live. The Bible says that continued blessings depend on faithful obedience.

Prayer *Father, we praise you for your steadfast love. Forgive us of our sins. For Jesus' sake. Amen.*

Day 132   Read 2 Chronicles 8-12

DIVISION OF THE KINGDOM

While the writer of 2 Kings tells of both Solomon's strengths and weaknesses, the writer of 1 Chronicles only focuses on his strengths. If we are honest with ourselves we must admit that we tend to notice the faults of others more than their good points.

Another difference between 2 Kings and 2 Chronicles is that, while 2 Kings keeps shifting back and forth between descriptions of the kings of Israel in the north and those of Judah in the south, 1 Chronicles only deals with the southern kingdom.

Solomon dies and is replaced with his son Rehoboam. Having described the folly of Rehoboam in deciding on a policy of being harsh, which the young men advised, the Chronicler goes on to focus on Rehoboam's good points. He plans to fight Israel but listens to the Word of the Lord through his prophet and changes his plans. He does a great deal of constructive building. He attracts the Levites and the common people from the northern kingdom who "set their hearts to seek the LORD" (11:16), so that they move into the southern kingdom.

Finally, the Chronicler considers the sins of Rehoboam. Even here the emphasis is on how he humbled himself and repented. Yet the final verdict must still be: "he did evil" (12:14).

Prayer   *Father, help us to learn from the failure of the kings to obey you. In Jesus' name. Amen.*

Day 133 Read 2 Chronicles 13–16

RELYING ON THE LORD

This section of Scripture deals with two kings, Abijah and his son Asa. They had this in common: they relied on the Lord (13:18; 14:11). Oh, that this might be the common bond between us and our children, that we all rely on the Lord our God for all of our needs, physical and spiritual!

Abijah was outnumbered by Jeroboam, king of Israel, two to one. But Judah was victorious and the writer makes the reason clear: "They relied upon the Lord."

Regarding Asa, we read that he "did what was good and right in the eyes of the Lord his God" (14:2). Our fellow human beings only see part of us. God sees us through and through, and what is important is that we do what is right in his sight.

Asa broke down idolatrous altars. We must stand in opposition to all that is wrong, using our influence to rid the world of evil, using means appropriate to righteousness. He commanded others to seek the Lord. We are not kings with power to command, but we do have many opportunities to influence others, especially our own children. When an Ethiopian army of a million strong came against him, Asa was given the victory because he relied on God. May our reliance also be upon him.

Prayer   *Father, give us the grace to rely on you in every circumstance of life. For Jesus' sake. Amen.*

Day 134 Read 2 Chronicles 17-20

A MIXED VERDICT

We have seen how Asa relied on the Lord. Yet near the end of his life a prophet said, "Because you relied on the king of Syria, and did not rely on the LORD your God, the army of the king of Syria has escaped you . . . You have done foolishly in this" (16:7-9). Asa was so angry that he threw the prophet in prison. So often in the Old Testament, men who had been strong in the Lord earlier in life slipped toward the end. We must be constantly on our guard, lest as time passes we drift away from reliance on God.

Now Jehoshaphat, Asa's son, becomes king. The Chronicler's description is given: "He walked in the earlier ways of his father" (17:3). Jehoshaphat is commended for what he did, "sought the God of his father and walked in his commandments" (v. 4) and also for what he did not do: "he did not seek the Baals" and he walked "not according to the ways of Israel" (v. 3). In doing what is right, we must avoid the sins of others around us.

Jehoshaphat sought to use his influence to encourage others to live godly lives. He sent priests to teach the Word of God throughout Judah. But he had his faults. He made an alliance with wicked Ahab, and in spite of the warning of the faithful prophet Micaiah, he joined with Ahab in a disastrous battle. Later he entered another alliance. There is only One who receives no mixed verdict—Jesus Christ.

Prayer   *Father, we all fall short of being all you want us to be. Forgive us. For Jesus' sake. Amen.*

Day 135   Read 2 Chronicles 21–22

INFLUENCED BY FAMILY MEMBERS

The Bible emphasizes the importance of the family. It says, "Believe in the Lord Jesus Christ, and you will be saved, you and your household" (Acts 16:31). Our faith has a tremendous influence upon others, especially those who live in the same home. Many are saved through the influence of parents. We can set a good or a bad example for others in our family.

Our Scripture today tells about two kings, both of whom were influenced to do evil by members of their family; in the one case a wife, in the other case a mother. Jehoram was an evil king, and the Bible gives this explanation, "He walked in the way of the kings of Israel, as the house of Ahab had done; for the daughter of Ahab was his wife" (21:6). How important it is to choose the right marriage partner. The Bible says, "Do not be unequally yoked with unbelievers" (2 Cor. 6:14 ESV). Young people, be godly and choose only godly persons as your best friends. You may not like that advice, but it is for your own good.

Ahaziah was also wicked. Here the explanation is "for his mother was his counselor in doing wickedly" (22:3). How sad, for a mother to be a bad influence upon her child! Parents, you play an important role in the lives of your children. What kind of example are you setting for them?

Prayer   *Father, give us the strength to set a good example for the other members of our family. In Christ. Amen.*

Day 136   Read 2 Chronicles 23–25

REJECTING GOD'S PROPHETS

Joash did well until Jehoiada, who had influenced him for the good, died. Then he turned away from God. But God was still very concerned about him, sending prophets to bring him and others back. "But they would not give heed" (24:19). When Zechariah, filled with the Spirit of God, spoke prophetically, they stoned him to death. As a result, God caused the Syrians to defeat Joash even though they had a smaller army. Joash was then murdered by his own servants.

Amaziah, his son, started out well. He hired soldiers from Israel to fight for him; but when a prophet told him to forfeit the money he had paid rather than continue his plan, Amaziah did so, even though he lost the money. The prophet had said, "The LORD is able to give you much more than this" (25:9). Whatever we sacrifice to do God's will, God will restore, with more besides.

However, when Amaziah defeated the Edomites, he began to worship their idols. When a prophet told him how foolish he was, the king threatened to kill him if he didn't keep still.

When Jesus spoke about Israel's stubbornness, he referred to the fact that God's people had a history of failing to obey the prophets. Finally, because they would not listen to his servants the prophets, God sent his own Son, and they crucified him!

Prayer   *Father, work in our hearts by your Holy Spirit, that we may obey your Word which is preached to us. In Christ. Amen.*

Day 137 — Read 2 Chronicles 26–28

INTERPRETING HISTORY

The biblical writers provide us with reliable historical facts, but that is not their primary interest. They are inspired by the Holy Spirit to interpret history, providing lessons for our instruction.

Notice how often the word "because" is used. "Jotham became mighty, *because* he ordered his ways before the LORD" (27:6). Pekah "slew a hundred and twenty thousand in Judah . . . *because* they had forsaken the LORD" (28:6). "The LORD brought Judah low *because* of Ahaz, king of Israel, for he had dealt wantonly in Judah and had been faithless to the LORD" (28:19). God causes some things to happen to people because of the way they live. The same is true of nations. That is how God dealt with people, both in the days of the kings and today.

As we have noted before, what counted most was whether a king did what was right in the sight of the Lord. The Bible is above all God's self-revelation; it shows us what kind of a God he is by showing us how he acts and reacts to human behavior. He is the same yesterday, today, and forever. He acts now as he acted in the past and as he will act in the future. Paul says that the Old Testament stories are given for our instruction, that we may not make the same mistakes the people made in the past (Rom. 15:4; 1 Cor. 10:11). This is how the Word of the living God speaks to us.

Prayer — *Father, help us to learn from the mistakes of others and therefore receive your blessings. In Christ. Amen.*

Day 138　　　　　　　　Read 2 Chronicles 29–32

DOING GOOD

Hezekiah did what was right in the sight of God. He restored temple worship. He renewed the covenant with God. He led the people to worship with joy. He encouraged them to give generously. He reinstated the Passover. He sent missionaries to the Israelites, most of whom mocked the missionaries. When some came to partake of the Passover being ritually unclean but sincere in heart, he prayed for them and they were forgiven. He broke down altars dedicated to idols. When the king of Assyria threatened to attack, he prayed and God destroyed many of the Assyrians. When he sinned through his pride, he humbled himself before God, thereby averting God's wrath.

Because we are not in as influential a position as a king, we may not be able to do as much good as Hezekiah. But every one of us has many opportunities to do good. By the way in which we live our lives, we can be a blessing to our family, our neighbors, our church, and our community. What is your goal in life? To see how many luxuries you can enjoy? Or is your goal to do all the good you can to all the people you can in every way you can? God blessed Hezekiah. "Every work that he undertook in the service of the house of God and in accordance with the law . . . prospered" (31:21). God blesses faithfulness.

Prayer　　*Father, help us to aim not at our pleasure but at ministry by which we can be a blessing. In Christ. Amen.*

Day 139   Read 2 Chronicles 33–34

TOO LATE

Manasseh was especially wicked. "He did *much* evil in the sight of the LORD, provoking him to anger" (33:6). In both the Old Testament and the New, we read of God's love and of his wrath. Many churches today do not mention God's wrath, thus distorting the biblical message. Sin fills God with righteous indignation. He punishes it with the severity it deserves.

When brought into captivity in Assyria, Manasseh repented; and God in his mercy brought him back to Jerusalem. Although he undid some of his wickedness, the evil he had done produced so much rotten fruit in the lives of the people that it was now too late. Amon, the son of Manasseh, worshiped the idols of his father and he did not repent, thus sealing the fate of the nation.

Amon's son Josiah sought God from childhood. How much better to be godly from childhood than to do much wickedness and then later repent! We are sometimes impressed by the conversion stories of people who have lived in wickedness. Praise God for his grace in saving them! But how much more wonderful when the Holy Spirit causes someone to be born again at an early age. Our constant prayer should be that this take place in the lives of many. Josiah learns of God's Word, but it is too late for the nation—Judah is doomed.

Prayer   *Father, we pray for our nation, that there be national repentance before it is too late. In Christ. Amen.*

Day 140　　　　　　　Read 2 Chronicles 35–36

THE END, BUT . . .

Because of his godliness, Josiah had been promised that the punishment which would come upon Judah would not come in his day. He died. But after his son had reigned only three months, he was deposed by the king of Egypt. The next king, Jehoiakim, did evil in God's sight and was taken into exile in Babylon. Jehoichin, his son, reigned only three months. Having done evil in God's sight, he also was taken into exile. Zedekiah did evil and did not listen to the word of the prophet Jeremiah. God in his mercy sent other prophets but they would not listen "till there was no remedy" (36:16). They were taken into exile, the temple was burned and the walls of Jerusalem broken down "to fulfill the word of the Lord" (v. 21).

The exile lasted for 70 years, as had been predicted by Jeremiah. The implication is that the Sabbaths which had been neglected by the ungodly nation would now be made up by the rest given the land during the exile. Yet, by the grace of God, it was not the end. The Babylonians had a policy of exiling the nations they conquered. But they in turn were conquered by the Persians whose King Cyrus had a different policy. He apparently felt that the more people who were praying for him, the better, plus he seemed to feel obligated to make amends with the gods of the peoples under his rule. So he sent back people, including the Jews, to rebuild their temples where they could pray for him. It was not the end!

Prayer　　*Father, we thank you that when this world comes to an end there will be a new world. In Jesus' name. Amen.*

Day 141   Read Ezra 1-4

REBUILDING

The first verses in Ezra are the same as the last verses in 2 Chronicles, making it clear that this is a continuation of the story. Ezra tells us of the return of the Jews from exile to rebuild Jerusalem and the temple. The church needs constantly to be rebuilt, to be reformed anew according to the Word of God, so there are lessons to be learned here.

Renewal requires dedicated people. Many Jews had prospered in Babylon and had no interest in returning, but there were those "whose spirit God had stirred to go up to rebuild" (1:5). May God fill us with the desire to see the church revived.

Renewal required funds. Some not interested in going back were willing to give (1:6) and those who did return "made freewill offerings . . . according to their ability" (2:68-69). Renewal involves missionary activity and this requires finances, which we are to provide as God has blessed us.

Renewal required leadership. The first exiles were led back by Jeshua the priest and Zerubbabel the governor. May God raise dedicated persons to lead the church in spiritual revival today.

Renewal faces discouragements. The Great Reformation under Luther and Calvin faced many difficulties, as did the people who returned from exile. We can expect the same.

Prayer   *Father, we pray for a great revival of biblical faith in our day. For Jesus' sake. Amen.*

Day 142 Read Ezra 5–7

RETURN TO REBUILDING

Under pressure from neighbors who opposed it, the work of rebuilding the temple was halted. Good work must not only be started; it must be continued until the goal is reached. Is there any good work which you began but have laid aside? Take it up again. The Bible says, "Do not be weary in well-doing" (2 Thess. 3:13).

Under the prodding of two prophets, Haggai and Zechariah, they returned to rebuilding the temple. Pastors, those who speak God's Word today, ought to be in the forefront of revival in the church.

When the neighbors again object, the Jews do not stop their work but continue, while they send for a clarification to the king of Persia. The decree of Cyrus to rebuild is discovered, and those who had tried to stop the work are commanded to support it. Finally the temple is completed with great joy.

Ezra had not gone with the first group to return from exile, but now he is the leader of a second group. He is a scribe, a man familiar with the Hebrew Scriptures that had been written up to this point. He receives the support of the king and recognizes this as the work of God. "Blessed be the Lord, the God of our fathers, who put such a thing as this into the heart of the king, to beautify the house of the Lord" (7:27). May God work in the hearts of many in our day who will work for revival in the church.

Prayer *Father, help us to return again and again to the important task of working for revival. In Jesus' name. Amen.*

Day 143　　　　　　　　　　　　　　　　Read Ezra 8–10

DRASTIC MEASURES

Having told the king of Persia that he trusted in God to care for him, Ezra does not dare to ask for military protection for the trip to Jerusalem. So he humbles himself before God and sets out in faith with the group he was bringing back from exile.

Arriving in Jerusalem, Ezra is shocked to find a great deal of intermarriage with unbelieving people. The leaders had been foremost in this unfaithfulness. The great danger of such intermarriage was that these pagan wives would lead the Jews astray, as had happened over and over again in their history. Because the Israelites had been led astray into idolatry, they had lived sinful lives that resulted in the exile. Now returned exiles were doing the same thing over again. This would once again lead to practices which were abominable in the sight of God.

Therefore, Ezra took drastic measures, which seem unbelievable in an age of tolerance we live in today. He forced the men to send their pagan wives away from them. Interestingly, in the New Testament, Paul says that those with pagan spouses should not separate, but rather be a Christian influence upon their unbelieving spouses. At the same time, the New Testament urges believers to marry only believers. Only where both husband and wife are believers will there be the spiritual bond needed.

Prayer　　*Father, work in the hearts of Christian young people that they may choose Christian life partners. In Christ. Amen.*

Day 144   Read Nehemiah 1-4

PRAYING, SAYING, AND DOING

Several groups have now returned from exile to Jerusalem. The temple has been rebuilt. But the walls have not been rebuilt, leaving the city vulnerable to the attack of enemies. God now leads Nehemiah to take up the work of rebuilding the walls.

Nehemiah sets an example in that he prayed and talked to others at the same time; he prayed and he built at the same time. An old Latin saying states: *Ora et labora*, "pray and work." We need both.

Of Nehemiah we read, "I prayed to the God of heaven. And I said to the king" (2:4-5). He had prayed beforehand, and now as he has the opportunity to speak to the king, he prays once again. Pray before you deal with people, and pray while you deal with people. Nehemiah receives permission from the king to go to Jerusalem to rebuild the walls. He is a spiritual man, but also a practical man. He inspects the walls so that he has first-hand knowledge of the situation. He then approaches the leaders of Jerusalem. As a result, the project of rebuilding the walls is begun.

The project was a matter of cooperation; each group was responsible for a section of the wall. It is now half built when the project is threatened by enemies. Nehemiah combines prayer and sound strategy. "We prayed to our God, and set a guard" (4:9).

Prayer   *Father, help us to have a healthy balance between prayer, conversation, and action. In Jesus' name. Amen.*

Day 145   Read Nehemiah 5-7

THREATS FROM WITHIN AND WITHOUT

Jerusalem was a struggling community. The people needed a sense of unity and brotherhood. Unity was threatened because the rich were demanding high interest of the poor, forcing them into slavery. Nehemiah sees that this is wrong. He calls them together and they are willing to right these wrongs. God never wants the rich to get richer by causing the poor to become poorer. Many passages throughout the Bible speak of God's concern for the poor. Nehemiah not only calls for justice for the poor; he reveals his own records to show that he has set an example by not taking advantage of them. Evangelical Christians need a greater concern for justice for the poor.

There were also external threats. Sanballat, Tobiah, and Geshem were always looking for ways to thwart Nehemiah's efforts. They tried to lure him outside the city, perhaps with the intent of assassinating him. They spread false rumors about his aspirations to become king. They tried to make him show his fear so as to discredit him. Nehemiah's hope was in God.

The church today is threatened from within and without. Let us trust God and use wise efforts to thwart these threats, as Nehemiah did. His concern was not for himself but for the cause to which he was committed. Our cause is the spread of the gospel of Jesus Christ.

Prayer   *Father, make the church strong to resist those forces within and without which threaten it. In Christ. Amen.*

Day 146   Read Nehemiah 8-9

THE BIBLE AND PRAYER

Spiritual renewal comes when we listen obediently to the Bible and pray earnestly. Ezra led in renewing the spiritual life of the Jews at this time, using these two means. He gathered the people together and not only read the Bible to them but gave explanations so they would understand it. Expository preaching, by which portions of the Bible are explained and applied, is one of the most important kinds of preaching. Such preaching is not expounding the views or opinions of the preacher, but opening God's Word.

Hearing the Bible read, the people realized they had failed to do what God wanted them to do and were sorry. The leaders, however, urged them to rejoice because they knew what God wanted them to do. They then kept one of the festivals appointed in Scripture for the first time since the days of Joshua.

Ezra also led in prayer. In this prayer he rehearsed God's gracious dealings with their ancestors, who had been so rebellious. He realized that they were in their present predicament as vassals to a foreign king because of sin. He acknowledged that sin, thus anticipating God's mercy. Then he renewed the covenant to which their ancestors had been unfaithful.

May our day be a day of spiritual renewal. It will be as we make faithful use of the Bible and of prayer.

Prayer   *Father, revive us again. Give your people renewed interest in Bible study and in prayer. In Christ. Amen.*

Day 147   Read Nehemiah 10–11

COVENANT RENEWAL

The details of the covenant mentioned in Nehemiah 8–9 are now spelled out. The first promise was to be obedient to all of God's commandments. The second was to avoid intermarriage with unbelievers, which had been a source of introducing pagan ways in the past. The third was the promise to keep the Sabbath. The fourth was to bring tithes and offerings faithfully for maintaining the temple and for the sacrifices to be made there.

Spiritual renewal in our day must take the shape which will be given to it by the Spirit of God. New days provide new opportunities. But the elements of Ezra's revival are applicable today. We must regulate our lives by the commandments of God rather than by the practices of men. We must build strong Christian homes, which is only possible when both husband and wife are dedicated to Christ. We must take time to be holy. God has given us one special day in seven not for sharing in the entertainment provided by the world but to refresh body and soul in worship. We must give generously because there are so many opportunities to spread the gospel. A church interested not only in maintaining itself but in Christ's global mission will be an obedient church.

Prayer   *We pray for spiritual renewal in the church that will enable us to meet the challenges of today. Amen.*

Day 148   Read Nehemiah 12-13

BACKSLIDING

One of the saddest moments I have had was to stand before the church served by the great revivalist Jonathan Edwards and read the sign: "Closed for the Summer." Revivals do not last. Ezra had led a great spiritual renewal with the approval of the governor Nehemiah. Then Nehemiah traveled back to the king of Persia, and upon his return he discovered that the practices of the people stood in stark contrast to the promises they had made a short time ago when they had entered into covenant to be faithful to God.

Someone had provided for Tobiah, a foreigner who had opposed Nehemiah every step of the way, a room in the very court of the temple. This was not only a personal insult; more seriously, it was contrary to the commandments of God. The Levites, who were to care for the temple, had not been paid, forcing them to return to their fields to provide for their families. Commerce was flourishing on the Sabbath. Intermarriage with unbelievers was again practiced. Nehemiah had to undo all of this evil.

Revival is necessary, but it is not one short campaign which will provide everything needed in the life of the church. Sinful human nature still dwells in the hearts of God's people, so there is a natural tendency to backslide. Renewal in the church must take place over and over again.

Prayer   *Father, we see so many evidences of backsliding today—*
                please turn the situation around. For Jesus' sake. Amen.

Day 149   Read Esther 1-2

WINNERS OF THE BEAUTY CONTEST

The Old Testament is often divided into three main sections: Historical Books, Books of Poetry, and Prophetic Books. Esther is the last of the Historical Books. Actually the events in this book occurred about 30 years prior to those described in Nehemiah.

Esther is a most unusual book. The name of God is never mentioned, yet the book describes God's providential protection of his people. It contains events which God overrules for the benefit of his people, although the events themselves fall short of biblical ethics. God works in everything for good, even in those things which he disapproves.

Ahasuerus holds a banquet for the rulers of his empire. During the banquet, having drunk too much, he calls for his wife to show off her beauty. She refuses to come and as a result is cast out of his harem. When a beauty contest is held to find a replacement, a young Jewish woman who went by the name Esther, enters the contest. She reaches the semifinals, in which the contestants take turns visiting the king. He is so pleased with her that he chooses her as his new queen. God surely must not have been pleased with many aspects of all of this, yet he uses these events to keep his people from being annihilated. One cannot approve Esther's involvement in this process, yet this put her in a place of opportunity during this time of exile for the Jews.

Prayer   *Father, use even the failures of your people to accomplish your saving purposes. In Jesus' name. Amen.*

Day 150 — Read Esther 3–6

THE PLAN OF PROVIDENCE UNFOLDS

The book of Esther is not only God's Word; it is delightful literature. What story has a more interesting plot? Haman is given a high position by the king, but his joy is spoiled because Mordecai will not bow to him. So he plans to kill all Jews. Mordecai's message to Esther is, "If you keep silence . . . deliverance will rise for the Jews from another quarter . . . [W]ho knows whether you have not come to the kingdom for such a time as this?" (4:14). Mordecai has faith that God will save his people in some way. Perhaps, however, he has placed Esther in her position to rescue the Jews.

It is dangerous for Esther to enter the king's throne room. If he does not lift up his scepter indicating his acceptance of her intrusion, she will be executed. He does raise the scepter and offers to give her anything she wants. She asked that he and Haman be her dinner guests. After dining with the royal couple, Haman is ecstatic, but his joy is spoiled when Mordecai will not bow before him.

The king has insomnia and thinks reading the chronicles of Persia will put him to sleep. Reminded from the selection read to him that Mordecai once saved his life but without being rewarded, he determines to honor him. He asked Haman what to do to honor a man. Haman thinks the king is speaking of him and proposes a public honor, which the king commands Haman to provide for Mordecai!

Prayer — *Father, protect your people. Thank you for the great ironies of your providence. In Jesus' name. Amen.*

Day 151   Read Esther 7-10

GOD'S PEOPLE ARE SAVED

The story now reaches its climax. When the king and Haman have come for dinner on the second day, Esther reveals Haman's wicked plot to the king. The king steps out of the room and comes back finding Haman falling over Esther on the couch pleading with her. It looks as if he is assaulting her. So in a classic illustration of poetic justice, Haman is hanged on the gallows he built for Mordecai.

The edict to kill the Jews, however, still stands. So Mordecai receives permission from the king to write to all the provinces giving the Jews permission to defend themselves, which they do with a great slaughter of their enemies. Mordecai is made an influential person in the kingdom of Persia.

The fourteenth and fifteen day of the month Adar are then made to serve as feast days celebrating this great victory, days which are to be celebrated annually. This is the basis of the Jewish feast days called Purim, since *pur* is the name for the lot, which had been cast by Haman to decide on what day to kill the Jews. At this feast the book of Esther is read.

This book does not mention the name of God yet is a powerful story illustrating his providential care of his people. The God who protected his people in that day is our God and will surely care for us.

Prayer   *Father, we rejoice that you are not only the God of the individual but are also sovereign over the nations. In Christ. Amen.*

Day 152 — Read Job 1–3

A GOOD MAN TESTED

We begin the second section of the Old Testament called the poetic books. These are also referred to as Wisdom Literature. Hebrew poetry does not have rhyme but rather parallelism; in its most common form, two parts of a verse say the same thing in different words.

The purpose of Job is to counteract a misunderstanding of the truth which we have seen emphasized over and over in the Old Testament so far, that the righteous are blessed and the wicked are punished. From this truth, people mistakenly argued backward that if someone was suffering, it must be because he had sinned in some way. To this false conclusion the book of Job gives a resounding "No!"

Job is a godly man. Satan tells God that this is because God has blessed him. If instead God would cause him to suffer, he would not be so godly. God gives Satan permission to bring trouble to Job. Satan causes Job to lose all of his possessions and all his children in one horrible day. Job's response is, "The LORD gave, and the LORD has taken away; blessed be the name of the LORD" (1:21).

Satan says to God that if God would allow him to harm Job personally, then his attitude would change. God permits Satan to smite Job with terrible boils. Job still remains steadfast. Following this prose introduction is the poetic body of the book and now Job is far from patient. He curses the day of his birth.

Prayer   *Father, give us patience in difficult times. Amen.*

Day 153   Read Job 4–8

WITH FRIENDS LIKE THESE . . .

When they heard of his trouble, three of Job's friends came to comfort him. And they surely did when they sat with him for seven days and said nothing. But then they began to talk, and Job realized he had been doing better without them. With friends like these, who needs enemies? His "friends" were convinced that Job was suffering because he had committed a serious sin. If he would just confess his sin, then he would be healed. They did not know what transpired between God and Satan. When we visit suffering people, we need to be sensitive to their feelings.

Every word of the book of Job is inspired by God. That is, he has given us a faithful record of what was spoken. But we should realize that not everything Job and his friends spoke to each other was entirely correct. To accept the whole book as inspired is not to say that the ideas of the friends or even of Job are always theologically sound. We must measure such soundness in the light of the rest of Scripture.

Eliphaz begins the dialogue by chastising Job for being so good at giving advice to others and faulting him for now becoming impatient. He stated his thesis when he said, "Who that was innocent ever perished?" (4:7). The implication is that since Job is perishing he must not be innocent. After Job's reply, Bildad stated the same thesis, "If you are pure and upright, surely then [God] will rouse himself for you" (8:5). The friends were so dogmatic—and so wrong!

Prayer   *Father, when we cannot understand your ways, assure us of your love. For Jesus' sake. Amen.*

Day 154 — Read Job 9–11

NEEDED: JESUS CHRIST

Job agreed with Bildad that "God will not reject a blameless man" (8:20). But then he added, "But how can a man be just before God?" (9:2). If Job had only been able to read Paul's letter to the Romans written centuries later! "A man is justified by faith apart from works" (Rom. 3:28). How blessed we are to live in the days following the writing of the New Testament, so we can read clear answers to some of Job's questions. How wonderful to know with certainty how to be right with God, through faith in Christ. But millions of people are still in Job's situation. In the midst of their heartaches, they do not know of Jesus Christ. We have yet to tell them the good news.

As he spoke about God, Job cried out, "There is no umpire between us" (9:33). One familiar with the New Testament thinks of the truth that there is one mediator between God and people, the man Christ Jesus (1 Tim. 2:5). How good to know what Job did not know and what millions of people do not know today. How important to send forth the good news.

Again, Job said to God, "There is none to deliver out of your hand" (10:7 ESV). But we who know the gospel of Christ may have echoing in our minds the hymn inspired by that gospel, "When by sin oppressed, go to Him for rest; our God is able to deliver thee."

Prayer   *Father, stir up Christians to be more urgent in sending forth the gospel of Christ. In his name. Amen.*

Day 155   Read Job 12-14

WHEN WE CAN'T UNDERSTAND GOD'S WAYS

Job's problem is that he cannot understand why God is treating him as he is. He knows the explanation of his "friends" is wrong, but he doesn't understand the right explanation. At times we cannot understand why God is dealing with us as he is, so we should be able to empathize with Job.

Each of his "friends" having spoken, Job now gives a rebuttal. They think they know it all, but Job refuses to accept the attitude that they know more than he does. He seems to have calmed down somewhat. When one deals with a problem over a length of time, the person's feelings change for better or for worse. Job points out that there are instances which show that sometimes the righteous suffer and the ungodly seem to get away with it. From our limited perspective God often seems to be using his omnipotence in ways which puzzle us.

Job turns from speaking to his friends to speaking to God. He recognizes that he is a sinner, but he is sure that he has not committed some terrible secret sin as his "friends" claim. He cried out to God, "Why?" and he did not get an answer. Job's problem was compounded by the fact that he does not seem at this point to have a bright hope of a world to come which we have. "We'll understand it all by and by."

Prayer   *Father, help us to believe in your love even when we cannot understand your dealings with us. In Christ. Amen.*

Day 156 — Read Job 15–19

MY REDEEMER LIVES

The second round of argument begins with Eliphaz, who repeats the same old tired arguments. Only before he was gentle; now he is blunt. Let us avoid argument, but when we find it necessary to argue, let us be gracious. It is possible to win an argument and to lose things which are much more important, such as friendship.

Job called his friends "miserable comforters" and said that if he was in their place, he could easily speak as they do. All around us people need comfort. Let us carry out a ministry of comfort. To do so we must have sensitivity. Compassion and sympathy both mean literally "to feel with." Job stated that God had worn him out for reasons he did not understand.

Bildad repeats his old arguments and Job expresses his despair. God has broken him down, and his family and friends look on him with loathing. He is in the deepest distress. Suddenly the Spirit of God moves him from despair to hope: "I know that my Redeemer lives, and at last he will stand upon the earth . . . I shall see God, whom I shall see on my side" (19:25-27). We need to realize that there was little hope of heaven in the Old Testament. It remained for Christ to "bring life and immortality to light" (2 Tim. 1:10). But occasionally God granted his people a glimpse of that wonderful life to come.

Prayer — *Father, we rejoice that Christ our Redeemer is very much alive and interceding for us. In his name. Amen.*

Day 157   Read Job 20–22

IT'S NOT THAT SIMPLE

Zophar makes the point that the "joy of the godless" is "but for a moment" (20:5). This is true in the light of eternity. But Job points out that in fact many wicked people "reach old age, and grow mighty in power" (21:7). The simplistic view of Job's "friends" will not stand up in the light of the facts. The wicked often prosper and die at ease. The fact is that regardless of their goodness or evil, some people die in quiet ease and others die a terrible death, but their final fate is the same: "they lie down alike in the dust" (v. 27). Again we must remember that there was little knowledge at this stage of God's revelation regarding the life to come. The knowledge we now have in the light of the New Testament regarding heaven and hell was not clearly known in Job's day.

Eliphaz responds to Job and also has a simplistic view which does not fit the facts. He accuses Job of wickedness. He charges him with mistreating people. If Job is suffering, this must have been the case. He distorts the facts to fit his theology. But Job had always been kind to people and had not mistreated them. Eliphaz again pleads for repentance on Job's part, which would have been excellent advice if he had done the things he was accused of, but he had not. If we have sinned against our fellow man, we certainly ought to repent.

Prayer   *Father, help us to hold views which are in keeping with the Bible and with reality. In Jesus' name. Amen.*

Day 158   Read Job 23-27

DOES GOD ANSWER PRAYER?

Job wishes he knew where he could find God, because he still believes that God would vindicate him if they could only meet. But he can't find God. How good that now that Christ has come, we can speak to God, knowing he will listen. But we must also admit that there are times when it seems as if God is not listening. At those times, let us be assured that he is, for Christ has said so.

Job also still has the faith that in the end things are going to turn out all right. "When he has tried me, I shall come forth as gold" (23:10). God sends trials that we do not understand, but he will use them for our spiritual benefit.

Job condemns those who mistreat the poor. Concern for the poor is emphasized in the Bible. Never forget that. But as the poor are mistreated, it often seems as if God is not listening to their prayer. But he is. If his answer is not "Yes," it is either "No, I have something better for you" or "Be patient, wait." But this last answer is hard for us to accept.

The "friends" are now running out of steam. Zophar does not take his turn and Bildad is short. Job's reply to him is rather sarcastic. He says in essence, "You have been so helpful," obviously meaning that they have not been helpful at all. Are we really being helpful to people in the depths of their needs?

Prayer   *Father, sometimes you do not seem to answer prayer. Give us faith to know the answer is coming. In Christ. Amen.*

Day 159   Read Job 28–30

THE PAST IS PAST

Job extols human technological achievements but points out that they do not bring wisdom, which only comes from God. What a message to our generation, which seemingly is so advanced in its technology! Yet with all our genius, people still do not have wisdom. Many have wealth and education but make a mess of their lives. Someone has said that this is a day of guided missiles and misguided men. Christ is the source of true wisdom; we need to share him with our generation.

Job continues by contrasting his present misery with the past when God was with him and all men showed him the highest respect. He claimed that he did what was right because he had concern for the poor: "I delivered the poor who cried, and the fatherless who had none to help him" (29:12). Yet now, "I cry to you for help and you do not answer me" (30:20 ESV). The loving God is not treating him as well as he had treated others, and he cannot comprehend this.

When we are going through trials, comparing our present situation to the wonderful past does no good. It only generates self-pity, which is one of the most destructive attitudes we can have. The past is past. Each phase of our lives must be handled. Things do not stay the same. Changes come, and we need to ask for grace to handle the problems of the present, instead of dreaming about the past.

Prayer   Father, help us to deal with our present problems with your help. In Jesus' name. Amen.

Day 160 — Read Job 31–33

BIBLICAL MORALITY

The three "friends" have charged Job with some sin which they think must be the cause of his suffering. Job now examines his life, and in doing so provides us with a good list of the morality which the Bible demands. God demands honesty (31:5). God demands sexual purity (v. 9). Job recognizes that if he had a sexual relationship with another man's wife it "would be a heinous crime" (v. 11). In a day when adultery is taken so lightly, we need to reaffirm the biblical standard and how wrong it is to break that standard.

God requires that we treat people who work for us with consideration (v. 13). He demands that we feed and clothe the poor (v. 16). He does not want us to put our trust in our money (v. 24). How careful we must be lest we do just that. We must not rejoice when people who hate us suffer misfortune (v. 29). We must take a responsible attitude toward natural resources (v. 38). Here we have a good summary of the kind of morality required by God in his Word.

Now, a certain young man who has been listening to the debate speaks up. Elihu has respect for age, and rightly so, yet he has been disappointed by what Job has said and equally disappointed in the arguments of the three "friends." But while he is rather pompous in his claim to have an answer, what he says sheds no light on the problem of Job.

Prayer — *Father, help us to examine ourselves by the standards found in your Word. In Jesus' name. Amen.*

Day 161   Read Job 34-37

MAN DOESN'T HAVE THE ANSWER

Elihu keeps saying, "Listen to me, I have the answer," but when we listen we find little help. The fact is that Job and the three "friends" and Elihu do not have the answer because none of them knows what transpired in the opening chapters of the book. There we learn that God allowed Satan to test Job to prove that Job served God, not because of what he received from God, but because he loved God.

There are difficulties in life which we do not understand because we only know part of the facts. In the meantime we need to trust in what we know about God, that he loves us and has some good purpose in it all, even when we cannot understand. "In everything God works for good with those who love him, who are called according to his purpose" (Rom. 8:28).

Elihu has emphasized the greatness of God. He called God "the Almighty" (35:13). He said, "God is mighty" (36:5). He said, "God is great" (36:26). This is true, but he fails to show how this sheds light on Job's situation. He says essentially the same things as the three "friends" did, although he does not seem to realize it.

Toward the end of his speech, however, Elihu begins to speak in terms similar to those God will soon use. He describes the greatness of God in terms of specific aspects of his great creation. God is great!

Prayer   *Father, often we do not understand how you are dealing with us. Give us faith in you. In Christ. Amen.*

Day 162   Read Job 38–39

GOD IS NO LONGER SILENT

All along Job has asked that God will enter into conversation with him. Finally God obliges. But he does not answer Job's questions. Instead he bombards Job with a series of his own questions. He intends, on the one hand, to take Job seriously, and on the other hand, to overwhelm him with a realization that God's wisdom and God's power put him in a league all by himself. In an age when people often act as if they could stand on the same plane as God, we need to realize that we are frail creatures of clay who know so little, that we should listen to God with a humble spirit.

Human beings often think they are smart, but in the light of God's perfect wisdom, we need to realize that often we do not know what we are talking about, yet we keep talking. God said, "Who is this that darkens counsel by words without knowledge?" (38:2). The barrage of God's questions is meant to put us all in our place. The scientist knows so little; good scientists realize that, but often second-rate ones do not. The Bible scholar knows so little; he often builds theories on slim evidence and later takes his theories as facts. God sends forth a barrage of questions to which we do not have the answers. This is meant to humble Job, and us. What an amazing world God has made. Let us stand in awe of our Creator.

Prayer *Father, you know everything. Show us what we need to know to serve you faithfully. In Jesus' name. Amen.*

Day 163   Read Job 40–42

A GOOD ENDING

God asks Job to answer his questions. Job, realizing how small he is, has nothing to say. God then describes his power in terms of his dealings with his creation. He concludes by describing his control of a great land animal, Behemoth (perhaps the hippopotamus), and a great sea animal, Leviathan (perhaps the whale). Job realizes God can do anything and that he himself doesn't know what he is talking about. He repents, not regarding sins he didn't commit, but for the arrogance of thinking he could win a debate with God.

Job realizes that before his difficulties he had had a secondhand knowledge of God, but now he has had a personal encounter with him. This puts his experience in a different light. Many of us have known about God through our parents; "I had heard of you by the hearing of the ear" (42:5 ESV). We need a personal relationship with God. Whatever difficulties it takes to produce that relationship will be worthwhile.

God vindicates Job to his "friends" and requires them to ask Job to pray for them. When he prayed for them, his fortunes were restored. If we expect God's blessings, we must not hold grudges. Job receives twice the blessings he had before. This is a good ending, but the ending of our story will be far better—trusting in Christ, we will be with him forever.

Prayer   *Father, cause us to know in our trials that the best is yet to come according to your promises. In Christ. Amen.*

Day 164 — Read Psalms 1–7

HEAR OUR PRAYER, O LORD

Although Job has taught us that we must not deal with this truth simplistically, the first psalm once again reminds us that God blesses godliness and punishes evil. The godly person loves God's Word, and as a result avoids getting involved in evil.

The second psalm is one of a number of psalms called *messianic*; that is, it deals with prophecies which are fulfilled by Christ. He will break down the proud resistance of those who rebel against him.

Psalm 3 tells of David's faith in God as he endures the trial produced by the rebellion of Absalom. The historical superscriptions which situate many of the psalms were added at some point after the psalms were originally written down, but they provide helpful insight. The fourth psalm is an evening prayer, setting us a good example, that we may place ourselves in the hands of God each night before we go to sleep.

The fifth psalm is a morning prayer. Let us begin each day with God, putting our trust in him to help us with all the problems we face that day. Psalm 6 is one of the psalms called *penitential*, in which the psalmist realizes he deserves the wrath of God, but pleads for his mercy instead. David had many enemies who were always threatening him, so in Psalm 7 and in many other psalms, he prays for protection from their attacks. We all have a great enemy, the devil. Let us constantly ask for God's protection against him. As Jesus taught us to pray, "Deliver us from evil [or the evil one]."

Prayer   *Father, help us to develop the same prayerful spirit expressed by the psalmist. In Jesus' name. Amen.*

Day 165   Read Psalms 8–14

SING TO THE LORD

The psalms were written to be sung. Notice that the headings of most of these psalms are addressed: "To the choirmaster." As mentioned on Day 164, the headings were not part of the original text of the Psalms, but they are so old that in the Hebrew Bible they are cited as verse 1. The biblical faith is a singing faith. When I have conducted funerals, part of the service includes the congregation singing. How different our mourning from that which we see in other parts of the world on news reports! In all the experiences of life, let us sing praises to our God, for he is good and his steadfast love endures forever.

Psalm 8 rejoices in the place we have in God's creation. "You have made him little less than God" (v. 5 ESV). Some psalms are acrostics: each verse begins with a succeeding letter of the Hebrew alphabet. This was probably to aid in memorization. Psalms 9 and 10 are tied together by this device, the acrostic starting in the ninth psalm and concluding in the tenth. Together they deal with a recurrent theme in the psalms: wickedness is prevalent, but God will help his people. The remaining psalms for today's reading continue to deal with that same theme.

The fourteenth psalm begins with a declaration that practical atheism (spoken in the heart and not in public) is folly. The Wisdom Literature, of which the Psalms are part, emphasizes the foolishness of sin.

Prayer   *Father, put a song in our hearts no matter what the circumstances, for we trust in Christ. In his name. Amen.*

Day 166 — Read Psalms 15–18

THE GODLY LOVE GOD

What kind of person pleases God? Psalm 15 answers this question by describing a person who "does what is right" and "speaks truth" (v. 2). He is also described in negative terms as a person who "does not slander" and "does no evil to his friend" (v. 3). We are saved by grace, but we are called to a life of godliness.

The godly are also people who love God. In Psalm 16 we read "I say to the Lord, 'You are my Lord'" (v. 2 ESV). "The Lord is my chosen portion" (v. 5). "I keep the Lord always before me" (v. 8). Salvation establishes a personal relationship with God.

But the godly are not without trouble. In Psalm 17, David again cries out to God for help as he faces people who desire to hurt him. In this difficult situation, David pleaded, "Keep me as the apple of your eye; hide me in the shadow of your wings" (v. 8 ESV).

Psalm 18 is similar to 2 Samuel 22, which provides the same historical introduction. When David has rest from his enemies, he is overwhelmed with thanksgiving to God. He begins by describing the role that God has played in his life, "I love you, O Lord, my strength. The Lord is my rock, and my fortress, and my deliverer, my God, my rock, in whom I take refuge, my shield, and the horn of my salvation, my stronghold" (v. 2 ESV). May God be those same things to us.

Prayer — *Father, help me to be godly and to rejoice in my relationship to you. In Jesus' name. Amen.*

Day 167 — Read Psalms 19–22

THE WORD OF GOD

This section contains outstanding psalms. Psalm 19 is divided into two parts. The first extols God's revelation in nature. The second gives even higher praise to the greater revelation in the written Word. It describes the greatness of God's Word and the wonderful effect it has on those who read it and apply it to their lives.

The twentieth psalm talks about the day of trouble and expresses the desire that God may answer prayer in such a day. "May he grant you your heart's desire, and fulfill all your plans!" (v. 4 ESV). The important thing is that we desire the right things and that our plans are of such a nature that they are worthy of being fulfilled. What is the greatest desire of your heart?

The 21st psalm tells of those prayers being answered, "You have given him his heart's desire" (v. 2 ESV). How wonderful to want the right things and to receive them. Then "We will sing and praise your power" (v. 13 ESV).

In amazing detail, Psalm 22 describes the crucifixion of Christ. He himself drew our attention to it when, being crucified, he cried out, "My God, my God, why have you forsaken me?" (v. 1 ESV). Other references to his crucifixion are, "All who seek me mock at me" (v. 7) "My strength is dried up" (v. 15) and "They have pierced my hands and feet" (v. 16).

Prayer — *Father, we praise you that your Word tells us of your Son Christ and of his crucifixion. In his name. Amen.*

Day 168   Read Psalms 23–28

SHEPHERD AND KING

We who have heard Jesus say to us "I am the Good Shepherd" see Jesus in this wonderful shepherd psalm. He is the One who leads us. He is the One who comforts us, and because of his goodness, we shall dwell with him forever.

The Shepherd is also the King of Glory described in Psalm 24. A psalm like this should fill our hearts with exultation. It is fitting that our hearts should burst forth in praise to so wonderful a Savior.

In Psalm 25, the author looks to God for protection, for guidance, for instruction. On the one hand, he is troubled, and on the other, he turns to God in a trusting spirit for help in that trouble.

Psalms 26–28 deal with the house of God. In Psalm 26, "O Lord, I love the habitation of your house, and the place where your glory dwells" (v. 8 ESV). In Psalm 27, "One thing have I asked of the Lord, that will I seek after; that I may dwell in the house of the Lord all the days of my life" (v. 4). In Psalm 28, "Hear the voice of my supplication, as I cry to you for help, when I lift up my hands toward your most holy sanctuary" (v. 2 ESV).

Today Jesus says to us that what counts is the attitude of our hearts, that we are to worship him in spirit and in truth. Yet how precious the actual place of our baptism, confession, and wedding.

Prayer   *Father, we rejoice that you have given us Jesus, our Good Shepherd, the King of Glory. In his name. Amen.*

Day 169   Read Psalms 29–33

PAIN AND PRAISE

In Psalm 29, God is praised as the writer considers the power of God expressed in thunder. Here we note one of the techniques of the psalms: repetition. The divine name "Lord" (Yahweh) is mentioned 18 times in 11 verses. The result is to focus our attention where it ought to be focused, on the Lord.

In the ESV and other translations, the heading of Psalm 30 speaks of the temple, since the Hebrew word is *bayith*, which means "house." But the occasion for the psalm must have been the dedication of David's palace. This beautiful home is a symbol of his present prosperity compared to his years of being persecuted. Indeed, "Weeping may tarry for the night, but joy comes with the morning" (v. 5). We may endure long years of difficulty, but we shall have joy for eternity.

"Into your hand I commit my spirit" from Psalm 31:5 (ESV) is quoted by Jesus among his last words on the cross. The line from verse 13, "Terror on every side" is quoted by Jeremiah five times.

Psalm 32 is another penitential psalm. For the psalmist, communion with God is the source of his greatest joy. He describes how terrible it is to have that communion destroyed by his sin and how wonderful when, as a result of heartfelt confession, sin is forgiven and fellowship is restored. Psalm 33 is a beautiful example of a song of praise to God.

Prayer   *Father, we confess our sin. Forgive us and give us the joy of fellowship with you. For Jesus' sake. Amen.*

Day 170   Read Psalms 34–37

WAIT PATIENTLY FOR GOD

When David fled from Saul, he sought refuge with Achish (Abimelech). However, when David realized he might be killed by Achish, he acted mentally imbalanced and so escaped. He then wrote this psalm, expressing his relief and gratitude for being spared from a dangerous situation. This psalm must have meant a great deal to the apostle Peter, who refers to it several times in his letters.

In Psalm 35, David is again faced with his enemies and pleads with God to rescue him. God's timetable is often slower than ours. He helps us, but not as quickly as we would like. So David cried out, "How long, O Lord, will you look on? Rescue me" (v. 17 ESV). It seems as if God is just looking at the situation, but is doing nothing about it. How often have we felt that way? But David knows God and therefore knows the time of delivery will surely come; "I will thank you in the great congregation" (v. 18 ESV). Psalm 36 provides a contrast between the wickedness of man and the goodness of God.

Psalm 37 is a call to wait patiently for God to act. It tells us not to get upset when we see wicked people prosper while we are suffering. The time will come when that will change. Ultimately, the wicked will perish and the righteous will be blessed. Therefore, "wait for the Lord, and keep to his way" (v. 34).

Prayer   *Father, help us to be patient, knowing your plan for us is far better than ours. In Jesus' name. Amen.*

Day 171	Read Psalms 38–41

CONTINUE TO WAIT FOR GOD

Psalm 38 is the third of the penitential psalms. The expression of repentance should have a significant place in our lives. Having acknowledged the sad consequences of his sin, the psalmist waits for the blessing of God which he knows will come to those with a penitent spirit.

In Psalm 39, David is overwhelmed by his frailty, but his response is, "And now, Lord, for what do I wait? My hope is in you" (v. 7 ESV). Our sin and our weakness need to be very real to us, but praise God, they are not the last word. That last word is the intervening grace of God. Praise the Lord!

The theme of waiting is found in Psalm 40, which begins, "I waited patiently for the LORD; he inclined to me and heard my cry. He drew me up from the desolate pit" (vv. 1-2). Our patience will pay off. God often tests us by not giving us what we want as quickly as we want it. But the result is spiritual growth. In this life, deliverance is not permanent. At the end of the psalm, David is again in distress, but he knows that the gracious God who has helped him in the past will help him again.

Throughout most of Psalm 41, David expresses disappointment with his circumstances, but he ends with praise. The psalms are divided into five books, each ending in praise.

Prayer   *Father, how we need patience, and faith that in the end all will be well, because of Jesus. Amen.*

Day 172 — Read Psalms 42–47

GOD IS THE RULER YET

Book 2 consists of Psalms 42–72. Most of the psalms in Book 1 are ascribed to David, but these have a variety of authors. Psalms 42 and 43 are obviously connected by these common sentences: "Why go I mourning because of the oppression of the enemy" (42:9; 43:2) and "Why are you cast down, O my soul, and why are you disquieted within me?" (42:5, 11; 43:5). The latter goes on to say, "Hope in God; for I shall again praise him, my help and my God." This is the conclusion of the matter. Our distress is not without hope; the assurance we have is that in due time God will deliver us.

Some psalms deal with national as well as personal situations. Psalm 44 deals with a national disaster which took place in spite of the faithfulness of God's people. National disasters often come as a result of sin, but not always. God is the Lord of the nations, but often his ways are beyond our understanding.

A royal wedding is the occasion of Psalm 45, but there is an application in terms of Christ. Psalm 46 was the inspiration for Luther's great hymn, "A Mighty Fortress Is Our God," and describes God's power as it is manifested in various areas of life. Psalm 47 describes a coronation scene. This is no earthly king; it is God himself, "For God is king of all the earth" (v. 7).

Prayer — *Father, we rejoice that you are Lord of all the earth and also our loving Father. Through Christ. Amen.*

Day 173 — Read Psalms 48–53

GOD'S DELIVERANCE

Psalm 46 expresses David's joy on an occasion of deliverance. God's rescuing us should be reason for expressing our gratitude. Surely "great is the LORD and greatly to be praised" (48:1).

We have pointed out that the poetic section of the Old Testament is called Wisdom Literature. In Psalm 49, we see a connection between the psalms and other books in this section. In the first few verses, there are a number of words such as "wisdom," "proverb," and "riddle," which are also in the opening verses of the book of Proverbs. The transiency of human achievements as described in the twice-used line of this psalm, "Man cannot abide in his pomp, he is like the beasts that perish" is another way of stating the theme of Ecclesiastes, "All is vanity."

While God is a deliverer, he is also a judge. In Psalm 50, God's people are reminded that both those who are spiritually careless and those who have hardened themselves in wickedness will be called before his judgment seat.

Psalm 51, another penitential psalm, describes the wonder of deliverance from the guilt of sin. Psalm 52 is a condemnation of Doeg: he betrayed the priest, Ahimelech, who had helped David when he fled from Saul. Psalm 53 is almost identical to Psalm 14 and is another plea for deliverance.

Prayer — *Father, in your grace deliver us from all our sins and trials. For the sake of Christ. Amen.*

Day 174   Read Psalms 54–58

WHEN IN DANGER

Psalm 54 is David's cry to God for help when he was betrayed by men of his own tribe who had told Saul where he could find David. From time to time all of us find ourselves in difficult situations. The place to turn is where David turned, to God. While the occasion is not specified, Psalm 55 is another response of David when he feels betrayed. Again he cries out to God for help. The fact that it was a close friend who betrayed him reminds us of the painful experience of Christ, betrayed by one of his own disciples.

David was so desperate at being hunted by Saul that he fled to Gath, the home town of Goliath, of all places. There he was seized by the Philistines and again in great danger. He cried out to God for help in Psalm 56: "When I am afraid, I put my trust in you" (v. 3 ESV). Every one of us has fears. Here is what we should do with them.

Hiding in a cave while Saul is seeking to find him to kill him, David writes Psalm 57, and once again expresses faith that God will take care of him in this dangerous situation.

In Psalm 58, David cries out against the injustice perpetrated by evil leaders. Because he believes in a God who is righteous, he is assured that the time will come when these tyrants will fall.

Prayer   *Father, in our times of fear, remind us of your wonderful promises to take care of us. In Christ. Amen.*

Day 175   Read Psalms 59–65

FROM DANGER TO VICTORY

Psalm 59, apparently written after David became king, looks back at that episode when he had to slip out of a window to avoid being captured by his enemy, Saul. He had been in danger, but now he was enjoying victory, which was only because of God's blessings. Look back and see God's merciful hand at work in your life. Give him the praise.

The background of Psalm 60 was this: David and his troops were in the north when an enemy attacked the land from the south. The psalm begins with David's feelings of sadness at hearing this news, but ends with the assurance that God will help him solve this problem too.

In Psalm 61, David is again pleading for God's help. Being assured of that help, he promises to praise God every day. The God of David is alive today. He will help us. Let us express our gratitude daily.

Psalm 62 shows us how difficulties driving us to God can end in enriching our lives as we learn to trust him for everything. Psalm 63 shows how God was ever central in the thoughts of David. He should have that same place in our lives. Psalm 63 focuses on God with the enemy in the background, but Psalm 64 focuses on the enemy with God in the background. Psalm 65 is a psalm of thanksgiving because God has provided a bountiful harvest.

Prayer   *Father, be with us in our struggles and give us assurance that by grace victory will come. In Christ. Amen.*

Day 176   Read Psalms 66–72

MY GOD, LORD OF THE WORLD

Psalm 66 calls the whole world to thank God, but ends on this personal note: "I will tell what he has done for me" (v. 16). The Lord with whom we have a personal relationship is Lord of all the earth. The next psalm contains the same truth but moves in the opposite direction: may the God who blesses us be praised by all the peoples of the earth. The more God means to us, the more we will be missionary minded, wanting others to share these blessings.

Psalm 68 rejoices in the way God brought his people from Egypt to Jerusalem. Since Ephesians 4 uses this wording to describe the ascension of Christ which led to the sending of the Holy Spirit, this psalm has often been used at Pentecost.

The New Testament quotes Psalm 69:9 as describing Christ's zeal for God's house and verse 21 predicts Christ being offered vinegar as he hung on the cross. Psalm 70 is almost identical to part of Psalm 40.

The author of Psalm 71 is obviously old. He has had a hard life and continues to have difficulties. But since childhood he has trusted in God and continues to do so. May we turn to the Lord early in life so we may experience his help all our life long, and as a result let us praise him "all the day long" (v. 24).

The final psalm of this second book tells of a great king who inspired the hymn "Jesus Shall Reign."

Prayer   *Father, we thank you for what you mean to us. May such blessings flow to others across the world. In Christ. Amen.*

Day 177 — Read Psalms 73–77

FROM SADNESS TO JOY

Book 3 of the Psalms begins with psalms written by Asaph, founder of a temple choir. Psalm 73 describes his jealousy of the wicked who prosper. Then he describes how entering the temple made him realize that in the end the wicked would lose.

The destruction of Jerusalem by the Babylonians seems to be the occasion in Psalm 74, since it reflects language similar to that of Lamentations. The psalm begins with a note of great sadness. In the middle of the psalm there is a note of triumph, but it ends once again with a plea for deliverance.

Psalm 75 describes God as judge. With ideas similar to those expressed in the Virgin Mary's *Magnificat* in Luke's Gospel and those of the Song of Hannah, it tells how God brings low the mighty and lifts up the humble. Perhaps this is meant to be an answer to the pleas with which Psalm 74 ends.

The theme of judgment continues in Psalm 76. God by his judgments will "save all the oppressed of the earth" while he "cuts off the spirit of princes" (vv. 9, 12). Remember that "Although the wrong seems oft so strong, God is the ruler yet."

The beginning of Psalm 77 focuses on "I" and expresses depression, like Romans 7. But the later part focuses on God and his power, even as Romans 8 expresses victory as the focus is on the Holy Spirit.

Prayer — *Father, give us faith to believe that in the end those who trust in you will triumph. In Jesus' name. Amen.*

Day 178   Read Psalms 78-79

THE GOD OF HISTORY

Psalm 78 is one of several psalms recounting God's dealings with his people in the past. It describes the "glorious deeds of the LORD" (v. 4), emphasizing the importance of passing on the story to our children. It tells how God brought the Israelites out of Egypt and cared for them in the wilderness, "yet they sinned still more against him" (v. 17). In response, God provided food for them, but also punished them. "In spite of all this they still sinned" (v. 32). They forgot the plagues which fell on Egypt on their behalf and how God had brought them to Sinai. Later God rejected the northern kingdom but continued to work with Judah, choosing David as king.

How good to know that the story continued. God did even more glorious deeds on behalf of his people. He brought them back from exile. He sent his Son to become one of them, to die on the cross as the atoning sacrifice, to rise from the dead, to ascend to heaven, and to send his Holy Spirit upon his church. When his church became corrupt, he raised up reformers whose spiritual descendants we are to this day. Let us not, like Israel, forget the glorious deeds of our God. Let us not like them rebel against him. Psalm 79 tells what happens when rebellion continues. It is a psalm describing the grief of those who experienced the destruction of Jerusalem.

Prayer   *Father, as we consider your glorious deeds on our behalf, fill us with gratitude. In Jesus' name. Amen.*

Day 179 — Read Psalms 80–85

JOYS AND SORROWS

Psalm 80 probably describes the distress of those in Jerusalem as they hear of the fall of Samaria. Three times the refrain "Restore us" is heard. They had been rival groups, but there is no note of glee, only one of sorrow. "Restore us" may express the desire that the old united kingdom be brought back into existence. So with us, problems in other denominations ought never to be a source of joy, but only one of sorrow.

The tone of Psalm 81 is different. It is probably to be sung at the Feast of Tabernacles commemorating God's care for his people as they traveled through the wilderness. God reminds them of how he cared for them at that time in their history and how he would love to care for them now if they would only listen.

In Psalm 82, the Lord is calling the "gods" into judgment. It is not absolutely certain who these "gods" are, but in the context they are probably the rulers of the people who have failed to carry out their responsibility of providing justice for the powerless. In the Judgment Day, all officials will be held accountable for injustice.

In Psalm 83, God's people are surrounded by their enemies. The prayer is not only for their defeat but that they may realize the greatness of God. Psalm 84 describes how blessed it is to be in God's house. It is also a prayer for revival.

Prayer   *Father, revive your church and fill all of its people with the joy of your salvation. In Jesus' name. Amen.*

Day 180 — Read Psalms 86–89

THE CRY OF THE HEART

In Psalm 86, David cries out for help. He sees no evidence that his prayer is being answered, but he continues to pray. Perhaps you have some problem today. There seems to be no answer. Keep trusting, keep praying. God will help you. Do not give up.

Zion was a name for Jerusalem. Christians naturally apply to the church the good promises made to Jerusalem. Psalm 87 inspired John Newton to write the great hymn "Glorious Things of Thee Are Spoken" which makes such application. Since the church is the body and bride of Christ, our longings also should be for its welfare. Those longings should express themselves in faithful service on behalf of the church.

Heman the Ezrahite, the author of Psalm 88, is in deep distress. In the midst of his despondency, he cries out to God. He does not understand why God is not answering him, but he continues to pray day and night.

In 2 Samuel 7, God had promised that sons of David would sit on his throne forever. In Psalm 89, Ethan the Ezrahite stresses the point "forever." This is God's covenant promise. But the current events of his time seem to contradict this promise. Ethan pleads with God to explain this to him. We, too, often have situations where God does not seem to be keeping his promises. But of this we can be sure: he will keep his word. We need to wait patiently.

Prayer — *Father, give us faith to believe in your promises and patience to wait for their fulfillment. In Christ. Amen.*

Day 181   Read Psalms 90–95

O WORSHIP THE KING

Most of the psalms in Book 4 seem to be intended for public worship. While most are anonymous, Psalm 90 is ascribed to Moses. It is commonly used at funerals. Isaac Watts loosely paraphrased it in the familiar hymn "O God, Our Help in Ages Past."

Psalm 91 expresses faith in God's care in time of danger. It echoes the Song of Moses in Deuteronomy 32 and some of the psalms of David. Psalm 92 is entitled "Song for the Sabbath" and shows that the Sabbath was not only a day of rest but also of corporate worship, a "holy convocation" as it is called in Leviticus. It reminds us that this day is intended to be a day of joy, not a burden. It is also a test of faith, since increasingly others use it for work and play rather than for rest and worship. God wants Sunday to be a day in which we receive spiritual blessings.

Psalms 93 and 95–99 emphasize God as king. Several of them begin with the line "The Lord reigns." In the midst of these psalms, Psalm 94 emphasizes God as judge and calls upon him to execute his judgment upon the wicked.

From ancient times the church has used Psalm 95 as a call to worship, entitling it "Venite," which is Latin for "O come." Hebrews 3 and 4 pick up the theme of the urgency of response to the Word of God by stressing the word *today*.

Prayer   *Father, may our worship be more meaningful and give us grace to respond to your Word today. In Christ. Amen.*

Day 182   Read Psalms 96–101

THE KING IS COMING

At the arrival of the ark of the covenant in Jerusalem, a song was sung, part of which was Psalm 96. The psalm emphasizes giving glory to the Lord. It repeats the phrase "The LORD reigns" and says he is coming to judge the world. Psalm 97 again repeats this phrase and emphasizes God's majesty and his judgment. Psalm 98 urges everyone to sing praises to God and commands the physical world to join in. Psalm 99 emphasizes the holiness of God but also rejoices in his forgiveness.

Psalm 100 is commonly used as a call to worship and inspired William Kethe's paraphrase "All People That on Earth Do Dwell" and Isaac Watt's "Before Jehovah's Awful Throne." In Psalm 101, David determines to have nothing to do with evil men. It is a challenge to all in government to be honest.

All of the psalms which emphasize God as king who will come to judge remind us that Jesus Christ is King of kings and is coming to judge the living and the dead. The immorality all around us is evidence that the world pays no attention to this great truth. We who believe it should be motivated to live not like the world, but as those who know that God rules and that everyone must give account of his or her whole life before him. We must also make this part of the message we proclaim to the world.

Prayer   *Lord Jesus, come soon that the struggle between truth and falsehood may come to an end. Amen.*

Day 183　　　　　　　　　　　Read Psalms 102–104

BLESS THE LORD, O MY SOUL

Like Job, the author of Psalm 102 struggles with unexplained suffering. He grieves because of personal problems and the problems of Zion (his "church"). He compares the brevity of life and God's eternity. This comparison is applied to Christ in Hebrews 1. May our concerns be not only for ourselves but also for the welfare of the church for which Christ died. Let us face these concerns in faith, knowing that Christ has come to bring victory for his people.

Psalms 103 and 104 are joined by the fact that they both begin and end with the words "Bless the LORD, O my soul." Psalm 103 echoes earlier Scriptures and in turn is echoed in Isaiah and Jeremiah. Its repeated use of the words "steadfast love" reminds us that God is faithful to his covenant from generation to generation. The God of the Old Testament is the God of the New Testament. He is the God of church history and he is our God today. This psalm inspired Henry F. Lyte's hymn, "Praise, My Soul, the King of Heaven."

The structure of Psalm 104 parallels that of Genesis 1 very closely. It tells of the events of the days of creation in order and in some cases returns again to that sequence. It inspired Robert Grant's "O Worship the King" and William Kethe's "My Soul, Praise the Lord." May it inspire us to worship and praise God as he should be praised.

Prayer　　*Father, we worship and praise you for the greatness of your creation and your salvation in Christ. Amen.*

Day 184 — Read Psalms 105–106

THE STORY OF GOD AND PEOPLE

Psalms 105 and 106 both begin with "O give thanks to the LORD" and end with "Praise the LORD!" Psalm 105 recounts the mighty acts of God from the call of Abraham to the entrance to the Promised Land. Sentence after sentence begins with "He" and tells what God did for Israel.

Psalm 106 recounts the history of God's people from the exodus to the judges. It tells the human side, how Israel again and again failed God. Sentence after sentence begins with "They" and tells how the people sinned. The reason it gives is, "They forgot God." God blessed them, but they soon forgot what he had done and lived in ways which displeased him. While the psalm describes the sinfulness of people, it ends on a positive note. While the people forgot God, "he remembered for their sake his covenant." We forget God, but he does not forget us. He remembers the promises he made to our spiritual forefathers that for their sake he would bless their descendants.

Parts of Psalms 105 and 106 were combined with Psalm 96 to form the psalm of praise at the reception of the ark of the covenant in Jerusalem.

What a powerful message: God does great things for his people. We sin against him because we forget him, but he remembers his promises. Therefore, praise the Lord!

Prayer — *Father, we rejoice in your grace; keep us from forgetting your goodness that we may be faithful. In Jesus' name. Amen.*

Day 185   Read Psalms 107–110

THE LORD'S STEADFAST LOVE

Psalm 107 describes four scenes where people are in trouble. Then come the words, "Then they cried to the LORD in their trouble, and he delivered them from their distress." Then there is a description of how the Lord delivered them, followed by the refrain, "Let them thank the LORD for his steadfast love, for his wonderful works to the sons of men!" After the fourth scene, there is a description of how God blesses people, with the final conclusion, "Let men consider the steadfast love of the LORD."

The words "steadfast love" are a translation of the Hebrew term *chesed*, one of the most beautiful words in the Bible. It speaks of God's faithfulness, of his covenant love, which is absolutely dependable. Let us consider that marvelous love of God and let it motivate us to praise him in song and through obedient lives.

Psalm 108 consists of the endings of Psalms 57 and 60. Both of these psalms begin with stress and end on a positive note. Psalm 109 is one of those psalms that cries out for vengeance. Such psalms fall short of the forgiving spirit of the New Testament, but they do express the honest feelings of people who have been terribly mistreated.

Psalm 110 is quoted 21 times in the New Testament. It speaks of both the lordship and priesthood of Christ, who is now seated at the right hand of the Father.

Prayer   *Christ, reign in our hearts and may all of your enemies be defeated and righteousness prevail. Amen.*

Day 186   Read Psalms 111–118

HALLELUJAH

Most of the psalms in this section begin with "Praise the LORD" which in Hebrew is *Hallelujah*. This is to be the constant attitude of our hearts. Psalms 111 and 112 are both acrostics (each having 22 lines beginning with successive letters of the Hebrew alphabet). Psalm 111 describes God with a mention of his "works" in half the verses. God is an active God, revealing the kind of God he is by what he does. So also our actions show what kind of people we are. Psalm 112 describes the godly, and in several cases uses the same words to describe God and the godly. To be godly is to be like God.

    The rest of the psalms in this section are called the Egyptian *Hallel*, since they were used at the Jewish Passover to express gratitude for the rescue of God's people from Egypt. The first two were sung before the Passover meal, the last four after it. Psalm 114 describes the rescue vividly; our rescue from sin is likewise cause for such excitement. While Psalm 114 looks to the past, Psalm 115 emphasizes that God is the God of the present. Psalm 116 tells us that we best express our gratitude to God by receiving the salvation he offers us. Psalm 117 commands all nations to praise God. Think of it: these were the psalms Jesus and his followers sang the night before his crucifixion.

Prayer   *Father, we praise you for the rescue far more wonderful than that of the exodus. Through Christ. Amen.*

Day 187   Read Psalm 119

THE WORD OF GOD

Every verse in this lengthy psalm speaks about the Word of God, using various designations such as "law," "testimonies," "precepts," "statutes," "commandments," "ordinances," "word," and "promise." The psalm is an acrostic in which the first eight verses begin with the first letter of the Hebrew alphabet, *aleph*, the next eight with the second letter, *beth*, until the end of the alphabet is reached.

Over and over, the psalmist tells us how much he loves the Word of God. Surely we should love that Word too, and by reading it, let it shape our thinking and therefore our lives. The Scriptures fill the psalmist with awe as he considers how dependable they are. When we read the Bible, it must not be a ritualistic duty but rather a listening to the voice of God, which provides us with the directions we need.

Again and again the psalmist considers how God's Word provides true freedom, how it gives insight into the situations we deal with, how we experience fullness of life as we obey God who speaks in his Word, and how that Word provides us with comfort, stability, and hope.

The psalmist reminds us to keep God's Word in a world that often disdains it. This Word is to be kept in the midst of the struggles of daily living. May we be able to say, "O how I love thy law!" (v. 97).

Prayer   *Father, thank you for the Bible. Speak powerfully to us through its pages. In Jesus' name. Amen.*

Day 188   Read Psalms 120–131

PREPARE TO WORSHIP

Psalms 120–134 are called the "Songs of Ascent" and were probably sung by people who traveled a distance to worship in the temple at the annual feasts. Psalm 120 is the cry of one who is in distress still in a distant land. The traveler was sometimes in danger, so Psalm 121 is a confession of faith in God as One who *keeps* his people in safety.

In Psalm 122 Jerusalem has come into sight, and the call is to pray for the peace of that city. May there be peace in the Middle East, but even more importantly, may there be peace in the church, which in a spiritual sense is Jerusalem for the Christian. Let us pray and work for harmony in our congregation.

Psalm 123 looks beyond Jerusalem to heaven, which is the true dwelling place of God, and beyond that to God himself. Looking to God, we pray for his mercy. Psalm 124 considers that God's people would have been destroyed were it not for that mercy. As the pilgrim on the way to worship considers the scene around him, in which the mountains speak to him of stability, so he trusts in the ever dependable God (Psalm 125). Continuing to focus his thoughts on Mount Zion, the author of Psalm 126 considers how God has protected it in the past and prays for similar help in his own time. The rest of the psalms in today's reading express hope in God.

Prayer   *Father, help us to be filled with thoughtfulness and song as we prepare to worship you. Through Christ. Amen.*

Day 189   Read Psalms 132–137

IN VICTORY AND DEFEAT

Psalm 132 describes the devotion of David to God and of God to David. We are to serve God whatever the cost, but what he does for us is far greater than what we do for him. Psalm 133 exemplifies the biblical practice of using the most vivid of terms to compare spiritual realities with the physical, and here this literary form describes how refreshing it is to live together in harmony, which should be a very high priority for every Christian.

Like Psalm 132, Psalm 134 stresses the mutuality of our relationship to God, "Bless the LORD" (vv. 1-2), and "The LORD bless you" (v. 3). Again, his blessing is far greater than our blessing (or praise) of him.

Every verse in Psalm 135 either refers to a previous verse of Scripture or is mentioned in Scripture which follows. There are great themes which run through the Bible, and if we would be biblical, we must grasp those themes.

Notice the refrain in Psalm 136, "For his steadfast love endures forever" (ESV). True love, like the love God has for us, is not something one falls into or out of. Rather, it is covenant love, loyal love, love which remains faithful in every circumstance. Because God loves us in this way, we are to give thanks to him. In contrast, the sorrow of the Jews in Babylon led to a terrible hatred of the enemy in Psalm 137.

Prayer   *Father, grant to us a very personal relationship with you which will affect our attitudes. In Christ. Amen.*

Day 190 — Read Psalms 138–143

THE I–THOU RELATIONSHIP

David had a very personal relationship with God. In Psalm 138 this is especially noticeable with the constant use of "I," "me," "my" and even more "thou," "thee," "thy" (or more commonly today, "you" and "your"). This is biblical religion. It is also expressed in Psalm 139 where the psalmist is conscious that he lives his life in the presence of God.

In Romans 3:10-18, Paul draws most of his witness to the depravity of man from Psalm 140. In Psalm 141 David is conscious of his own temptation to sin and prays for God's help in this struggle.

Both Psalm 57 and Psalm 142 are noted as being written as a result of David's experience of hiding away from Saul in a cave. His emotions fluctuate as ours often do, for in the former psalm he speaks with exaltation while here he cries out of the midst of a spirit of depression. But again he ends with the assurance that his God will not abandon him.

Again in Psalm 143, at the beginning he is weighed down by his troubles, but toward the end he focuses on the need to be taught God's will so that he may do it. How thankful we can be that we can know God's will through a Bible which climaxes in the perfect revelation of that will in God's Son, Christ. May our relationship with God be very personal as we are conscious of his presence, commune with him, and pray to him to avoid sin and do his will.

Prayer — *Father, you are our God, we are your people; may we listen to you in Scripture and answer you in prayer. Amen.*

Day 191   Read Psalms 144–150

PRAISE THE LORD

Verses in Psalm 144 are similar to those in several other psalms, especially Psalm 18. Common themes run through the Psalter as well as through the whole Bible. Psalm 145 is the last of the psalms attributed to David and the last of the acrostic psalms. I have often read this psalm to the mothers of newborn infants, for birth is surely a "wondrous work" and parents are called to pass the faith on to the next generation.

The last five psalms all begin and end with "Praise the LORD." Psalm 146 inspired several German hymns as well as one in English by Isaac Watts. Psalm 147 has similarities to the questions of Isaiah 40 as well as the words of God to Job near the end of that book.

Psalm 148 calls upon the angels, the inanimate creation, the nations of the world and finally Israel to praise God, while Psalm 149 especially calls upon God's people to do so. Surely we Christians have more reasons to praise God than anyone else. But do we really praise him as we should? Are our worship services as full of praise as they ought to be?

Each of the five books in the book of Psalms ends with praise to God, but the final psalm of this final book is entirely one of praise. What a book is the book of Psalms! It expresses the wide range of feelings of the believer, even those feelings which are unworthy. May we read it frequently.

Prayer   *Father, we praise you for you are great. We especially praise you for your Son Jesus Christ. Amen.*

Day 192   Read Proverbs 1–3

MY SON, LISTEN

Proverbs are short sayings meant to tell the reader how to live. They show that the commands of God are proven to be valuable in practical experience. Like the Pentateuch and the Psalms, the book is divided into five parts. Solomon, who wrote some 3,000 proverbs, wrote most of those included here. He begins by calling attention to the fact that if we are to be truly wise, we must begin at the right point, which is a deep respect for God. He calls upon his pupil whom he addresses as "My son" to give attention to his instructions, for doing so will lead to joy, while failing to do so will lead to sorrow.

Wisdom is personified as a woman who is calling upon the pupil to practice what Wisdom teaches in order to enjoy the truly good life. The wisdom which the Lord gives is seen to be a shield and protection against danger. Of special concern is the need to avoid the wrong kind of sexual relationships, a warning that will be repeated again later.

It is important to trust in the Lord rather than to rely on one's own viewpoint. It is important to honor God with our material possessions, a teaching which will be repeated later in the book.

The section ends with a series of "do nots," for true wisdom is not only a matter of doing the right; it is also avoiding the wrong. Significantly, the "do nots" deal with our relationships to other people.

Prayer   *Father, help us to trust you rather than our own ideas, for we ask it in Jesus' name. Amen.*

Day 193 — Read Proverbs 4–7

MY SON, BE ATTENTIVE

Solomon wants to be sure that we take his message seriously. Again and again he calls his pupil to be attentive. He is concerned about the reception of his message because he is convinced that it will make a real difference in the life of the reader. And it will!

The major theme of this section is that we are to avoid adultery because of its tragic consequences. In vivid language we are warned about sexual sin. This warning needs to be heeded in our generation when so many, by their disobedience to God's commands in this area of life, are losing the joy God wants to give them. Proverbs 5:18-19 teach that nurturing one's marriage is the best defense against such temptation. "He who commits adultery has no sense; he who does it destroys himself" (6:32). All need to hear such advice in a day when television, film, and other media are constantly brainwashing us with the opposite message.

One of the minor themes is a warning against laziness. We are called to observe the activity of the ant by which it provides for the future. Scripture teaches us not to be anxious about tomorrow because God takes good care of us, but he does so through means, one of which is that we work hard preparing for the future. We are told that there are seven things that are an abomination to the Lord. God hates pride, lying, hurting other people, and causing trouble.

Prayer — *Father, may all who read these words see the wisdom of following them. For Jesus' sake. Amen.*

Day 194　　　　　　　　　　　　　Read Proverbs 8–11

WISDOM CALLS

In chapter 8 and the first part of 9, Wisdom continues to call us to follow her teachings so that we may avoid folly and experience blessings. In the last part of chapter 9, folly is also personified as a woman who calls in the same way, but who calls to the wrong kind of life, which ends in death. Both of them call, "Whoever is simple, let him turn in here" (9:4, 16). Still today, God calls us to his way, which is best for us, while the world calls us to a different way that ends in death; the broad road still leads to destruction.

The second section of the book of Proverbs begins with chapter 10, also written by Solomon, but in a different style. Each verse is an individual proverb not connected to the verses in the context. But there are some common themes. Many proverbs begin with "He who" in which the first line of the proverb gives the result of the right kind of living, while the second line shows the result of the wrong kind of living. For example, "He who walks in integrity walks securely, but he who perverts his ways will be found out" (10:9).

Just as is often found in Psalms, there are two kinds of people: "the righteous" and "the wicked," and the action of the first will result in blessing while that of the later ends in destruction. Jesus enlarges on the teachings of some proverbs; for example, 10:25 is similar to the conclusion of the Sermon on the Mount.

Prayer　　*Father, as voices call us from all directions, give us ears to hear and hearts to obey your Word. In Jesus' name. Amen.*

Day 195　　　　　　　　　　Read Proverbs 12–14

PORTRAIT OF A GOOD MAN

The proverbs describe a good man. He "loves discipline" and "listens to advice." He is not a know-it-all, but realizes he has much to learn. His thoughts "are just"; that is, his thought life is honest, not like the wicked whose thoughts are "treacherous." His words are true but also gracious, so that they "bring healing" in the relationships of human beings to each other. He "ignores an insult"; he does not allow the unkind words of others to disturb him. He "has regard for the life of his beast"; he treats animals kindly and therefore human beings with even greater kindness. He "tills his land"; that is, he is not lazy and does not "follow worthless pursuits" as does the person who "has no sense." He is among those who "act faithfully" and is one who "turns away from evil." These are the practical applications of the commandments of God which were revealed to us earlier in the Old Testament story.

Just as that earlier law said that obedience would result in blessing, so also here. A man who lives like this "obtains favor from the LORD." Being rooted in righteousness, he will "never be moved." He escapes from the trouble which befalls the evil man, for there is a just God in heaven. He is "satisfied with good." Such people "have joy."

Proverbs portrays the good person so as to call us to live such a life with its resulting rewards.

Prayer　　*Father, help us to be good people as you measure goodness and to reap the reward of righteousness. Amen.*

Day 196   Read Proverbs 15–17

A GENTLE TONGUE

Proverbs stresses the proper use of the tongue. A God-controlled tongue gives a "soft answer" and therefore helps in peacemaking. Such a tongue "dispenses knowledge" and "is a tree of life." Those who hear the speech of a good man benefit from it. His lips "spread knowledge" and in God's ears his prayer is "his delight." The rest of the Bible speaks similarly. We are taught to be careful how we use that powerful instrument, the tongue. It can do much good or much harm.

Proverbs also likes to make comparisons. A number of them start with the words "Better is." It is better to have a meal consisting of just a few vegetables and enjoy the meal because of the harmony around the table, than to have a big steak dinner with the people eating it angry with each other. What timeless advice! It is better to have very little in the way of material goods and have a deep reverence for God than to be wealthy and have a life full of trouble because of ignoring God's commandments.

There is also the "but the LORD" formula. A person may think he is good, "but the LORD" looks at his motives. A person may make plans, "but the LORD" has the final say as to how they all turn out. What God thinks counts. He is in control, not us. Because he is in charge, it doesn't pay to be "hot-tempered," "a sluggard," or "greedy."

Prayer   *Father, help us to guard our tongues and to follow the better way of life you have revealed to us. Amen.*

Day 197 Read Proverbs 18–21

THE POWER OF WORDS

Several proverbs talk about "a fool." In each case he shows his folly through his words. A fool is not interested in understanding but only in giving his opinion. What he says leads to his hurt. He is ready to give an answer to a question before he has really heard what the question is. Words are so important that "death and life are in the power of the tongue" (18:21). As someone has said, "Never forget that God gave you two ears and only one mouth."

Laziness comes in for its share of rebuke. Failing to work hard and destroying something fall in the same category (18:9), for in both cases others are shortchanged by the action. *Slothfulness* results in hunger (19:15). *The sluggard* fails to sow and then is surprised when there is no harvest (20:4).

The "Better is" formula is also used. It is better to be poor and have integrity than to show folly by a wrong use of words (19:1). Solitude is better than relationships that produce contention (21:19).

The words "Wine is a mocker, strong drink a brawler; and whoever is led astray by it is not wise" will be commented on more fully later. A book on wisdom cannot ignore the folly produced by the misuse of alcohol. This is the kind of advice needed by many today. There is a timelessness about the proverbs because human nature is ever the same.

Prayer *Father, keep us from letting alcohol make us foolish, and from speaking hurtful words. Amen.*

Day 198   Read Proverbs 22–24

AVOID ADULTERY, DRUNKENNESS, AND LAZINESS

Included in this passage is a departure from the common structure of Proverbs. Along with isolated sayings are longer sections dealing with one subject.

There is a section on adultery (23:26-28). I met a man who when he was young never went to church but read his Bible regularly, especially Proverbs. Once he and his friends were walking along when one suggested they visit a house of prostitution, but this young man refused to go with them because Proverbs had convinced him that this would be folly.

Another second section deals with drunkenness (23:29-35). It begins with a series of questions as to who has a number of related problems and then answers by saying the person who has such problems is the one who drinks too much. Alcoholic drink is so attractive to the physical senses of vision and taste, but "at the last it bites like a serpent, and stings like an adder." Today multitudes are suffering from that bite. Then follows a vivid description of the sensations of drunkenness concluded by the sad words, "I will seek another drink"! Personally, I am thankful I followed my father's advice, "Never take the first drink and you will never get drunk."

Another section deals with laziness describing the way in which it leads to poverty.

Prayer   *Father, deliver people from sexual sin, the misuse of alcohol and drugs and from laziness. In Jesus' name. Amen.*

Day 199　　　　　　　　　　Read Proverbs 25–28

COMPARISONS AND CONTRASTS

We now begin the third Section of Proverbs with chapter 25. These proverbs are a collection apparently discovered many years after their writing and copied by scribes in Hezekiah's court. In the first part of this collection are many proverbs beginning with the word "like." They compare a physical truth with a spiritual truth. Jesus in his parables expanded this form. Many of his parables begin with: "The kingdom of God is like."

A person who gives wise criticism is like gold jewelry (25:12). Cold snow and a faithful messenger both provide refreshing stimulation (v. 13). A similarity exists between clouds which promise rain but do not produce any and a person who promises a gift but doesn't follow through on his promise (v. 14). Both a drink of water given to a person who is thirsty and good news from a distant land provide a similar positive response (v. 25). A proverb told by a foolish person is as helpful as a lame leg (26:7).

We also have here more contrasts provided by the use of the word "better." As in several similar proverbs, to live in a little attic room is to be preferred to a companionship that is filled with dissension (25:24). A person who is not a blood relative but who is on hand to be of help is better than a brother too far away to be of help (27:10). An honest poor man is better than a rich stubborn person (28:6).

Prayer　　*Father, we thank you that we can understand spiritual truths through comparison to the physical. In Christ. Amen.*

Day 200 — Read Proverbs 29-31

LEARNING FROM OTHERS

Proverbs 29 is the last chapter written by Solomon in the book of Proverbs. It includes proverbs beginning with "if." One describes the uselessness of arguing with a foolish person. Another shows how corruption grows in government. Still another promises that a government concerned for the poor will be stable.

Agur is the author of chapter 30. He likes to speak about groups of four. There are four things he doesn't understand, including how a man courts a woman. There are four things which cause trouble, all four of them being ways in which people suddenly gain power which they cannot wisely handle. There are four small animals, all of whom show great wisdom.

The final chapter consists of wisdom taught to a king by his mother. In the first part of the chapter, she stresses the dangers of a king falling under the influence of his wives. This was certainly illustrated by the bad influence that pagan wives had on King Solomon. She also warns of the danger of alcoholic beverages. She concludes her advice to the king by reminding him that he must speak out on behalf of the oppressed.

The last part of the last chapter consists of a description of the ideal wife. She is a very industrious person with managerial skills and as a result she is praised by her husband and children.

Prayer *Father, give us the willingness to learn from the right sources that we may be a blessing. In Jesus' name. Amen.*

Day 201 — Read Ecclesiastes 1–4

RESULTS OF WRONG PRIORITIES

Some think Ecclesiastes was written by Solomon in his old age. It is the work of a man who has had the opportunity to live life to the full and ends up disillusioned. The theme is "all is vanity." It describes how a life of earthly success that leaves God out of the picture is ultimately meaningless.

The author put forth great effort to acquire wisdom but found the search unsatisfying. He tried pleasure, the accumulation of wealth, and hard work, and yet all his success in these areas did not bring him lasting happiness. Many people seek happiness in the same ways. But lasting happiness is not found by making these things the top priority in life.

At the end of chapter 3, he considers the role of God in life and comes to the conclusion that it is best simply to enjoy the gift of life which God gives us. In the chapter 4, he uses the "better" formula that we saw in Proverbs. Perhaps he is thinking about himself when he says, "Better is a poor and wise youth than an old and foolish king, who will no longer take advice" (4:13). Tragically, Solomon's spiritual life deteriorated over the years. This is true of a number of characters in the Old Testament, and it is a warning to us. Our spiritual life deepens over the years only if we nourish it through continuing to take the advice given to us in God's Word.

Prayer — *Father, fill our lives with meaning and purpose through our relationship to Christ. In his name. Amen.*

Day 202 — Read Ecclesiastes 5–8

THE BETTER WAY

This passage begins by cautioning against carelessness in worship. Again the "better" formula is used. When you come to God's house, "to draw near to listen is better than to offer the sacrifice of fools" (5:1). "It is better that you should not vow than that you should vow and not pay" (v. 5).

Next is a section on problems connected with the possession of riches. The author considers these "a grievous evil . . . under the sun" (5:13). The phrase "under the sun" is used in this book to describe life lived on the horizontal level, without giving due regard for God.

While all things are vanity, some things are better than others. "A good name is better than precious ointment" (7:1). It is better for the soul to recognize the lessons learned in mourning than to focus on shallow humor. A patient spirit is better than a proud spirit.

Wisdom is commended. "Wisdom preserves the life of him who has it" (7:12). "Wisdom gives strength to the wise man" (v. 19). "A man's wisdom makes his face shine" (8:1). Life may be frustrating, but a life directed by wisdom will be better than that of the foolish.

At several points in the book, the author commends enjoying one's food and work. A life of moderation, of enjoying simple things, is better than madly pursuing riches or pleasure only to be disappointed in the end.

Prayer — *Father, we thank you for the simple things of life that can be enjoyed when we are conscious of you. In Christ. Amen.*

Day 203 — Read Ecclesiastes 9–12

FEAR GOD

One disadvantage the writer of Ecclesiastes has as he seeks to understand the meaning of life is that he lived in a day when God had not yet revealed as much about what happens after death as we can know today. God's revelation throughout the Bible is progressive. The godly in Genesis did not know all there was to know about life and death. God slowly revealed more down through the centuries, and it remained for the coming of Christ to bring "life and immortality to light" (1 Tim. 1:10). The writer is pessimistic because he thinks "one fate comes to all, to the righteous and the wicked" (9:2), but in the New Testament we learn that the fate of the two is very different. The writer thinks that "the dead know nothing" (v. 5), while the New Testament reveals that at death the soul goes to heaven or hell.

The concluding chapter is a plea for young people to come to God now. This is followed by a vivid description of old age, when "the grinders cease" (we lose our teeth), "the windows are dim" (our eyesight diminishes), and similar things. Death is then described in terms of "the silver cord" being "snapped."

The conclusion: "Fear God, and keep his commandments; for this is the whole duty of man" (12:13). The reason given: God will judge every deed and all that we cannot see. This book shows how empty life is without God and how meaningful with him.

Prayer — *Father, we thank you that we know that death for the believer means entrance into Christ's presence. Amen.*

Day 204　　　　　　　Read Song of Solomon 1–4

TRUE LOVE

The Song of Solomon is called the Song of Songs or Canticles, and may have been written by Solomon or about Solomon. It describes the love of a bride and groom, and in so doing places God's approval on the physical aspect of marital love. In trying to find why it should be included in the Bible, the Jews allegorized it to represent the love between God and Israel. Some Christians followed this line by seeing in the book a description of the love between Christ and his church. There are passages of Scripture which compare God's love for Israel and then for the church in terms of the love between husband and wife, but there is no reason for not taking the book at face value as describing the love which should exist between a married couple.

A difficulty in understanding the book is that it appears to be a dialogue between the bride and the groom with a chorus provided by "the daughters of Jerusalem," and it is necessary to determine when the speech changes from one person or group to the other. The book has enriched our own language and literature by providing such attractive lines as "I am a rose of Sharon, a lily of the valleys" (2:1), which in a hymn is used to describe Christ, and "the little foxes, that spoil the vineyards" (v. 15), which shows how little things can spoil wonderful relationships.

Prayer　　*Father, fill the hearts of husbands and wives with unselfish love for each other. For Christ's sake. Amen.*

Day 205　　　　　　　　　Read Song of Solomon 5–8

WHAT IS LOVE?

Having read this passage, which speaks so much about love, it is well to ask ourselves, "What is love?" Love between a husband and wife is physical attraction, it is affection, but it must be much more than this if the marriage is to be a good one.

In the Old Testament, we read of "steadfast love." The emphasis is on faithfulness, on keeping the covenant. God has that kind of love for us; we are to have it for each other. A husband and wife have made a covenant with each other; let there be determination to be faithful to those covenant promises.

The Greek language has several different words for love, three of which are used in the New Testament. *Storgē* describes natural affection for family members, *erōs* refers to sexual attraction and passion, *philia* to human affection like that of a good friend, and *agapē* to a determination to act for the benefit of the one loved. It is this last kind of love that the New Testament most often uses to describe God's love for us and the love we are to have for him and for each other.

This is the kind of love described by the word *agapē*, which the New Testament says a husband and a wife are to have for each other. It is not primarily a matter of feelings, for emotions are very changeable. It is a matter of the will, a decision, always to treat one's marriage partner for that person's benefit. It is to wake up each morning and ask yourself, "What can I do to make my spouse happy?"

Prayer　　*Father, help us to be totally committed to our marriage partners. For Jesus' sake. Amen.*

Day 206　　　　　　　　　　　　　　Read Isaiah 1–2

SPOKESMAN FOR GOD

We now come to the prophets. The name means "one who speaks on behalf of another." The prophets spoke to the people on behalf of God. There are four major prophets (those who wrote long books) and twelve minor prophets (those who wrote short books). The books of the prophets are not arranged in chronological order but primarily in order of length.

Isaiah had a long ministry. He spoke primarily to the southern kingdom at the time when the northern kingdom was being overrun by the Assyrians, in the ninth century BC.

In the first chapter, he grieves over the rebellion of God's people against God, which is such an unnatural attitude, for even farm animals are attracted to their owners (1:3). They are "a sinful nation" for they have "despised the Holy One of Israel" (v. 4). The result has been a spiritual sickness affecting the whole being (vv. 5-6). Isaiah shows that God hates religious rituals that do not reflect a love of the heart. This love must be expressed by justice that prevents oppression.

But there is also hope in the message. When the call to repentance is heeded, great blessings will flow from God to his people. While the prophets addressed God's Old Testament people, there is a powerful message to us in their words. If we desire God's blessings, we must serve him from the heart.

Prayer　　*Father, help us to hate sin and to love you.*
　　　　　　For Jesus' sake. Amen.

Day 207 — Read Isaiah 3-6

WOE IS ME

The "woes" in chapter 5 are instructive to us as we seek to shape our behavior biblically. Woe to those who seek to swallow up every one else economically (5:8). Already in chapter 3, God condemns "grinding the face of the poor" (v. 15). Also in the coming day of judgment "the Lord will take away the finery of the anklets," and so on (3:18). Businesspeople must accept social responsibility, something which often does not happen even among Christians.

Woe to those who love alcohol (5:11-22). Again the message is contemporary. Woe to those who question that God is at work in human life (vv. 18-19). "Woe to those who call evil good, and good evil" (v. 20). Woe to those who are know-it-alls (v. 21).

Isaiah has a vision of God in all his majesty. He heard the angels chanting, "Holy, holy, holy is the LORD of hosts" (6:3). He cried out, "Woe is me." Before he had seen the sinfulness of others; now he sees his own sin. When he confesses that sin, God provides for forgiveness. Being forgiven, he hears the call of God to go out to be God's servant, and he responds, "Here am I! Send me" (v. 8).

We all need to realize that we are sinners. To receive God's forgiveness made possible by the blood of Christ. To hear the call to serve and to respond with a hearty yes. Has this happened to you?

Prayer   *Father, forgive us and give us grace to respond wholeheartedly to the call to service. In Christ. Amen.*

Day 208 — Read Isaiah 7–9

MESSIANIC PROMISES

Throughout the Old Testament, a number of passages speak of a great deliverer whom God will send. They promise that the Messiah will come to save his people. From the perspective of the New Testament, we see many such passages in Isaiah.

Many messianic promises have a twofold fulfillment, one in the days of the prophet or shortly thereafter and the second in Jesus Christ. God gives wicked King Ahaz a sign that a young woman will bear a child, and before the child grows up, the prophecy made through Isaiah will be fulfilled. But a much more important fulfillment is in the virgin birth of our Lord Jesus Christ. He will be called Immanuel, which means "God with us."

The northern province of Galilee was not an illustrious place, but the promise is that there "a great light" will shine. There was no greater light in the world than Christ, who grew up and had a great ministry in Galilee.

The promise is that a child will be born who will be called "Wonderful Counselor." What wonderful advice Jesus gives us. He will be called "Mighty God" and we now know that Jesus is truly man and truly God. "Of the increase of his government and of peace there will be no end" (9:7). Jesus is King of the kingdom of God, which shall continue forever.

Prayer — *Father, we thank you that the wonderful promises of the Old Testament are fulfilled in Jesus. In his name. Amen.*

Day 209   Read Isaiah 10–13

SOVEREIGN OVER THE NATIONS

God used Assyria to punish Israel. But the king of Assyria did not realize he was a tool in God's hands. He was filled with "arrogant boasting" and "haughty pride" (10:12), an attitude which God hates. He thinks he can destroy Jerusalem as he has destroyed Samaria, but God says he is mistaken.

In 10:20 an important concept is introduced, that of "the remnant." Although the majority of God's people may be unfaithful, God will always maintain a small faithful group whom he will protect.

In chapter 11 are more messianic promises. The Spirit rested on Jesus (11:2) when he was baptized, and he showed "wisdom and understanding" throughout his ministry. But in 1 Peter 4:14, Peter says that this will also be true of Christians. *Messiah* or *Christ* means "the Anointed One," and to be a Christian is to share in the anointing of the Spirit who filled Christ. What a promise! What a challenge!

When the Messiah comes, the old fears and animosities will be gone (Isa. 11:6-10). Here promises of the return from the exile are mingled with promises of the coming of Christ. The Babylonians who would bring Judah into captivity will be conquered, as in fact they were many centuries later by the Persians. Here is the concept "the day of the LORD" (13:6-9). This is the day of judgment within history and at the end.

Prayer   *Father, we thank you that you have shown us clearly that you rule over the nations. In Jesus' name. Amen.*

Day 210   Read Isaiah 14-17

PRIDE GOES BEFORE A FALL

Babylon had not yet become a world power, but her downfall is here predicted. The king of Babylon will go down to Sheol, the place of the dead. He who had said, "I will make myself like the Most High" (14:14) will then be dead and powerless. Of him who had been so filled with pride, the other dead will say, "Is this the man who made the earth tremble?" (v. 16). How foolish the pride of mortal man.

Beginning at 14:24, we see how God will crush the Assyrians. Back in chapter 10, we read of the king of Assyria's "haughty pride." But Philistia better not rejoice in the fall of Assyria, for she whose champion Goliath many years before had proudly taunted the Israelites will also fall.

Moab also would be laid waste. "We have heard of the pride of Moab, how proud he was; of his arrogance, his pride, and his insolence" (16:6). The Syrians whose capital was Damascus (17:1) and the Israelites whose main tribe was Ephraim (v. 3) had teamed up against Judah back in chapter 7 where they had said: "Let us go up against Judah and terrify it" (v. 6). But both of them also will be "brought low" (v. 4). Israel was especially guilty since she knew the true God, but the prophet said to her, "You have forgotten the God of your salvation" (v. 10). The message to us is: "Walk humbly with your God." Are you doing that?

Prayer   *Father, help us to see where the sin of pride is doing damage in our lives. In Jesus' name. Amen.*

Day 211 — Read Isaiah 18–22

PRESENT TENSE, FUTURE PERFECT

Yesterday's roll of nations that will be punished by God continues. Ethiopia must also prepare for the invading Assyrians. But the time is coming (18:7) when gifts shall be brought to God by the Ethiopians. Was not the trip of the Ethiopian eunuch in Acts a fulfillment of that prophecy? According to chapter 19, Egypt also will fall before the Assyrians. But "in that day," which is a term used in the prophets to speak of the time when their prophecies will be ultimately fulfilled, Egypt and Assyria will be joined with Israel in the worship of the true God (19:24-25). This must refer to the messianic age ushered in by Christ. In the early church, Alexandria, Egypt, was a powerful center for Christianity, and over the years thousands of people living in what was then Assyria have become Christians.

But back to the immediate future in chapter 20, the Assyrians will humiliate both the Egyptians and the Ethiopians. There follows in chapter 21 further prophecies against Babylon, Edom and Arabia. Now that Isaiah has the attention of Judah, who is reveling in the thought of coming judgment upon their enemies, chapter 22 says they too will be punished. We also stand under God's scrutiny!

Prayer   *Father, we thank you that in Christ you have prepared a way to escape the judgment we deserve. In his name. Amen.*

Day 212 — Read Isaiah 24–26

THE BEST IS YET TO COME

The theme changes from individual nations to the whole world. This seems to refer to the end of history. "The LORD will lay waste the earth" (24:1). Peter tells us in the New Testament that this old earth along with the heavens will be burned up (2 Peter 3). "On that day the LORD will punish" (Isa. 24:21). The New Testament tells us that at the end of the world will come the final judgment. "The LORD of hosts will reign" (v. 23). The New Testament tells us that at the end, the Lord will usher in his kingdom in all its fullness.

"He will swallow up death forever, and the Lord GOD will wipe away tears from all faces" (25:8 ESV). The book of Revelation reflects these words as it describes the heavenly life which shall be experienced by all who have been redeemed by Christ.

"In that day this song will be sung in the land of Judah: 'We have a strong city'" (26:1). The book of Revelation speaks of the New Jerusalem where God's people will dwell forever. "Your dead shall live, their bodies shall rise" (Isa. 26:19 ESV). The New Testament tells us that at the end of the world there will be the resurrection of the dead. Yes, the best is yet to come. What is predicted in Isaiah is predicted in greater detail in the New Testament. You who are suffering, who are dealing with difficult problems, hold fast to your faith; the best is yet to come.

Prayer *Father, may our assurance of future glory give us the courage to deal with our problems today. In Christ. Amen.*

Day 213 — Read Isaiah 27–29

PUNISHMENT AND SALVATION

As with many passages in the prophetic writings, here there is mingled together a description of Israel's sin and the punishment which will result, and the salvation which will come first in the return from the exile and then in the coming of Christ.

The punishment of Leviathan may refer to the destruction of nations who oppressed Israel, and ultimately to the defeat of the beasts in Revelation representing the enemies of God's people. "In the days to come . . . Israel shall blossom . . . and fill the whole world with fruit" (27:6). Through Israel, Christ was born and has caused the fruit of the Spirit to abound in people all over the world.

Ephraim is the main tribe of the northern kingdom which is filled with drunkenness and pride and therefore will be punished by God. They will not listen to the word of the prophet sent to teach them (28:9-10), so they will have to learn the hard way, through the enemy who speaks a foreign language.

But in the midst of the prediction of trouble, there is the promise of the Messiah, "Behold, I am laying in Zion for a foundation . . . a precious cornerstone" (28:16). Ariel represents Jerusalem whose sin is that "This people draw near with their mouth . . . while their hearts are far from me" (29:13). Let us be sure we draw near to God with our hearts.

Prayer — *Father, help us to learn from the mistakes of your Old Testament people that we may serve you aright. Amen.*

Day 214   Read Isaiah 30–32

AMAZING GRACE

Woe to those who put their trust in Egypt instead of in God (30:1; 31:1). They look to horses and chariots for their salvation, but not to God. We may do something similar, although in a quite different form. So often we place our hope in ourselves or in other human beings when we should be putting our trust in God. This will only lead to sorrow.

How wonderful the grace of God! "The Holy One of Israel" said, "In returning and rest you shall be saved . . . But you said, 'No!'" (30:15), yet a few verses later we read, "Therefore the LORD waits to be gracious to you" (v. 18). "He will surely be gracious to you at the sound of your cry" (v. 19). We say "No!" to God and he patiently waits. The moment we cry out to him from the heart, "he will answer you." Amazing grace! As soon as we are ready to listen, he says, "This is the way, walk in it" (v. 21).

God calls us from our complacency (32:9). Because of it, the "populous city" will be deserted. Spiritual indifference will be costly. But that is not the end of the story. These tragedies will occur "until the Spirit is poured upon us from on high" (v. 15). God will graciously take the initiative, as he did again and again, especially at Pentecost. As a result, "My people will abide in a peaceful habitation" (v. 18). Israel's history was one of their rebellion and of God's grace.

Prayer   *Father, we praise you for your marvelous grace. Help us to show our gratitude. In Jesus' name. Amen.*

Day 215   Read Isaiah 33–35

WHAT THE KING WILL DO

In this section, the Lord is seen as King. "Your eyes will see the king in his beauty" (33:17). "The Lord is our king; he will save us" (v. 22). As king, he will carry out his judgment on evil doers. It is probably the conquering Assyrians who are in mind when Isaiah says, "When you have ceased to destroy, you will be destroyed" (v. 1). God's judgment will surely fall on all who deal "treacherously."

How contemporary the condition described in 33:8, "Covenants are broken . . . there is no regard for man." Such conduct shall not escape judgment, for we read, "'Now I will arise,' says the Lord, . . . 'The peoples will be . . . like thorns cut down, that are burned in the fire'" (33:10-12).

But the King will also bless his people. And who are his people? "He who walks righteously and speaks uprightly" (33:15). For them "the desert shall rejoice and blossom" (35:1). "They shall see the glory of the Lord" (v. 2). "A highway shall be there, and it shall be called the Holy Way . . . The redeemed shall walk there" (vv. 8-9). "They shall obtain joy and gladness" (v. 10).

The prophets never tire of telling us that God will punish the wicked and bless the righteous, urging us to turn from sin and become righteous in the only way possible, through faith in Jesus Christ.

Prayer   *Father, remind us and others that we cannot avoid dealing with you, you who are King. In Christ. Amen.*

Day 216   Read Isaiah 36–39

A PRAYING RULER

This is a historical section of the book in which Isaiah deals with Hezekiah. The Assyrians have captured Israel; they are threatening Jerusalem. The representative of Assyria taunts Hezekiah that neither Egypt nor the Lord can help.

Going to the temple, Hezekiah sends a message to Isaiah and receives the reply that God will protect Jerusalem. Receiving a threatening letter from Rabshakeh, he knows what to do with it; he lays it before the Lord and prays. He makes an appeal to God which many other biblical characters make. He points out the fact that being spared will cause all nations to know "that you alone are the Lord" (37:20 ESV). Hezekiah receives God's answer through Isaiah. God will protect Jerusalem, and he does by sending an angel who slew 185,000 Assyrian soldiers.

Sometime after this Hezekiah gets sick. He prays for healing, and God says through Isaiah that he is adding 15 years to his life. In response, Hezekiah writes a psalm of praise. But Hezekiah was far from perfect. When Babylonian envoys come to congratulate him on his recovery, he foolishly shows them all his possessions. When God says that as a result someday the Babylonians will take away those possessions, he rather selfishly rejoices that it will not happen in his own day. Let us learn from his strengths and weaknesses.

Prayer   *Father, help us to have a stronger and stronger prayer life. For Jesus' sake. Amen.*

Day 217   Read Isaiah 40–41

THE MESSAGE OF COMFORT

The first 39 chapters of the book of Isaiah were addressed to Judah prior to the captivity. They are primarily warnings that unless there is repentance, tragedy will follow. Mingled with these warnings are words of hope.

At chapter 40, there is a new emphasis. The messages are addressed to the people who have been suffering in exile. The good news is that now God is about to act on their behalf. The section begins with a note of joy: "Comfort, comfort my people, says your God" (40:1). "Behold, the Lord God comes with might . . . He will feed his flock like a shepherd, he will gather the lambs in his arms" (vv:10-11). These words were fulfilled when God brought the Jews back from exile in Babylon, but with the figure of the Good Shepherd we can see an even greater fulfillment in Christ. "In the wilderness prepare the way of the Lord" (v. 3) is quoted by the Gospel writers describing John the Baptist's ministry preparing for the arrival of Jesus on the public scene.

There is comfort because God has the power to deliver his people, for in his sight "the nations are like a drop from a bucket" (40:15). There is comfort because God's message to his people is "Fear not" (41:10, 13-14). Are you downhearted? Look to God to lift you up. He is able! Share the message of comfort with a downhearted friend.

Prayer   *Father, we praise you because you will comfort all those who look to you in sincerity. In Jesus' name. Amen.*

Day 218   Read Isaiah 42–43

SERVANT OF THE LORD

Beginning in chapter 42, the focus is on the servant of the Lord. The New Testament sees this servant as our Lord Jesus Christ. In Matthew 12:17-21, the actions of Jesus are described: "this was to fulfill what was spoken by the prophet Isaiah" (ESV), and Isaiah 41:1-4 is quoted by Simeon and twice by the apostle Paul. Jesus Christ is the great Servant of God who acts to deliver God's people.

But interestingly, the servant concept is also referred to Israel, who failed so miserably in that role that the prophet said, "Who is as blind as my dedicated one, or blind as the servant of the LORD?" (42:19). In spite of God's gracious dealings with Israel, "yet you did not call upon me, O Jacob; but you have been weary of me, O Israel . . . You have burdened me with your sins" (43:22, 24).

Yet now God has chosen to act graciously to his servants who have failed him. "I, I am he who blots out your transgressions for my own sake, and I will not remember your sins" (43:25 ESV).

Israel was to be God's faithful servant, a witness to the nations of his greatness. But she had failed again and again. Yet from within Israel, God brought forth his Son Jesus Christ to be the Savior. Now we Christians are called to be the faithful servants of the Lord.

Prayer   *Father, we praise you for your grace shown so wonderfully in your Son Jesus Christ. In his name. Amen.*

Day 219   Read Isaiah 44-45

GOD USES HUMAN INSTRUMENTS

God promises that the Jews will be brought back to Jerusalem. But the Jews must realize that only God can do this, not the idols they had worshiped in the past. Again and again, God affirms that he is the only God. "I am the first and I am the last; besides me there is no god" (44:6). "I am the LORD, and there is no other" (45:5-6, 18). Idolatry is ridiculed; a man cuts down a tree, uses part of the wood to warm himself and another part to make an idol: "Shall I fall down before a block of wood?" (44:19).

God will bring his people back to Jerusalem, but he will do it through a pagan king who does not even know him. That pagan king was Cyrus the Persian who conquered the Babylonians through the power given him by God.

The passage ends with a call to all nations to turn to God to be saved. There the Lord said concerning himself, "To me every knee shall bow, every tongue shall swear" (45:23). The fulfillment in Christ is an evidence of Christ's deity. Of him Paul said "that at the name of Jesus every knee should bow, in heaven and on earth and under the earth, and every tongue confess that Jesus Christ is Lord" (Phil. 2:10-11).

God has a great plan to redeem his people through Jesus Christ. He uses human instruments to bring that salvation to people across the world.

Prayer   *Father, we bow before Jesus Christ and confess that he is Lord and ask that you use us as your instruments. Amen.*

Day 220   Read Isaiah 46–49

ISAIAH AND REVELATION

Many things can be said about this passage, for example, the repeated use of the words "Listen to me," which remind us how important it is to hear and obey God, and the constant refrain "Thus says the Lord," reminding us that this is not the word of human beings but the Word of God. But let us focus on the constant use of this passage in the book of Revelation.

Isaiah 47:8-9 quotes Babylon as speaking haughtily of her security and then predicts that she will fall with great suddenness. Revelation 18:7-8 reflect similar words regarding Babylon, which in the book of Revelation is probably a code word for pagan Rome. Nations filled with great pride may persecute God's people, but God will bring them down to destruction.

In Isaiah 48:12, the Lord says that he is the first and the last, and in Revelation 1:17; 2:8 and 22:13, these words are spoken by Jesus, again evidence of his full deity.

In Isaiah 49:10, the Lord promises that his people will no longer be hungry or thirsty or scorched by the heat, and very similar words are used of God's people in heaven in Revelation 7:16.

Isaiah 49:13 calls upon the heavens to rejoice because God is freeing his people and wreaking havoc upon their oppressors, and Revelation 12:12 and 18:20 do the same thing.

Prayer *Father, we praise you that the Old and New Testament alike tell of your power in rescuing your people. Amen.*

Day 221 — Read Isaiah 50–52

ISAIAH AND PAUL

When Paul said, "Who shall bring any charge to God's elect? It is God who justifies" (Rom. 8:33), he was reflecting the words of Isaiah 50:8-9: "He who vindicates me is near. Who will contend with me? . . . Behold, the Lord God helps me; who will declare me guilty?" Both teach the truth that if God accepts us, no one can condemn us.

In Romans 10:15, when Paul was speaking about the necessity of preaching the gospel, he said, "How beautiful are the feet of those who preach good news!" He was quoting Isaiah 52:7 where the prophet is rejoicing in the fact that the good news of their deliverance is being brought to the exiles.

In Isaiah 52:11 the prophet is urging the Jews to take advantage of the offer to return from the exile by saying, "Depart, depart, go out from there; touch no unclean thing" (ESV). Paul uses these words to urge Christians to make a clean break with the practices of the unbelievers around them in 2 Corinthians 6:17.

In Romans 15:21, Paul loosely quotes Isaiah 52:15, which says, "For that which has not been told them they shall see, and that which they have not heard they shall understand" as a reason why he goes to preach the gospel of Christ where it has never been heard before.

One of the reasons Paul is able to quote from Isaiah often is because the Holy Spirit showed Isaiah so much about Christ.

Prayer — *Father, we rejoice that both the inspired prophet Isaiah and the inspired apostle Paul tell us of Jesus Christ your Son, our Savior. In his name. Amen.*

Day 222 — Read Isaiah 53–55

THE SUFFERING SERVANT

Isaiah 53 is the highlight of the book of Isaiah, for with remarkable foresight and even detail it describes for us the substitutionary atonement of Jesus Christ, which is the basis for our salvation.

Indeed Jesus came as "a root out of dry ground," for the Judaism of his day, dominated by Phariseeism, was spiritually sterile. "He was despised," both in being rejected by the majority of his generation and especially in being crucified on the cross, a form of the death penalty considered worst of all by Jew and Gentile alike.

But above all, he was wounded for our transgressions, he was bruised for our iniquities; upon him was the chastisement that made us whole, and by his stripes we are healed. In our place, Christ suffered the punishment for our sins, so that we might be "made whole" and "healed" spiritually.

The story does not stop with Christ's death. "He shall see the fruit of the travail of his soul and be satisfied" (53:11). Christ is in heaven rejoicing as he sees the result of his atonement: people from all nations trusting him and experiencing eternal life.

The atonement making salvation possible, the invitation goes forth to accept what Christ offers. "Come, everyone who thirsts" (55:1 ESV). That message will be successful, for "my word . . . shall accomplish that which I purpose" (v. 11). Spread the word about Christ.

Prayer — *Father, we praise you that Jesus was willing to suffer so that we might have eternal life. In his name. Amen.*

Day 223 — Read Isaiah 56–59

PREACH ABOUT SIN

God said to Isaiah, "Declare to my people their transgression" (58:1). Sin is taken so lightly today. God wants pastors to preach against sin so people may repent and avoid the tragic consequences of disobedience. To preach against sin, using the Bible as our guide, is therefore an act of love.

One great sin is injustice. "The LORD saw it, and it displeased him that there was no justice" (59:15). God is not only concerned about personal sins; he is also concerned about social sins. Being a God of justice, he demands justice. We must cry out against the unfair treatment of oppressed people everywhere.

God is also concerned about sins regarding worship. Failure to worship, failure to spend time in his house with him, to use Sunday for pleasure instead, is sin. "If you turn back . . . from doing your pleasure on my holy day, and call the Sabbath a delight . . . then you shall take delight in the LORD, and . . . I will feed you" (58:13-14 ESV). But God hates worship by those who do not treat others justly. "Is not this the fast that I choose: to loose the bonds of wickedness . . . to let the oppressed go free . . . to share your bread with the hungry" (58:6-7). God also condemns the personal sins of drunkenness (56:12) and lust (57:5). Paul quotes from these chapters (59:7-8) when he teaches the universality of sin in his letter to the Romans.

Prayer — *Father, may pastors preach about sin and as a result people repent and avoid its consequences. In Christ. Amen.*

Day 224　　　　　　　　　　　　Read Isaiah 60-62

ZION, CITY OF OUR GOD

Zion is another name for Jerusalem, the site of the temple of the Lord. Jerusalem failed God again and again. The New Testament transfers to the church many of the things the Old Testament says about Zion. Christians therefore see the wonderful descriptions of this passage in Isaiah as applying to themselves. This is reflected in the great hymn of John Newton, "Glorious Things of Thee Are Spoken." But as seen in the book of Revelation, these glories will reach their fulfillment in the New Jerusalem, the church in its future perfect state.

God's glory will shine where previously there was darkness and all nations shall share in this light. Christ is the source of that light. In the midst of this section of Scripture there is a passage which Christ applied to himself (61:1-3) as reported in Luke's Gospel. He sees this description as his agenda "to bring good tidings to the afflicted; . . . the oil of gladness instead of mourning," and so on. But is not the church the body of Christ; is not his agenda to be ours? Are we not to continue his words of grace and works of mercy? The church has great blessings, but it also has great responsibilities.

"For Zion's sake I will not keep silent, and for Jerusalem's sake I will not rest, until her vindication goes forth as brightness" (62:1). Let us not rest until the church becomes all God wants it to be.

Prayer　　*Father, we rejoice in the blessings you have showered upon the church and dedicate ourselves to its work. Amen.*

Day 225　　　　　　　　　　Read Isaiah 63–66

THE COMING OF THE LORD

From the parallel language of Revelation 19:15, we learn that he who "comes from Edom" (Isa. 63:1) is Jesus Christ. The loving Savior is also the One whose wrath falls on the ungodly. He "became their Savior" (v. 8), but they "rebelled and grieved his Holy Spirit" (v. 10). Paul warns us that we must be careful not to grieve the Holy Spirit by our sin.

The plea is to "look down from heaven and see" (63:15), so that seeing, God will "rend the heavens and come down" (64:1). Throughout the history of Israel when God heard the plea of his people and saw their plight, he acted on their behalf. So it will be for us if we have a humble spirit, for the one in this passage cried out, "We are the clay and you are our potter" (v. 8 ESV). To this God said, "This is the one to whom I will look: he who is humble and contrite in spirit" (66:2 ESV). Meet God's requirements and he will keep his side of the bargain.

God wants us to cry out to him. "I was ready to be sought by those who did not ask for me" (65:1 RSV). The Lord will come, but it will be in judgment (66:15-16). When he comes he will create "new heavens and a new earth" (65:17; see 66:22). This idea is enlarged upon in 2 Peter and in Revelation. The Bible tells us that Christ comes to us in grace and judgment within history and in his final coming at the end of the world.

Prayer　　*Father, hear our cries and see our needs and come to us as we humble ourselves before you. Amen.*

Day 226   Read Jeremiah 1–2

CALLED TO BE A PROPHET

Jeremiah was clearly called by God: "I appointed you a prophet" (1:5). He made the excuse that because he was young he could not speak (v. 7). People should not choose to be pastors but rather sense that they are clearly called by God, and even more important, they must speak not their own ideas but the Word of God, which he has given us in the Bible.

Jeremiah's task was not easy. He had to call the people to God as they stood on the brink of destruction caused by their unfaithfulness to God.

As soon as Jeremiah is called, he sees a vision of an almond tree and is told that God is watching over the word he will give Jeremiah so that it will accomplish God's purpose for it. There is a play on words here. In Hebrew *shaqed* means "almond" and sounds like *shoqed*, which means "watching." A second vision soon follows, that of a caldron from the north representing the Babylonians who will soon destroy Jerusalem.

There follows a message from God in chapter 2 in which he condemns Judah because of her unfaithfulness. Her spiritual and civic leaders are especially responsible. They are soon to suffer greatly but "have you not brought this upon yourself by forsaking the LORD your God . . . ?" (2:17). This same message is addressed to us today; the nations have turned away from Christ and the results are tragic.

Prayer   Father, raise up those who will preach your Word with the power of the Spirit. For Christ's sake. Amen.

Day 227 — Read Jeremiah 3–5

SINKING INTO SIN

Sometimes the term "Israel" is used for the whole nation, sometimes for the 10 northern tribes. Here it refers to the northern tribes which had long since been taken into captivity by the Assyrians. One would think that the southern kingdom of Judah would have learned a lesson from seeing what had happened to sinful Israel. Instead she continued to sink further into sin. Now the Babylonians are advancing upon them and the call is to turn to God so that he will protect them. But Jeremiah is deeply distressed because he sees that this is not happening. In fact, sin is rampant.

A righteous person cannot be found either among the people or their leaders. Adultery has become common and therefore there will be great punishment. In the light of this fact, what is going to happen to our own nation today? People have come to believe that God will not punish evil. Are there not many people like that even in the churches today? Dishonesty had become commonplace in ancient Judah. Religious leaders preached a soothing message rather than cry out against sin and that is the way the people like it to be! Again, how contemporary!

Complacency is a great enemy of the soul. It was Jeremiah's task to rouse people from their acceptance of sin, and this is part of the task of all who would be true preachers of God's Word today.

Prayer *Father, help us to see how much you hate the sins which have become acceptable in our society. In Jesus' name. Amen.*

Day 228   Read Jeremiah 6-7

REPENT! REPENT!

Jeremiah describes what will happen in the near future. Jerusalem will be besieged because "this is the city which must be punished" (6:6). This happened later in Jeremiah's own lifetime. Again and again he said "thus says the Lord" and then described the results of the people's failure to repent.

Judah had come to believe that Jerusalem could not be destroyed because the temple was there. Jeremiah is instructed to stand at the temple and tell them that they are mistaken. Only if they will amend their ways, that is, truly repent, will Jerusalem be spared. They must execute justice, stop oppressing the weak members of their society, stop the murders which were taking place, and stop worshiping gods who in reality were no gods. Sounds like a good agenda for us today.

Instead they were stealing, murdering, committing adultery, swearing, and worshiping false gods and then going to church thinking everything would be all right. Jeremiah reminds them that although Shiloh had been the site of the tabernacle, it was destroyed. Church buildings on every corner will only be a witness against the ungodly in the day of judgment.

They worshiped the "queen of heaven," that is, Ashtoreth, the main female deity of the Canaanites. They sacrificed their children in the valley of Hinnom, which later became the name for hell (Gehenna).

Prayer   *Father, grant unto each of us a repentant spirit, a genuine sorrow for sin and a turning from it. For Jesus' sake. Amen.*

Day 229   Read Jeremiah 8–10

BROKENHEARTED PROPHET

Sometimes a prophet could see the future so clearly that he could speak of it as though it already had taken place. The false prophets are especially to blame because they keep telling the people everything will be all right when it will not be. We must, above all, preach about the love of God, but if we never mention his wrath we are false prophets. In some churches sin and punishment are never mentioned; this omission distorts the Word of God.

In spite of their evil, Jeremiah loves the people so much that he weeps continually because he sees that they are closing their ears to the message God has given to him to proclaim to them. Do we really love people so much that their sin causes us to cry, or do we look down our self-righteous noses at them? Jeremiah would like to just walk out on the people (9:2), but he cannot because he has too strong a sense of duty. So he continues to plead and plead with them, but it is in vain. Let us be just as faithful in continuing to proclaim God's Word to the world, even if we see little results.

Jeremiah ridicules idolatry in the hope that this will open the eyes of the people. "Their idols are like scarecrows . . . They have to be carried, for they cannot walk" (10:5). Millions of people who worship idols need to hear the gospel.

Prayer   *Father, may all who preach be true prophets, preaching about your love and your wrath. In Jesus' name. Amen.*

Day 230   Read Jeremiah 11–13

WHEN THINGS GO WRONG

The concept of covenant is a very important one in the Bible. In fact, the Bible is the story of two covenants, the old one with Israel and the new one with the church. Covenant describes a relationship between God and humanity. God will be faithful to his side of the relationship and he calls upon us to be faithful to our side. But Israel constantly broke the covenant; she was unfaithful to God. Occasionally she would repent, only to turn back to the same old sins her forefathers had committed. Now as a result she is in serious trouble.

To be faithful does not mean we escape trouble. In chapter 12, Jeremiah is complaining to God. The wicked are still prospering, while Jeremiah is having difficulties. Instead of comforting Jeremiah, God basically said, "You haven't seen anything yet." Still more difficult times lay ahead for Jeremiah. God does not promise that life will be easy. But he calls us to faithfulness, promising that in the end all will be well.

Jeremiah sometimes used visual aids to make his point. Commanded by God he takes his waistcloth and places it in a damp place. As a result, it becomes soiled and moldy and then he wears it as a sign to Judah that God will "spoil the pride of Judah and the great pride of Jerusalem" (13:9). The message to ancient Judah and to us today is "Be not proud . . . Give glory to the LORD your God" (vv. 15-16).

Prayer   *Father, give us grace to be faithful and humble no matter what difficulties we must endure. In Jesus' name. Amen.*

Day 231   Read Jeremiah 14–16

LIMITS TO GRACE

God is gracious and longsuffering. For centuries he had been merciful to Israel in spite of constant backslidings and stubbornness. But now the time of judgment had come. Many people would like to believe that there are no limits to God's grace, but both the Old and New Testaments tell us there are.

In spite of how terribly they had treated him, Jeremiah prays fervently for the people in the midst of a devastating drought. But God tells Jeremiah to stop praying for them. He says that even if spiritual giants like Moses and Samuel were alive to pray for them, it would do no good (15:1). God said, "I am weary of relenting" (v. 6). Over and over, God had warned that destruction was coming because of sin. Again and again, he had relented and given them one more chance. But this is it! Now destruction is coming to Judah.

The people said, "Why has the LORD pronounced all this great evil against us?" (16:10). God's answer is, "Because your fathers have forsaken me . . . and because you have done worse than your fathers" (vv. 11-12). We rejoice in the love and mercy of God. But there is a danger that we take grace for granted, that in our eyes it becomes "cheap grace" as one theologian has said. Some say, "God will forgive, that's his business." But God only forgives if there is repentance; if not, punishment will come.

Prayer   *Father, keep us from the complacent attitude that you take sin lightly. For Jesus' sake. Amen.*

Day 232   Read Jeremiah 17-19

EXILE AND RETURN

The time of punishment has come for Judah. Now the nature of that punishment is foretold; they will be taken away into exile (17:4). They often trusted in other nations to rescue them rather than in God; such behavior results in God's curse (v. 5). On the other hand, "Blessed is the man who trusts in the LORD" (v. 7). Such a person is "like a tree planted by water" (v. 8), which is an obvious reference to Psalm 1.

A sin which especially troubled the Lord was that of working on the Sabbath. Under the new covenant, we are not to keep the Sabbath in a legalistic fashion, yet we must take time to rest and worship, to commune with God and to praise him with our fellow Christians. Those who do not take such time show their lack of interest in the Lord and in his plans.

Jeremiah is taught a lesson at the house of the potter where he sees this craftsman in the process of making a vessel of clay. Part way through a flaw is discovered in the clay, so the potter crumbles up the clay and reshapes it into another vessel. So it would be with Judah. God would crumble her in exile, but that would not be the end, he would begin anew to remake her. But while people are like clay in one way, in another they are not in that they must make choices. So the call to repentance goes out once again, "Return, every one from his evil way" (18:11).

Prayer   *Father, we pray that many may repent before it is forever too late. For Jesus' sake. Amen.*

Day 233   Read Jeremiah 20–22

JUSTICE AND RIGHTEOUSNESS

Pashhur the priest, a religious ruler in the Lord's temple, should have done justice. Instead he beats Jeremiah and throws him in the stocks. Therefore he will be among those carried captive into Babylon. As a result of this painful experience, Jeremiah pours out his heart to God in anguish that he must suffer for preaching God's Word. He decides to stop, but he cannot do so. He reflects the words of Job wishing he had never been born.

At a later date, Jeremiah has a message from the Lord to king Zedekiah, "Do justice and righteousness" (22:3). To king Jehoiakim he gives a similar message: "Woe to him who builds his house by unrighteousness" (v. 13). He reminds him that his father did "justice and righteousness" (v. 15) and that, as a result, he was blessed. "But you have eyes and heart only for your dishonest gain" (v. 17).

God requires that we deal honestly with people in all our transactions with them. When we do not do so, he sees it and will not let us get away with it very long. Businesspeople should examine all of their practices. Are they absolutely honest? God cares. Those who are in government are especially responsible. Corruption is abominable in God's sight, and he will not let such actions go unpunished. This biblical truth should cause us to be honest and give us comfort that injustice will be punished.

Prayer   *Father, help us to be absolutely honest in all of our dealings with others. In Jesus' name. Amen.*

Day 234 — Read Jeremiah 23–25

GOOD AND BAD SHEPHERDS

The Lord calls the religious and secular leaders of Judah shepherds. He condemns these shepherds for failing to care for the flock properly. He then promises to act as a shepherd himself and appoint new shepherds who will care for the sheep. Such language reminds us of Psalm 23, "The LORD is my shepherd," and the words of Jesus, "I am the good shepherd." God promises he himself will be a shepherd, and this is fulfilled in Christ. In Jeremiah 23:5, the metaphor is changed. A king is promised in the future, and again it is Jesus who fulfills that promise.

In the section that follows, these bad shepherds, the false prophets, are further condemned. These men claim to speak the word of the Lord, but it is their own word. Preachers today must be tested to see if they really preach the Bible or their own ideas.

The true prophet, Jeremiah, is given a vision of two baskets, one filled with good figs, the other with bad. The people who remain in Jerusalem think of themselves as good, but Jeremiah tells them that the bad figs represent them. False prophets speak soothing words. True prophets challenge the hearers to change as God wants them to change.

Jeremiah prophesies that the exile will last for 70 years, a prediction which was fulfilled many years later when Cyrus gave Jews the opportunity to return.

Prayer — *Father, we praise you that Jesus is the Good Shepherd. Enable us to be good undershepherds. In his name. Amen.*

Day 235   Read Jeremiah 26–28

WEARING THE YOKE

The priests and the prophets decide to kill Jeremiah, but the princes come to his aid. Not so fortunate was Uriah, another prophet with a message similar to that of Jeremiah. They killed him. One is reminded of the time just before the Reformation. Hus was burned at the stake, but Luther, proclaiming the same message, survived because the German princes protected him.

Now Jeremiah is commanded once again to use visual aids. He wears a yoke, symbolizing the fact that Judah and the nearby nations will soon be brought under the yoke of Babylon. The false prophet Hananiah comes with a different message, saying that God will break the yoke of Babylon within two years. To underline his message, he breaks the yoke Jeremiah is wearing. Jeremiah's response to this is that the Lord says he will replace this wood yoke, which Hananiah has broken, with an iron one. Jeremiah further predicts that Hananiah will die within the year and he does.

We must make our message clear and vivid. The current use of various visual aids in the educational program of the church is an attempt to do just that.

The yoke reminds us of the words of Jesus that we are to take his yoke upon us because it is light. The yoke controlled the direction of the oxen; so also we are to surrender to the lordship of Christ. His yoke is light compared to the legalism of the Pharisees.

Prayer   *Father, give us wisdom to use methods which will make the message of Christ clear. In his name. Amen.*

Day 236   Read Jeremiah 29-32

BETTER TIMES AHEAD

Jeremiah writes a letter containing God's message to the exiles in Babylon. It instructs them to settle down to normal life with the promise that in 70 years the exiles will have opportunity to return. It assures them that God has a good plan for their future.

Jeremiah is also instructed to write in a book the prediction that God will restore his people. There are to be better days ahead. They are not to be afraid, for "I will save . . . your offspring from the land of their captivity" (30:10). They will pay a price for the centuries of sinning, but "I will restore health to you . . . the city shall be rebuilt" (30:17-18). Because of these promises they should rejoice.

Part of the wonders of the future will be that God will make a new covenant with his exiled people. Jesus deliberately focused our attention on this promise when he gave us the Lord's Supper and said, "This cup is the new covenant in my blood" (1 Cor. 11:25). The writer to the Hebrews quotes the entire passage, Jeremiah 31:31-34, when he writes of the new covenant which Christ has made for us (Heb. 8:8-12).

To assure the people that real estate will once again have value in Judah, Jeremiah is instructed to buy a field. The Bible is a book full of hope, giving us the assurance that the best is yet to come for those who are God's people.

Prayer   *Father, cause those who feel hopeless to fix their hearts on your promises of the good which lies ahead in Christ. Amen.*

Day 237   Read Jeremiah 33–35

KEEPING PROMISES

The siege of Jerusalem by the Babylonians has begun. Through Jeremiah, God predicts the downfall of the city but also future restoration. He assures them that the promise of a king always sitting on the throne of David and an everlasting priest will be fulfilled. Jesus is the eternal king and priest ever ruling over and interceding for his people. The promise of eternal burnt offerings is not kept literally but in a more wonderful way through the everlasting results of Christ offering himself. If a father promises a boy a bicycle and instead gives him an automobile, the promise has been kept, only at a higher level. The promises made to God's people of the Old Testament are fulfilled in a more wonderful way through Christ.

People often do not keep their promises. The Jews under siege promised to set free fellow Jewish slaves that they held as was to be done every seven years. But having set them free, they reneged and again made them slaves. Here was one more sin assuring the fall of Jerusalem.

There was a clan in Judah which had promised their father that they would never drink alcoholic beverages. They faithfully kept that promise. Therefore the Lord pointed out to Judah that while the Recabites kept their promise to their father, Judah did not keep its promises to God. Keep the vows you made at marriage and when you confessed your faith.

Prayer   *Father, assured that you keep your promises to us, give us grace to keep our promises to you and to each other. Amen.*

Day 238   Read Jeremiah 36–38

IMPRISONED FOR FAITHFULNESS

Many people have been imprisoned because of their faithfulness to God. Some examples are John the Baptist, the apostle Paul, and John Bunyan. Jeremiah suffered a similar fate.

Under house arrest, Jeremiah was commanded by God to write in a book all of his prophecies. Baruch, his secretary, read the book to the princes, who in turn told the king about it. King Jehoiakim had one of his underlings read it to him, and as he did, the king took the pages which had been read, cut them up with a knife and threw them into the fire. Jeremiah was ordered by God to rewrite the book with further additions.

While trying to leave Jerusalem, Jeremiah was thrown in prison, accused of deserting to the enemy. The king had him moved to the court of the guard. Later, however, he was thrown into a cistern where he lay in the mud. An Ethiopian eunuch, a black man, showed him kindness by having him pulled out of this pit and placed back in the court of the guard where he remained until the fall of Jerusalem. There the king conferred with him secretly and once again Jeremiah urged him to surrender to the king of Babylon, which in this case was the will of God. If he didn't, he and his family would be captured and the city would be burned.

God calls upon us to be faithful to him, whatever the cost. In our culture that cost may be more subtle.

Prayer   *Father, we pray for all those who are being persecuted for their faithfulness. In Jesus' name. Amen.*

Day 239   Read Jeremiah 39–43

THE FALL OF JERUSALEM

The day had come. Before this some Jews had been taken to Babylon. The Babylonian king had controlled Judah, but now the final blow was the destruction of Jerusalem. Zedekiah had his eyes put out and was taken to Babylon. Only the poor remained in the land, and with them Jeremiah.

Jeremiah was treated well by the Babylonians. He could go to Babylon or stay anywhere in Judah he chose. He decided to stay with Gedaliah, who had been appointed governor by the Babylonians. A fascinating archeological discovery throws light on this event. In 1935, in the ruins of Tell ed-Duweir were found letters written from Lachish before it was destroyed. This happened at the time we are now considering. Among them was found an inscription, "Belonging to Gedaliah, the one who is over the house."

Gedaliah was assassinated by Ishmael, one of his chief officers, who was forced to flee after most of his soldiers abandoned him when Johanan prepared to attack them. Johanan's people asked Jeremiah to pray for them and inquire from God what they should do. God commanded them not to go to Egypt but live peacefully in Judah. Having asked God's advice, they proceeded to do just the opposite and went down to Egypt, forcing Jeremiah to go with them. Let us seek God's will through Scripture, prayer, and godly advice and then do it.

Prayer   *Father, cause us to understand your will as we study Scripture and to do your will. In Jesus' name. Amen.*

Day 240   Read Jeremiah 44–45

REFUSAL TO REPENT

Jeremiah is with the remnant of Jews who fled to Egypt. God reminds them that their forefathers had continued in sin although he had sent one prophet after another to call them to repentance. Now that they are in Egypt they are continuing to worship idols, and therefore he will continue to punish them.

The reply of both the men and the women is that they intend to continue in their idolatry no matter what the Lord's prophet says to them. They will continue to burn incense to the queen of heaven (Ashtoreth, whose worship was accompanied by acts of immorality). Therefore the Lord says through his prophet that he will punish them because Nebuchadnezzar will invade Egypt.

This occurred at the Egyptian city Tahpahnes which was excavated in 1886. The palace where Jeremiah was told to hide the stones in chapter 43 was discovered there. Nebuchadnezzar invaded Egypt 18 years after Jeremiah's prediction, and inscriptions tell that he carried Jews captive from Tahpahnes.

In chapter 45, God addresses Jeremiah's secretary, Baruch, who evidently had some unwise ambitions, for God says to him, "Do you seek great things for yourself? Seek them not" (v. 5). God promises to protect him, but rebukes his pride. The Christian is not to seek his own ambitions but to seek God's will.

Prayer   *Father, ever give us a humble and repentant spirit,*
           looking to you for daily blessings. In Christ's name. Amen.

Day 241 — Read Jeremiah 46–48

LORD OF THE NATIONS

The prophets are very sure that God is not only the Lord of the individual but also of the nations. Here Jeremiah receives messages from God concerning the nations which surround Judah.

The first message is about Egypt, the nation in whom Judah often put her trust, rather than trusting God. Egypt will be defeated by the Babylonians who will later invade their land. This event is seen as "the day of the Lord" (46:10), a phrase used especially by the minor prophets to describe God's judgments both within and at the end of history. Through the prophets, the Lord would often give descriptive names to people. Here Pharaoh is called "Noisy one who lets the hour go by" (46:17). Let us be sure that our use of our time will be such that this will not describe us. Having spoken of the downfall of Egypt, Judah is assured that while other nations will come to an end, she will not, a promise which is fulfilled in the church being the new Israel.

The Philistines are also told that they will fall to the Babylonians, described as "waters . . . rising out of the north" (47:2). Moab will also fall "because you trusted in your strongholds and your treasures" (48:7) and "because he magnified himself against the LORD" (v. 26). Historical events are seen to be the results of attitudes toward God.

Prayer — *Father, help us to see that you are Lord both of the individual and of the nations. In Jesus' name. Amen.*

Day 242   Read Jeremiah 49–50

THE SIN OF PRIDE

Throughout the Bible God condemns sexual sins. But he condemns one sin even more vigorously. It is the sin of pride. Jeremiah continues to receive messages from the Lord regarding the fall of nations. In most cases the fall is traced to the sin of pride.

In the condemnation of the Ammonites we find these lines, "Why do you boast . . . O faithless daughter, who trusted in her treasures, saying, 'Who will come against me?'" (49:4). Boasting and trusting in one's possessions are expressions of pride. God hates pride. Again and again Scripture says that God will bring down the proud and lift up the humble.

In the case of Edom, God speaks of "the pride of your heart" (49:16). One reason for Edom's pride was her geographical position, "you who live in the clefts of the rock." Petra, their capital, was literally carved out of the face of a cliff, which seemed impregnable from a military viewpoint. But this will not help them because God has set his face against them. "'I will bring you down from there,' says the Lord."

Kedar refers to the Bedouins who lived in the Arabian desert. Their fall will also come because of their smug complacency. For Kedar is described as "a nation at ease, that dwells securely" (49:31).

While Babylon was used as God's instrument to punish the other nations, she too will be punished.

Prayer   *Father, help us to see our areas of pride and by your grace to be truly humble. In Jesus' name. Amen.*

Day 243   Read Jeremiah 51–52

BABYLON IS FALLEN

Chapter 51 continues the theme that Babylon also will fall because of her pride. "I am against you, O proud one, says the Lord God of hosts" (50:31). Her fall is also linked to her terrible treatment of Jerusalem. She was God's instrument in the fall of Jerusalem, but she will be punished because her own motives were sinful.

The Medes are predicted to be the instruments of God in bringing about the fall of Babylon, and the Medes and the Persians did conquer Babylon the night that Daniel interpreted the handwriting on the wall to the king of Babylon.

Babylon is a symbol of the sinful world in the New Testament. Here Jeremiah tells the Jews to leave Babylon because she will be destroyed. In 2 Corinthians, Paul uses similar language to tell Christians to separate themselves from the sinfulness of the world.

The book of Revelation picks up this language telling of the destruction of Babylon referring to the fall of Rome, which is probably called Babylon in Revelation because to use the name Rome would endanger Christians who had the book.

Chapter 52 is a historical appendix showing that Jeremiah's predictions of the fall of Jerusalem came true. We can be sure that God's word to us will also come true.

Prayer   *Father, we thank you for the assurance that nations which oppress others today will also be punished. Amen.*

Day 244   Read Lamentations 1–2

WEEPING OVER JERUSALEM

The book of Lamentations consists of five poems which are traditionally attributed to Jeremiah after the fall of Jerusalem. Four of the poems are acrostics, that is, they have sections starting with the 22 letters of the Hebrew alphabet consecutively.

Great sorrow is expressed at the condition of Jerusalem, although it is recognized that this is the fault of the inhabitants. In part of the poetry, Jerusalem herself is speaking. While the words "Is it nothing to you, all you who pass by?" (1:12) refers to the city, one cannot help but think that such must have been the thoughts of Jesus as he was being crucified. One tradition states that Jeremiah wrote while sitting at the foot of the hill that later became Calvary.

Although the actual destruction was carried out by Babylonian soldiers, the second poem pictures this as the action of God carried out because of his anger at the sin of Jerusalem. The question is asked of Jerusalem, "Who can restore you?" (2:13). The answer given elsewhere by the prophets is that God will restore Jerusalem after the punishment of the 70 years of exile. But during this period repentance will come, so that the people of Jerusalem are urged to "Pour out your heart like water before the presence of the Lord!" (v. 19). Let us with a similar spirit pray for the church, that God will bring revival.

Prayer   *Father, we weep as we see error and complacency in your church. Restore her to vibrant faith. In Jesus' name. Amen.*

Day 245 — Read Lamentations 3–5

GREAT IS THY FAITHFULNESS

Jeremiah complains because of how God has treated him. Then his mood changes as he realizes that "The steadfast love of the LORD never ceases" (3:22). This new mood is expressed in words which form the basis for part of the hymn "Great Is Thy Faithfulness." Then he uses words which are the basis for part of the prayer in the Funeral Service in the Liturgy of the Reformed Church in America, "He does not willingly afflict or grieve the sons of men" (v. 33).

This renewed realization of God's goodness, even when we cannot understand his dealing with us, inspired a call for self-examination and a return to God (3:40). As he thinks of the past, Jeremiah remembers how he was cast into the muddy pit (v. 53) but also how God rescued him. He cannot forget the terrible famine in Jerusalem in the last days of the siege (4:4, 9-10). He again sees this tragedy as the result of the sins of the spiritual leaders (v. 13). As he considers what caused the downfall, he focuses on the sins of their forefathers (5:7), but later realizes that their own sins had been the major cause (v. 16).

He concludes with a reminder that the Lord is on the throne and therefore with the pleas "Restore us to yourself, O LORD, that we may be restored" (5:21 ESV). May our desire also be that the Lord will once again fill the church with vitality.

Prayer — *Father, work by your Spirit in your church that it may be filled with new life in Christ. In his name. Amen.*

Day 246   Read Ezekiel 1-3

CALLED TO BE A PROPHET

Ezekiel was part of a group of Jews taken into exile in Babylon about 10 years before the fall of Jerusalem, so that his ministry is in Babylon at the same time Jeremiah is serving in Jerusalem. Near Babylon he has a great vision of the glory of God. A passage such as chapter 1 is called apocalyptic literature. It is a great message from God expressed in symbolic language intended to give a vivid impression of truth which cannot be fully comprehended by the mind. Historical sections of the Bible must be taken literally, but to take literally apocalyptic passages is to miss the great truth portrayed. Truly God is beyond description in human words, which in part is why Ezekiel is overwhelmed by this vision.

Being confronted by such a great God, Ezekiel falls down in worship and then hears the call of God to be his prophet. He is forewarned that he can expect great opposition because the people are a rebellious people. He is given his message in the form of a book which he is to eat. This may indicate that he must digest his message so that it becomes a part of himself. He is to speak God's message faithfully whether the people listen or not. Further preparation for his ministry is that he must sit among his people.

God has given us a message, the gospel of Christ. We are to discern and sense where people are in order to proclaim that message effectively.

Prayer   *Father, cause all Christians to sense the call of sharing in the proclamation of the gospel. In Jesus' name. Amen.*

Day 247   Read Ezekiel 4–7

GETTING ATTENTION

We must never seek to draw attention to ourselves. John the Baptist is our example here. He pointed away from himself to Christ. But God wants us to draw attention to the message he has given us. It is so important that people listen, that sometimes extreme means must be taken.

Ezekiel is commanded to exhibit some strange behavior so that the Jews in Babylon will realize that their complacent attitude in thinking that soon the exile will be over may be removed. Ezekiel is to make a crude model of Jerusalem, showing it under a long siege. He is to eat bread and water baked by the kind of fuel that will make it ritually unclean to make vivid the terrible famine in Jerusalem which will occur as a result of the siege. He is to shave off his hair, burn part of it, strike part of it with a sword and blow the rest away to show the varied tragic fates which will befall the inhabitants of Jerusalem.

Then Ezekiel is to prophecy against the mountains of Israel where the people had built idols to false gods, which was the cause of this terrible suffering. Because of all this sin will come "Disaster after disaster!" (7:5). The purpose of all of this is "They shall know that I am the LORD" (v. 27). Because God loves people, he will get their attention so they may hear the message to repent.

Prayer   *Father, please work by your Spirit so people will hear the message to repent and believe. In Jesus' name. Amen.*

Day 248   Read Ezekiel 8–12

GREATER ABOMINATIONS

Ezekiel is given a vision which transports him to Jerusalem so that he may see what great evils are being committed there. Then he will understand that the Lord must punish these things which are abominations in his sight.

God shows Ezekiel one scene of wickedness after another, in each case saying, "You will see still greater abominations" (8:6, 13, 15). People today say, "How could God punish people? Is he not a God of love?" But they fail to realize how abominable sin is in the eyes of a holy God. Right in the temple, the leaders of Jerusalem were worshiping the ugly idols of the pagan nations. In some cases, they were doing it in the dark, saying, "The LORD does not see us" (8:12). God will not be mocked, either by ancient people or by our culture. Much that is happening in our society today is an abomination in the eyes of a holy God.

Because of all of this, Jerusalem was bound to fall. But what about our present civilization? One could make a long list of those things which are abominable in the sight of God, practices for which people make all kinds of excuses. Can a holy God just ignore these things? Scripture here and in many other places tells us that he will not. Yet there is always the message of hope. "I will give them one heart, and put a new spirit within them" (11:19).

Prayer   *Father, work mightily in many hearts that people may turn from the abominable to the good. In Jesus' name. Amen.*

Day 249 — Read Ezekiel 13–16

FALSE, HYPOCRITICAL, AND UNFAITHFUL

Today the emphasis is on positive thinking, and there is much to be said for having a positive outlook when one has true faith in Christ. Trusting in the sovereign Lord, we ought to be optimistic. But there is much emphasis on the negative in the Bible also. It describes the tragic results of sin vividly so that people will be strongly motivated to turn away from sin.

The true prophets were always battling the false prophets. The false prophets encouraged the complacency of the people. They lulled them to sleep spiritually. So it is today when preachers give people the hope of salvation even though they have not turned in wholehearted faith to Christ as their Savior. The true prophet prods the conscience and makes people feel uncomfortable regarding their sin. So it must be with the true preachers of God's Word today.

In chapter 14, certain people who were worshiping idols came to Ezekiel rather hypocritically to inquire of the Lord. Regarding such people, God's word was, "I will . . . cut him off from the midst of my people" (v. 8). So it will be with hypocritical people today also.

Chapter 16 compares Jerusalem to a bride whose husband lavished luxury upon her. Yet she became a prostitute. But the relation of God's people to himself is so personal that no rivals can be tolerated.

Prayer   *Father, help us to see any falseness, hypocrisy, or unfaithfulness in our lives and change them. In Christ. Amen.*

Day 250 — Read Ezekiel 17–19

TWO EAGLES AND A LIONESS

Ezekiel is given a riddle by the Lord. An eagle representing Babylon came to a cedar tree and took the top twig representing Jehoiachin, king of Judah, and carried it away. He then takes Zedekiah and plants him and he becomes a vine. The vine then turns to a second eagle, Egypt, and in doing so breaks his covenant with Babylon. God is so opposed to someone not keeping a covenant that he will punish Zedekiah for doing so. Let us make sure we keep the vows we make (especially with our spouses and with God). God will not take it lightly if we fail to do so.

Chapter 18 deals with blaming parents for one's behavior. While parents have great responsibilities, each person is responsible for the decision that he or she makes about how to live life, regardless of how parents have acted. Environment, especially home environment, is an important factor in life, yet each person must choose to act as God wants us to act, and not make excuses.

In chapter 19, we find a poem lamenting the fate of the last kings of Judah. The lioness is Judah who has mothered these kings. Human institutions seem to carry within them the seeds of their own destruction. We, too, are to lament the tragic results of sin which we see in our present society. But we must do more than this. We must proclaim, as did Ezekiel, the solution: returning to the Lord our God.

Prayer — *Father, help us to see where we are making excuses for our behavior and to accept responsibility. In Jesus' name. Amen.*

Day 251   Read Ezekiel 20–21

HISTORY OF GOD AND HIS PEOPLE

The elders come to Ezekiel inquiring of the Lord, but instead of giving them an answer, he gives them a history lesson and recounts the way God dealt graciously with Israel, despite how Israel responded with unfaithfulness. This approach, recounting the history of God's dealing with his people, is very common in the Bible.

    We should consider the history of the church. God called into being the church. He built it upon the foundation of Christ. But, in a few centuries, the church departed from sound doctrine and from godly life. God produced a great Reformation, under the leadership of Luther and Calvin. This led to the establishment of the Protestant church based on three principles: (1) The Bible as the final authority for faith and practice. (2) Justification by faith in Christ alone as the way to be right with God. (3) The universal priesthood of believers, the recognition that clergy and laity alike have privileges and responsibilities. Since the Reformation, much of the Protestant church has drifted from these principles.

    But God is not interested in just teaching us history. He wants us to realize that in our generation we are responsible to be faithful to him. He will be faithful, but we must be obedient. Let us each do what we can to make the church as biblical as possible.

Prayer   *Father, we rejoice in your faithfulness in dealing with your people. Help us to be faithful also. In Jesus' name. Amen.*

Day 252   Read Ezekiel 22–24

GOD OUR HUSBAND

Having named and condemned the sins of Jerusalem once again, God compares Jerusalem and Samaria, the capitals of Judah and Israel respectively, with two sisters. They were God's "wife" so to speak, but they both behaved like prostitutes. They should have had an exclusive relationship to God, but instead they built intimate relationships with other nations in whom they put their trust along with idols. This was a matter of spiritual adultery which would lead to terrible punishment.

Physical adultery has not only become widespread in society today, but increasingly acceptable. God's Word makes it clear that such behavior will never become acceptable in his sight. Marriage is a covenant between a man and a woman, which the New Testament compares to the relationship between Christ and his church. Faithfulness to the covenants we make is strongly emphasized in Scripture. The church must make it clear to its members that sexual immorality will not be tolerated by God. Those who break God's commandments pay a high price.

But spiritual adultery is a more serious sin. The church is the bride of Christ. We are to be faithful to him as he is faithful to us. To allow other things to take the central place in our hearts which only he should have is spiritual adultery. There is a high price to be paid for such sin.

Prayer   *Father, we thank you for the intimate relationship we have to you. Help us to be faithful. In Jesus' name. Amen.*

Day 253   Read Ezekiel 25–28

LORD OF THE NATIONS

While the message of the prophets was primarily addressed to their own people, they also had a message regarding other nations, for they knew that their God was sovereign over the whole world. The prevalent idea of the time was that each nation was ruled by a different god, but the prophets knew there was only one God, who controlled all nations.

Ammon, Moab, Edom, and Philistia had rejoiced at Judah's downfall at the hands of Babylon. They were told they would suffer the same fate. The nationalistic spirit prevalent in our world causes nations to rejoice when something bad happens to another nation. We Christians know that the people of all nations are precious human beings each created in the image of God. We are to have compassion when some difficulty befalls them, and to do what we can to help.

A much lengthier message is directed toward Tyre, a city located about 60 miles northwest of Nazareth. Tyre had a prominent place in Mediterranean shipping. Here we find the prediction of the Babylonians laying siege to her and thus overthrowing her proud king as well as Sidon, a city 20 miles to the north.

The final word is that, although the neighboring countries will disappear, Israel will be restored. The Jews did come back to Jerusalem and formed the basis for the church.

Prayer   *Father, as sovereign ruler of the nations, graciously grant us peace in our day. In Jesus' name. Amen.*

Day 254   Read Ezekiel 29-32

THE FALL OF EGYPT

Throughout its later history, Israel was caught between two major world powers, Egypt, to its southwest and to its northeast first Assyria, then Babylon, and finally Persia. At this time, Babylon is pressing hard upon Judah, and the temptation is to trust in Egypt rather than in God. This section shows that Egypt was a poor ally, and will fall before Babylon.

It looks to the secular historian that little Israel is in the hands of the mighty nations around her, but the prophet sees that these nations are in the hands of the Almighty God of Israel. Here we find six messages predicting the downfall of Egypt. The prediction is that she will no longer be a world power, a prediction which came true. In fact, all the mighty nations around Israel have lost the great prestige they once had.

Today, the church stands in the midst of mighty nations. We make the mistaken assumption that these world powers will always be at the center of history. But the lessons of history, especially as they are interpreted in the Bible, should make us realize that nations rise and fall. The church seems unimportant perhaps, but when all nations have perished she will still be at the center of God's plan.

Israel failed to be true to its calling as she stood in the midst of the nations. The church must be sure to be salt and light to the world around it.

Prayer   *Father, may the church make a greater impact on society as it proclaims and lives the gospel of Christ. In his name. Amen.*

Day 255   Read Ezekiel 33-34

RESPONSIBILITIES OF LEADERSHIP

The prophet was like a watchman or sentinel who must warn of impending danger. So the prophet must warn people to flee from the wrath of God. If he does so and the people do not heed, their blood is on their own heads; but if he fails to warn them, he stands guilty. Today, the preacher stands in the place of the prophet. He has a serious responsibility. May all pastors so carry out their duties that their people "will know that a prophet has been among them" (33:33).

The shepherds were the prophets, priests, and princes. The prophets were false and the priests and princes were only interested in their own gain. Therefore they were condemned by the Lord. Amidst the condemnations is a wonderful promise. God will be their shepherd, "I myself will search for my sheep and will seek them out" (34:11). "I myself will be the shepherd of my sheep . . . I will seek the lost" (34:15-16).

When Jesus says, "I am the good shepherd" and when he says he will seek the lost sheep, he is proclaiming his deity. This means that we can rejoice that where human beings have failed, God has stepped in because he loves us and he will meet our deepest needs. In ourselves we are wandering sheep. We need a shepherd and that shepherd is Jesus.

Prayer   *Father, we praise you for sending your Son to meet our deepest needs. In his name. Amen.*

Day 256   Read Ezekiel 35–36

JUSTICE AND MERCY

Edom (Mount Seir) rejoices when Judah falls to the Babylonians. It thinks it might take over the land. But it receives God's justice: it falls to the Babylonians never to rise again. Israel (Judah), on the other hand, receives God's mercy. It too deserves justice, that its destruction should end its existence as it did for Edom. But instead, after a period of exile, it will be brought back to its land by the grace of God. Once again it will be fruitful and multiply.

God will do this, not because of any good in them, but in order to show the world his wonderful character (see Deut. 9:4-6). God will not only bring Judah back from exile; he will work in their hearts. "A new heart I will give you, and a new spirit I will put within you" (Ezek. 36:26). This wonderful covenant relationship will be restored: "You shall be my people, and I will be your God" (v. 28). Their land will become "like the garden of Eden" (v. 35). The return from exile fulfilled this.

God still deals with people in justice and mercy. The lost suffer the consequences of their sins, receiving what they deserve. Those who are saved, who by God's grace believe in Christ as Savior, receive God's mercy. We who are saved do not deserve to be saved. We too deserve justice, which means eternal punishment. Salvation is all of grace. Let us take no glory to ourselves but give all glory to God.

Prayer   *Father, we praise you for your mercy made possible by the atonement of Christ. In his name. Amen.*

Day 257   Read Ezekiel 37–39

ALIVE AGAIN

Judah's problem is not only that it is in exile, but much more seriously that it is spiritually dead. The deadness is emphasized by the fact that the bones are "very dry." The question "Can these bones live?" is meant to imply a "no" (37:3). Humanly speaking the cause is hopeless, but what human beings cannot do, God can do. Through the word ("prophesy to these bones") and the Spirit (the Hebrew *ruach* can mean either "breath" or "spirit"), God causes the bones to become living people once again. God causes people who are spiritually dead to become spiritually alive. What a miracle!

The referral is to what God will do in bringing the people from exile and causing them to be much more spiritually alive than they had been for centuries. But this also illustrates the fact that God can bring from death to life. Jesus did this for Lazarus. God raised his Son from the dead. We are by nature spiritually dead, but by his Word and Spirit, God gives spiritual life to his people. At the end of the world, by his miraculous power, he will cause all who are physically dead to live again. Praise God!

God is a God who rescues his people though they do not deserve it. He did that for Judah, but on a far greater scale he does that for us today. Praise God from whom all blessings flow!

Prayer   *Father, we were spiritually dead. You have made us spiritually alive and cared for us. We praise you. In the wonderful name of Jesus. Amen.*

Day 258   Read Ezekiel 40–42

WORSHIP PERFECTED

Ezekiel describes the rebuilding of the temple. How is this to be interpreted? The perfection described indicates that most likely it symbolizes the glorious eternal state when God's people will worship him perfectly. This is apocalyptic literature, meant to leave a vivid impression upon us of truth beyond description rather than to be taken literally, at face value only. It cannot be taken literally since the renewal of animal sacrifices after the one perfect sacrifice of Christ is unthinkable.

Like the visions of heaven described in the book of Revelation, where God's glorious throne is at the center, we see here how important worship will be for eternity. The most wonderful feature is the presence of God, from whom all blessings flow. This is a description of the perfection of worship in which God's people will be involved in the new heaven and the new earth.

But the descriptions of the perfection in eternity show us how God wants things to be. We cannot bring perfection on earth, but we can see what our goals are to be. For Jesus teaches us to pray, "Your will be done, on earth as it is in heaven." God is to be at the center of our lives now. We are to rejoice in his glorious presence. Worship, both in the sanctuaries of our churches and wherever we may be, is to be very important to us. What can you do to cause this ideal to be more fully realized here and now?

   *Father, we rejoice in the perfection which will take place when Christ returns. Be at the center of our lives now. Amen.*

Day 259   Read Ezekiel 43–45

GLORY AND HOLINESS

At the beginning of his ministry, Ezekiel had seen a glorious vision of the Lord. Now at this new temple, he sees the same vision. We speak of the glory of God and we say that the "chief end of man is to glorify God and to enjoy him forever," but what does the word "glory" mean? The glory of God refers to his inherent greatness which is now manifested. It is his majestic splendor which now becomes visible. How do we glorify God? By showing to the world how great he is. Though it pales in comparison, his wonderful character must be reflected in our character, so that people will look to him and take him most seriously. Jesus says that he glorified his Father by the work he did.

Another important word mentioned here is the word "holy" which is also found throughout Scripture. God's name is holy, but it had been defiled by Israel in the past (43:7). The whole area around this new temple is to be "most holy" (v. 12). The priests are to teach the people the difference "between the holy and the common" (44:23). They are to keep God's Sabbaths "holy" (v. 24). The word "holy" in Hebrew comes from a root that means "separated." God is holy because he is separated from sin; he is completely pure. For us to be holy means that we are to be separated to God, and therefore separated from that which is sinful. In the world to come, everything will be holy; let us seek to be holy now.

Prayer   *Father, give us grace to glorify you by reflecting your holy nature in daily living. In Jesus' name. Amen.*

Day 260   Read Ezekiel 46–48

THE LORD IS THERE

In these closing chapters of the vision, the similarities to the holy city of the book of Revelation become more and more evident. Water flowing from the temple becomes a mighty river, like that of "the water of life . . . flowing from the throne of God" (Rev. 22:1). There are trees on both sides of the river in both cases, trees which bear fruit every month and have leaves with healing power. In both cases the city has three gates on each side representing the twelve tribes of Israel. Great blessings flow from the presence of God. Now fruit trees only give fruit for a short season. Yet there the blessings will be continuous, and all the hurts of life will be healed.

But the most wonderful part of this eternal reality is found in the very last words of this book, "The LORD is there" (Ezek. 48:35). And in the book of Revelation, the most wonderful thing about the holy city is the glorious presence of God and of the Lamb. The pearly gates and the golden streets are symbolic of how wonderful a place the new heaven and the new earth will be, but by far the most wonderful feature is this: "The LORD is there." As Revelation says, "Behold, the dwelling of God is with men. He will dwell with them, and they shall be his people, and God himself will be with them" (Rev. 21:3). By faith Jesus is with us now; then we shall see him face to face!

Prayer   *Father, may the assurance of future glory enable us to face the difficulties of today. For Jesus' sake. Amen.*

Day 261   Read Daniel 1–2

DARE TO BE A DANIEL

The purpose of the book of Daniel is to inspire God's people to be courageous in the face of opposition. "Dare to be a Daniel, dare to stand alone." Whatever your age, do not yield to peer pressure, but rather be faithful to the Lord. Daniel and his friends were among the first exiles. Because they were well qualified, the Babylonians decided to educate them for places of government leadership. They refused to eat the food given to them, probably because it had been dedicated to idols, but God caused them to flourish on a simpler diet.

The king had a dream that his wise men could not interpret, especially since he could not remember the dream. Daniel was given ability by God to know the dream and its interpretation. In his dream the king had seen an image with a head of gold, chest of silver, abdomen of bronze, legs of iron, and feet made of a mixture of iron and clay. Then a stone, not cut by human hands, crashed into the image, destroying it.

The head represented the present Babylonian empire, the chest the Persians who would replace it, the abdomen the Greeks, the legs the Romans, and the feet the nations into which the Roman empire was divided. During this last period, Christ came and destroyed Rome as the center of civilization, replacing it with the influence of his church.

   *Father, you know all things. We praise you for revealing to us in the Bible what we need to know. In Jesus' name. Amen.*

Day 262   Read Daniel 3–4

FAITH AND COURAGE

True faith produces courage. If we really believe that God will take care of us, we need not be afraid. The story of the three friends of Daniel is given to us as an example of that truth.

Nebuchadnezzar built a 90-foot image of gold. Calling all government officials to him, he demanded that they bow before it. If not, they would be thrown into the fiery furnace. The three friends of Daniel refused to do so. Their reply is noteworthy. They said that they knew their God had the power to deliver them and they believed he would. But even if he didn't, they would remain faithful to him, though it meant death. They not only remained alive within the flames, but were joined by One who was "like a son of the gods" (3:25).

Later the king had another dream, that a tree would be cut down and its stump would suffer. Daniel explained that this meant the king would become insane and be cast out into the fields. He counseled the king to repent with the hope that this would stall off the fulfillment of the dream. But one day the king looked over the skyline of Babylon and was filled with pride that he was the builder of so great a city. Immediately he became insane, and was cast out into the fields. When he recovered, he gave God the glory. The lesson for us is that the Sovereign Ruler of heaven and earth is our God, so what have we to fear?

Prayer   *Father, strengthen our faith so that we will have courage when we face difficulties. In Jesus' name. Amen.*

Day 263   Read Daniel 5-6

WEIGHED IN THE BALANCES

This section contains two stories which are both great literature and powerful lessons to us. Both show the sovereignty of the God whom we serve and therefore challenge us to be faithful and courageous.

The Babylonian king Belshazzar throws a drinking party for 1,000 of his officials. He gets the drunken idea that it would be fun to use the sacred vessels taken from the temple in Jerusalem as drinking mugs.

Suddenly handwriting appears on the wall written by a disembodied hand. "The king's color changed . . . and his knees knocked" (5:6). Daniel is asked to interpret the words, and they mean "weighed in the balances and found wanting" (5:27). That night the Babylonians are overthrown by Darius ushering in the Medo-Persian empire. God weighs each of us in the balances and we too are found wanting, but the righteousness of Christ is applied to those who trust in him and we are accepted by God.

Darius makes Daniel one of his chief officials. The others are jealous and pass a law that no one is to pray to anyone but to the king. Daniel courageously continues to pray to God before his open window. As a result he is thrown into the lions' den, but is unharmed. The reason is given: "because he had trusted in his God" (6:23). Trust in God and remain faithful to him no matter how difficult it may be.

Prayer   *Father, we rejoice that although we fall short, we are accepted for Christ's sake. In his name. Amen.*

Day 264   Read Daniel 7–9

VISIONS OF THE FUTURE

The rest of Daniel consists of the records of visions Daniel had. The first pictures four beasts apparently symbolizing the same empires as were represented in the image made of various metals: Babylonia, Persia, Greece, and Rome. But as in the book of Revelation, which takes much of its symbolism from Daniel, there is not only the earthly scene where God's people are in trouble, but also the heavenly scene where God rules. God is described in terms which are applied to Christ in the book of Revelation, yet another evidence of his deity. In the presence of God is the Son of Man, a name which Jesus used again and again to describe himself. As John in his Gospel said in essence, The Word was with God, and The Word was God (John 1:1).

The vision of chapter 8 tells of conflict between beasts identified as representing the Medo-Persians and the Greeks. The Greek kingdom will be divided into four parts. This happened and one of the four resulting regencies centered in Syria and another in Egypt putting the Jews in the middle. "A king of bold countenance" (8:23) probably refers to Antiochus Epiphanes, who would do great harm to the Jews.

In the vision of chapter 9, Daniel is given information which may indicate the time when Christ would come to earth. God's timetable includes the first and second comings of Christ.

Prayer   *Father, in the spirit of the New Testament, we pray*
             "Come quickly, Lord Jesus." In his name. Amen.

Day 265   Read Daniel 10-12

CAUGHT IN THE MIDDLE

Daniel is given a revelation of what will happen during the period between the Old and New Testaments, when the Greek empire will break into four parts. One part would be centered in Syria (the kings of the north) and the other in Egypt (the kings of the south). The Jews would be caught in the middle, first ruled by the Egyptian Ptolemies, then by the Syrian Seleucids. One of the Syrian rulers, Antiochus Epiphanes, would desecrate the temple (11:31). During these critical times it was important for Jews to maintain their faith and identity. "The people who know their God shall stand firm and take action" (v. 32).

In many situations we are "caught in the middle." If we really know God, know of his sovereign power, know that he calls upon us to be faithful no matter what may happen, then we too will stand firm. As we said before, the purpose of this book of Daniel is to give God's people the courage to remain faithful.

Daniel 12 tells about the length of time that the desecration of the temple will last. The final word implies resurrection. "You shall rest, and shall stand in your allotted place at the end of the days" (12:13). We grow weary amidst the struggles between the forces of good and evil. But we shall have rest, and the final word is resurrection. Trusting in God we know we are on the side which will eventually win.

Prayer   *Father, give us courage to be faithful to you in our day when the struggle is often very subtle. In Christ. Amen.*

Day 266   Read Hosea 1-5

UNDERSTANDING WITH THE HEART

Hosea is the first of the twelve minor prophets. They are called "minor," not that they are unimportant, but because they wrote short books compared to the longer ones we have been studying.

God's heart was broken by the unfaithfulness of Israel. How could he prepare a prophet to describe how he felt? God used a drastic method. He commanded Hosea to marry a wife who would prove unfaithful, leaving him to become a prostitute. As Hosea continued to love his wife but hate what she had done, he realized how God felt and he was able to represent God to the people with a heart understanding of how God felt. He knew the pain in God's heart because of the pain in his own heart. He could proclaim God's word with the deep feeling with which that word needs to be proclaimed.

If we are to represent God to people, and that is the calling of every Christian, then we must have an understanding that is far more than rational, but which is from the heart. We must try to understand how people feel and we must try to understand how God feels if we are to be effective in our calling to witness. Jesus, being truly God, understands how God feels. Being truly man, he understands how we feel. So he is the perfect communicator of God's truth to us.

Prayer   *Father, help us to understand how people feel and how you feel, so we may be effective witnesses. Amen.*

Day 267   Read Hosea 6-9

WANTED: STEADFAST LOVE

The prophecy of Hosea teaches a truth which we also find in other parts of Scripture: our relationship to God is like our relationship to our marriage partner. Both relationships are covenant relationships, requiring dependable love on both sides, a love which does not waver, but which continues in the changing circumstances of life. God says to his people: "I desire steadfast love" (6:6). But the love of Israel for God was not that kind of love at all. "Your love is like a morning cloud, like the dew that goes early away" (v. 4). Israel claimed to love God, but it didn't last long. They fell out of love, because to start with their love was not of the stubborn commitment variety, which is the only kind that works both in our relationship to God and to our marriage partner.

Therefore Israel "transgressed the covenant; there they dealt faithlessly with me" (6:7). The kind of love needed is faithful love, but Israel's was faithless. Because of their failure to be faithful to God, their lives were half-baked, "Ephraim is a cake not turned" (7:8). They acted foolishly. "Ephraim is like a dove, silly and without sense" (v. 11). The shallowness which brings a harvest of pain in the lives of so many today is rooted in this lack of faithfulness to commitment to God and to each other. "For they sow the wind, and they shall reap the whirlwind" (8:7).

Prayer   *Father, give us the strength to be faithful to our commitment to you and to each other. In Christ. Amen.*

Day 268   Read Hosea 10–14

ADVICE TO SINNERS

Sin is not just a few external actions. The basic problem is, "Their heart is false" (10:2). Sin is putting one's trust in other things rather than in God: "you have trusted in your chariots" (10:13). Sin is breaking our relationship with God: "my people are bent on turning away from me" (11:7); "they forgot me" (13:6).

God still loves sinners. Israel is his people, and though they have turned their backs on him, God has not turned his back on them or on us! Amazing grace! God says, "How can I give you up . . . !" (11:8).

God's grace demands a response. His advice to sinners is, "It is the time to seek the Lord, that he may come and rain salvation upon you" (10:12b). What is involved in seeking the Lord? "Sow for yourselves righteousness, reap the fruit of steadfast love; break up your fallow ground" (v. 12a). If you have drifted from God, this is God's word to you: "It is time to seek the Lord." Seek him by faith in Jesus Christ, realizing that true faith will motivate you to "sow righteousness." The harvest will be experiencing the blessings of steadfast love. What a wonderful relationship is built up through years of faithfulness to God. What blessings result from faithfulness year after year to a husband or a wife. We cannot enjoy the harvest if we fail to sow the right kind of seed.

Prayer   *Father, speak to the hearts of people who have drifted away from you. Bring them back. In Jesus' name. Amen.*

Day 269 — Read Joel 1–3

THE DAY OF THE LORD

The minor prophets used this term, "The day of the LORD," frequently. Joel uses it five times in this brief book. He begins by speaking of a terrible plague of locusts which has either just happened or is soon to occur. The prophets were so sure that God's predictions would come true that they sometimes spoke of the future as if it already happened.

The day of the Lord is a great day of judgment, either within history or at the end of history. This plague is a day of the Lord, a reminder that God comes suddenly in judgment, a foretaste of that ultimate judgment day which stands at the end of history.

The proclamation of the day of judgment is always a call to repentance. God will spare from the impending disaster those who come to him in the right spirit. It is not too late now, but unless action is taken at once, suddenly it will be too late. "'Yet even now,' says the LORD, 'return to me with all your heart . . . and rend your hearts and not your garments.' Return to the LORD, your God, for he is gracious and merciful" (2:12-13). Have you done so?

The fact that there is a day of the Lord demands a clear-cut decision on our part *now*, and then to live a life which proves it.

Prayer   *Father, draw many people to Christ before it is forever too late. Use us as instruments of salvation through our words and deeds. In Christ's name. Amen.*

Day 270   Read Amos 1–4

PREPARE TO MEET YOUR GOD

Amos is a prophet from Judah who is called to preach to Israel. He knows how to get attention. He begins by condemning the sins of the neighboring nations. Then he moves on to the sins of Judah. The Israelites are listening with approval. But then Amos shifts to preaching about their sins.

Their foremost sin was oppressing the poor (2:7a). Amos preaches social righteousness. He makes it clear that God condemns those who take advantage of the powerless. It is wrong to live in luxury and not try to change the system to help the poor.

The second sin was that of sexual misconduct (2:7b). Today one wing of the church calls for social righteousness while another calls for personal godliness. God calls for both.

The third sin was misuse of alcohol (2:8). Amos calls the women who live in luxury while their husbands oppress the poor, asking their husbands for a drink, "cows" (4:1). That must have gained their attention.

Because of sin, God sends national disasters, one after the other, but the refrain after each is "'yet you did not return to me,' says the Lord" (4:6, 8-11). Because of all this the prophet says, "Prepare to meet your God" (v. 12). Through Christ we are prepared, but that doesn't relieve us of responsibility for godliness.

Prayer   *Father, our only hope is in Christ, but help us also to work for righteousness in all of life. In Christ. Amen.*

Day 271   Read Amos 5-9

SEEK GOD AND LIVE

Woe to those who have an attitude of spiritual complacency, living in luxury as do so many of us but not deeply concerned about the sad condition of the church and the nation. "Woe to those who lie upon beds of ivory . . . sing idle songs . . . drink wine in bowls . . . but are not grieved over the ruin of Joseph!" (6:4-6). Amos calls for social justice. "You trample upon the poor" (5:11), "you . . . who take a bribe, and turn aside the needy in the gate" (5:12).

The evangelistic call is to turn from such a way of life and turn to God. "For thus says the Lord to the house of Israel: 'Seek me and live'" (5:4). "Seek the Lord and live" (5:6). What does it mean to seek God? Certainly it means coming to him and asking for forgiveness, but it also means living according to his righteous demands: "Let justice roll down like waters, and righteousness like an ever-flowing stream" (5:24). Are we complacently living in luxury while we are indifferent to the injustices rampant in society? Then this prophecy is especially addressed to us.

There is hope for the future. In the end the Lord and his righteousness will prevail. "The days are coming . . . when the plowman shall overtake the reaper . . . I will restore the fortunes of my people Israel" (9:13-14). The New Testament teaches that the church is the new Israel. Its future is bright.

Prayer   *Father, give us a deep concern about injustice.*
                Work mightily in areas where we feel so helpless.
                In Jesus' name. Amen.

Day 272 — Read Obadiah

WINNERS AND LOSERS

The Bible teaches that all deserve punishment, and that God graciously intervenes in the lives of some, while he allows others to continue in the way in which they choose to go and suffer the consequences. Obadiah illustrates that concept. Both Edom and Israel deserve destruction. For Edom that destruction is permanent, as they justly deserve. For Israel, there is a period of punishment, but they will be restored.

The Edomites were the descendants of Esau. They felt very secure because their capital, Petra, was a seemingly secure city carved out of the rock at the top of the cliff. "The pride of your heart has deceived you, you who live in the clefts of the rock" (v. 3). But when God opposes people because of their sin, military security is of no avail. When Jerusalem was plundered, the Edomites joined in the plunder. We must not have "an eye for an eye" attitude, but perfect justice is for people to get exactly what they have given to others. "As you have done, it shall be done to you" (v. 15). God dealt with Edom in justice in the day of the Lord about which the prophets never tired of speaking.

Not so with Israel; it also deserved destruction. But having punished it for a time, God then restored it. This was grace, undeserved mercy. So also with us who are saved by Christ: we experience grace.

Prayer — *Father, as we experience your grace, fill our hearts with gratitude. For Jesus' sake. Amen.*

Day 273   Read Jonah

DISOBEDIENT PROPHET

The Lord says to Jonah, "Go to Nineveh." How often in the Bible we hear God saying to someone, "Go." We are inclined to sit back comfortably in the status quo, but the Lord says to us, "Go, I have something for you to do; be up and doing it."

Nineveh was the capital of Assyria, a cruel nation that was a great threat to Jonah's nation. Jonah was patriotic. He knew if the Assyrians continued in their sins they would fall, but if he preached to them and they repented, God would spare them and they would remain a threat to Jonah's country. So he disobeyed.

Some people have a problem with Jonah being swallowed by a sea creature (a whale or a fish or a specially created monster) and then being spit out again. But for the sovereign God, who with one word of his power created the whole universe out of nothing, this was a little miracle. The purpose of the book is not to tell us that God could do this; we should know that. The purpose is to show us that God wants us to change some of our narrow ideas. Too often, we are only interested in our own little circle, like the man who prayed, "Lord, bless me, my wife, my two sons, us four and no more." But God is interested in the lost people of Nineveh, and of the whole world. He does not want us to be like Jonah; he wants us to go into all the world and preach the gospel.

Prayer   *Father, stretch our circle of concern to be as wide as yours and to do something about it. In Jesus' name. Amen.*

Day 274   Read Micah 1-4

POWERFUL PREACHING

The prophets were powerful preachers speaking with conviction, "Thus says the Lord." The key to that power is found in Micah 3:8, "I am filled with power, with the Spirit of the Lord, and with justice and might, to declare to Jacob his transgression and to Israel his sin." A preacher must be filled with the Spirit to preach effectively. How can this happen? Filling with the Spirit is a result of wanting to be filled and praying earnestly for such filling. It is a result of desiring more than anything else to be a channel through whom the Spirit will work. If you are a pastor, make this your heartfelt prayer, and God will use you effectively. Lay people ought to be constantly praying that their pastors may be filled with the Spirit so that there will be powerful preaching, convicting people of sin and causing them to turn wholeheartedly to Christ.

But all of God's people need to be filled with the Holy Spirit, for every Christian is called to be a witness for Christ. Pray constantly that God will empty you of self and fill you with his Holy Spirit so that your life will be a powerful sermon accompanied by the courage to speak humbly about Christ. We realize the urgency of this task in the light of God's Word to Micah, which said that sin would lead to destruction. The lost are in great peril. "Only one life, 'twill soon be past, / Only what's done for Christ will last."

Prayer   *Father, fill us with your Spirit so that our witness may have power and fill our preachers also. In Jesus' name. Amen.*

Day 275   Read Micah 5–7

WHAT THE LORD REQUIRES

Today's Scripture includes two famous passages. The first predicts that the Messiah will be born in Bethlehem. It was a passage which the Jewish Bible scholars of Jesus' day knew so well that they could tell the wise men where to find the newborn King of the Jews. It was not a prominent place. God prefers to use the lowly.

The second passage is a request to know what God wants of us. Does he want us to make many sacrificial offerings? (6:6b-7). No. Does he want us to sacrifice our children on the altar as the pagans did? (v. 7b). No.

"He has showed you, O man, what is good; and what does the LORD require of you but to do justice, and to love kindness, and to walk humbly with your God?" (6:8). If we do not live the way we should, it is not out of ignorance. God has revealed how he wants us to live. First, we are to do justice. We are not just to talk about it, we are to do it. We are to be absolutely fair in all our dealings with our immediate family and with all with whom we have any kind of dealings. Second, we are to *love* kindness. We are to be kind as we meet people in the everyday affairs of life. Beyond that, we are to love kindness. We are not to be kind so that we can get more out of people, but because we cherish that attitude. Third, we are to walk with God, humbly. We are to be conscious of his presence and realize how great he is.

Prayer *Father, as we respond to your grace, help us to live in ways which are all pleasing in your sight. In Jesus' name. Amen.*

Day 276 — Read Nahum

RESULTS OF TEMPORARY REPENTANCE

Nahum's message is that God will destroy Nineveh, the capital of Assyria, because of its sin. One hundred fifty years earlier, Jonah brought a similar message. As a result the Ninevites repented and were spared. But it didn't last long. Threatened by the preaching of Jonah, they said they would serve Jonah's God, but they soon forgot. About 60 years later, they did what Jonah had been afraid they would do: they took Israel into captivity. They were used of God to punish Israel, but they did so with unnecessary cruelty. Because their repentance had only been temporary, Nahum declares the word of God that they will be punished.

Revivals are wonderful. We need them, but they tend not to last very long. Jonathan Edwards, a leader in the Great Awakening, was pastor of a church in a town in Massachusetts. I went there to see his church, only to discover to my sorrow that it was closed for the summer. We need spiritual awakenings. Oh that one would take place in our generation. But we also need to keep spirituality alive. We need to pass a living faith from one generation to the next.

How can we pass on our faith to our children? By seeing that they have biblical knowledge. By praying for them. But especially by showing them in our own lives what it means.

Prayer *Father, give us a living faith in Christ and give the same faith to our children. In Jesus' name. Amen.*

Day 277 — Read Habakkuk

LORD, WHY?

Habakkuk was deeply disturbed. There was so much evil in his land of Judah, and God didn't seem to be doing anything about it. Do you know the feeling? "Why do you make me see iniquity, and why do you look idly at wrong?" (1:3 ESV). God's answer is that he is preparing to do something. He will soon send the Babylonians to punish Judah. "For behold, I am raising up the Chaldeans, that bitter and hasty nation" (v. 6 ESV).

"Wait a minute," says Habakkuk, "they are even worse than us. How can you do such a thing, Lord?" So now Habakkuk waits to see how God will answer that question. "I will take my stand . . . and look forth to see what he will say to me" (2:1). God's answer is, "The righteous shall live by his faith" (v. 4). We do not always see what God is doing, but we need to trust God, that he will surely do the right thing.

Habakkuk 4:4 is quoted by Paul in both Romans and Galatians to buttress his argument that we are saved, not by our works, but by trusting in Christ alone. In the Middle Ages, the church had obscured this fundamental teaching of Scripture. Many believed they would be saved by doing the good things the church told them to do. Martin Luther tried that but found that it gave him no assurance of salvation. Then he began studying Paul, and eventually realized that we are saved by faith in Christ alone. Thus began the great Reformation.

Prayer — *Father, give us assurance of salvation as we trust in Christ for our salvation and everything else. In his name. Amen.*

Day 278 — Read Zephaniah

FACING THE JUDGMENT DAY

Zephaniah also speaks about the day of the Lord, which anticipates the day of judgment that falls upon a nation within history and the final judgment day. Zephaniah emphasizes the nearness of that day. "The day of the Lord is at hand" (1:7) and "The great day of the Lord is near" (v. 14). We do not know when the final judgment will come. But there is a judgment at death which will come to each of us within the relatively few years of our lives.

How can we be ready? Zephaniah tells us how not to be ready. "At that time I will search Jerusalem with lamps, and I will punish the men who are thickening upon their lees, those who say in their hearts, 'The Lord will not do good, nor will he do ill'" (1:12). What is "thickening upon their lees"? In wine making, the lees was the solid matter at the bottom of the container. If the wine stayed in contact with it too long, it would have a bad taste. The Israelites tasted bad to God because they were complacent. They said that since God does not judge, it doesn't matter how you live.

Zephaniah also tells us how to prepare. "Seek the Lord, all you humble of the land, who do his commands; seek righteousness, seek humility; perhaps you may be hidden on the day of the wrath of the Lord" (2:3). How thankful we can be that the "perhaps" is turned to certainty through Christ. Trusting in him we can be sure we will be accepted by God.

Prayer — *Father, use us to convince others to turn to Christ so that they will be ready for the judgment. In his name. Amen.*

Day 279 — Read Haggai

GET YOUR PRIORITIES STRAIGHT

Those who returned from the exile were the cream of the crop. Those more interested in continuing their successful businesses stayed in Babylon. Those who returned did so because they had a spiritual vision, to rebuild the temple of the Lord. But soon they were faced with problems which caused them to give up on completing the building of the temple. So they settled down and built themselves houses which were increasingly luxurious. Haggai and Zechariah were two prophets sent by God to inspire them to renew their vision, to put first things first, and to get back to building the house of God rather than their own houses.

Haggai's argument is that because they had lost their vision, and centered on their own prosperity, God had withheld that prosperity from them. They had worked hard to get ahead but in vain. Haggai says this was because they did not have their priorities straight. Jesus said something similar, "Seek first the kingdom of God and his righteousness, and all these things will be added to you" (Matt. 6:33 ESV). The best way for us to prosper financially is to put God first in the use of our resources. Try it. It works.

As the temple was built, those who remembered Solomon's temple were disappointed, but the prophet assured them this temple had a great future, and it did because Christ came to it.

Prayer   *Father, give us the grace to put your kingdom first in the use of our money, knowing you will bless so we can be a blessing to others. In Jesus' name. Amen.*

Day 280   Read Zechariah 1-8

BEGINNING OF A GREAT FUTURE

Haggai and Zechariah work together to get back to the important task of building the temple. Haggai prods them by telling them that their lack of prosperity has been due to not putting first things first. Zechariah uses a different approach. He inspires them by sharing with them visions God has given him of the glorious future of the project in which they are involved. Today also, we need to be motivated to serve God with zeal. One motivation is to realize the blessings we miss by not being faithful (Haggai). Another is to realize that we are part of something great, so that we find a sense of purpose for our lives (Zechariah).

Zechariah is apocalyptic literature, like parts of Ezekiel and Daniel and Revelation. It vividly describes truths using symbolic language. The vision of four horses (1:7-8) is interpreted by the angel to teach that the Lord now promises that this is the beginning of a great future for those who are rebuilding the temple. The four horns (v. 18) teaches that the power previously used to scatter the Jews will now be used to cast down the nations who have been their enemies. The vision of the man measuring Jerusalem (2:1-2) shows that Jerusalem, at the time such a weak little city, will have a great population in the future. Though the church today may seem feeble in its efforts to make an impact on the world, it has a great future.

Prayer   *Father, inspire us to be faithful in serving Christ, knowing that a wonderful future awaits us. In his name. Amen.*

Day 281   Read Zechariah 9-14

PROPHECIES OF HOLY WEEK

Zechariah may not be a very familiar book to us, but it was to the writers of the New Testament. There are many references to Zechariah in the book of Revelation. Of even greater significance is that in the narratives of what happened to Jesus during the last week of his life on earth, the Gospel writers cite Zechariah more than any other prophet.

It begins with Palm Sunday. Jesus comes riding into Jerusalem on a donkey. Matthew and John both remind us that this happened to fulfill what is mentioned in Zechariah 9:9. Zechariah 11:12 mentions 30 pieces of silver and the Gospel of Matthew tells us that this was the amount of money given to Judas to betray Jesus. On the night before the crucifixion, Jesus himself quoted Zechariah 13:7, "Strike the shepherd, that the sheep may be scattered." Jesus refers to this prophecy in order to prepare his disciples for what will soon happen.

The Old Testament looks forward to the New, which we will begin studying in a couple of days. We needed to spend all of these days on the Old Testament in order to rightly understand the fulfillment of the plan of God in the New. The Old Testament is like a bud, the New like the flower which develops from the bud. The Old Testament says, "The Messiah is coming." The New Testament proclaims, "He is here."

Prayer   *Father, we praise you that we live in the time when the promises have been fulfilled in Christ. In his name. Amen.*

Day 282 — Read Malachi

GET READY, GOD IS COMING

This is the last book of the Bible before God comes in the person of his Son, Jesus Christ. But the people are not ready. They show that they do not take God seriously by three practices of theirs which displease him:

(1) They are bringing animals with defects to offer to the Lord. They will not give such defective animals as a gift to a government official, yet they will bring them to God although he had specifically commanded that animals offered in sacrifice to him should be without blemish (1:7-8). But are we often careless in our worship? Do we come to church with our hearts prepared? Do we give God top priority in the use of our time and our talents? Are we ready to meet God?

(2) They are breaking their marriage vows (2:14). Marriage is a covenant where two people promise to be absolutely faithful to each other. But they are not doing that. And such infidelity is probably more common today than it was in the day of Malachi. God is faithful and we are to be faithful to God and to each other.

(3) They are remiss in stewardship. God accuses them of robbing him. When they ask how they are doing this, he mentions their failure to tithe. He challenges them to give the full tithe, 10 percent of their income, and see if the Lord of hosts will not respond opening "the windows of heaven for you and pour down for you an overflowing blessing" (3:10). Try it, it works.

Prayer — *Father, prepare us for the second coming of our Lord Jesus Christ to earth. In his name. Amen.*

Day 283   Read Matthew 1–3

THE PROMISED ONE ARRIVES

New Testament means "new covenant." The Old Testament is the story of the mutual commitment between God and Israel. But Israel failed to keep its commitment. So God made a new covenant with the church, and the story of that covenant is told in the New Testament.

The New Testament begins with four accounts of the life of Christ. They are called Gospels, which means "good news." Here is the greatest news human beings ever heard. All the wonderful promises God made to his people in the Old Testament, that he would send them a great deliverer, are now beginning to be fulfilled in the arrival of his Son on earth.

The good news begins by describing the birth of a child, who turns out to be God in human flesh. He is born uniquely of a virgin. His human stepfather is told ahead of time that he will be called Emmanuel, which means "God with us." Jesus is God with us. He is not far away. He has come down from heaven to visit us to save us from our sin. The name *Jesus* means "Yahweh is salvation." We cannot rescue ourselves from the bondage of sin; salvation from sin is all of the Lord, all of grace.

The fact that Jesus comes to save not just the Jews but people from every nation is foreshadowed by the call of God to the wise men (*magi* in Greek) from a foreign land in the East to worship the King of the Jews. Wise men still seek him and worship him!

Prayer   *Father, thank you for the amazing plan for our salvation centered in your wonderful Son, Jesus. Amen.*

Day 284   Read Matthew 4–6

IN WORD AND DEED

The structure of the Gospel of Matthew is that he intersperses sections describing the actions of Jesus with those reporting his teachings. Thus Jesus reveals to us what God is like. We must tell people about Jesus in word and deed, and thus model a lifestyle which shows the world how God wants them to live.

Having been baptized as a sign that he identifies himself with the people, even though being sinless he does not need a baptism of repentance, Jesus is led by the Spirit into the wilderness to be tempted. Significantly, he answered each temptation by quoting from the Old Testament, prefacing each rebuttal with "It is written." The Spirit leads him to face these temptations ahead of time. This is a good lesson for us: before we face specific temptations, we must make our decision to say "No."

Now we turn to the words of Jesus in the Sermon on the Mount. In this sermon, he shows us how those who are saved by grace ought to live. He begins with the Beatitudes, the blessings that come to those who live their lives in the same spirit as he lived his life.

Jesus gives us a model prayer called the Lord's Prayer. Note that we are first to pray for God's glory and then make petitions that he meet our needs. Notice we are not instructed to pray for "I" and "me" but for "us" and "we." We are a part of the church, and we are to pray for each other.

Prayer   *Father, may your name be honored and may our needs be met by your grace. In Jesus' name. Amen.*

Day 285   Read Matthew 7-9

JESUS THE MIRACLE WORKER

The Sermon on the Mount concludes with the famous parable about the man who built his house on the rock and the one who built his house on the sand. This teaches that while believers are saved by Christ's atoning death, how we will face the trials of life will depend on how fully we put the teachings of Jesus into practice in our lives. Salvation is more than justification (having our sins forgiven). It also includes sanctification (growing to be more like Jesus in character and conduct) and glorification (receiving the complete victory over the results of sin in both soul and body).

Having finished preaching, Jesus meets people with special needs and solves their problems through his power. He cleanses a man of leprosy, that dread disease that not only destroyed the body but cut the sufferer off from society. He restores the servant of a centurion who was suffering from paralysis, marveling at the faith of the centurion. He takes the fever away from Peter's mother-in-law, who then gets up from her sick bed to serve him. He stills the storm when the disciples are caught in the middle of the lake in a small boat. He brings two men possessed with demons back to normalcy. He not only heals a paralytic but forgives his sins. Greatest of all, he brings a little girl back from the dead. While we are to use the means God has provided for healing, let us pray to him who alone can heal.

Prayer   *Father, through Christ, heal us of our physical and spiritual ailments. In his name we ask it. Amen.*

Day 286   Read Matthew 10–12

FOLLOWING JESUS

Jesus had hundreds of disciples. A disciple is one who learns with the desire to be like his master. Does that definition describe you? From his many disciples Jesus chose 12 to be apostles. An apostle is one who is sent forth. Put together, an apostle was a disciple who was trained to go forth with the message of his master. Today, Christians have this responsibility. Working individually and together, we are to spread the gospel. Jesus equipped his apostles by teaching and by practical experience. So it must be with us.

Jesus invites others to become his disciples. At the end of chapter 11, he said, "Come to me, all who labor and are heavy laden, and I will give you rest. Take my yoke upon you, and learn from me" (vv. 28-29). Everyone who has a burden is invited to come to Christ to receive help. One way disciples learn is by asking questions. A question the disciples had concerned the unpardonable sin. In my ministry, several people have asked me if they had committed this sin. My answer has been that they have not, because those who have committed this sin couldn't care less. It is good to be troubled by our sin, but we should then ask for forgiveness with the assurance we will receive it.

At the end of chapter 12, Jesus says that his disciples who do what he teaches are closer to him than his relatives. How close are you to Jesus?

Prayer   *Father, help us to learn from Jesus and to share what we have learned. For his sake. Amen.*

Day 287   Read Matthew 13–14

PARABLES OF THE KINGDOM

A parable is an earthly story with a heavenly meaning. Jesus uses the physical to illustrate the spiritual. The parables tell us what the kingdom of heaven is like. Jesus came preaching the kingdom. He taught us to pray, "Your kingdom come." The kingdom is the rule of God in the lives of people. The kingdom of heaven comes in two stages. When Christ came to earth, the King came; the kingdom was established. All who trust in him are citizens of his kingdom. When he comes in clouds of glory, the kingdom will come in its fullness and will last forever.

In the parable of the sower, Jesus teaches that the right response to his word is crucial, and that a response that is based on understanding will produce good fruit in the life of the hearer. In the parable of the good seed, he teaches that there is opposition to the sowing of the good seed, but in the end that opposition will be conquered. In the parable of the mustard seed, he teaches that though the beginnings of the kingdom may be small, the final results will be great. In the parable of the leaven, Jesus teaches that his influence is to permeate all of life. In the parables of the hidden treasure and the pearl of great price, he teaches that a share in the kingdom is so valuable that every necessary sacrifice must be made to see to it that we are included in the kingdom. Are you?

Prayer   *Father, we rejoice that Jesus is King; may he rule in every area of our lives. In his name. Amen.*

Day 288 — Read Matthew 15–18

PHARISEES AND FOLLOWERS

The Pharisees appear frequently in the Gospels. Their original purpose had been good. In the period between the Old and New Testaments, the great threat to true religion was the infiltration of pagan Greek culture in the life of God's people. The Pharisees emerged as first-century theological conservatives and sought to maintain the true faith. But they used the wrong method, that of emphasizing obedience to the letter of all of their traditions, so that by the time Jesus arrived on the scene they were legalistic and hypocritical. They are severely criticized by Jesus, and we are not to be like them in their faults. Rather, we are to be like the Gentile woman of humble faith (15:28). Significantly, the Sadducees, who were theological liberals in their day and the enemies of the Pharisees, yet team up with them in their opposition to Jesus.

Unlike them, the disciples are led to confess, "You are the Christ, the Son of the living God" (16:16). Jesus reveals to his followers that a true disciple must "deny himself and take us his cross and follow me" (16:24). Here is a paradox: only those willing to lose even their lives for Christ will experience what true life really is. Among his followers are those to whom he reveals himself in a special way, in the transfiguration (17:2), so that they will be able to deal with difficulties. Being a disciple involves experiencing Christ's glory but also the willingness to forgive (18:22).

Prayer — *Father, keep us from hypocrisy and help us to lose ourselves for Christ and thus experience true life. Amen.*

Day 289   Read Matthew 19–20

PRACTICAL ISSUES

Divorce is one of the greatest causes of heartache today. Jesus emphasizes the permanence of marriage, yet there are illustrations in the Gospels of his gentleness toward those who had failed in that area. On the one hand, we must do everything possible to encourage people to be faithful to their marriage vows. On the other hand, we need to minister lovingly to people who have fallen short of God's perfect will in this area of life as well as in other areas.

Children are important. The disciples tried to keep children away from Jesus, but his attitude was entirely different. He welcomed them and pointed out that unless we come to him like a child, that is, in humility and sincerity, we cannot be part of his kingdom.

Wealth can be a hindrance, preventing us from following Jesus as we should. But whether we are rich or poor, we cannot enter the kingdom in our own strength, but only by the grace of God. That grace is further demonstrated in the parable in Matthew 20:1-16. The owner of the vineyard chooses to give each of the laborers a denarius, one day's wage, what was needed for a man to feed his family. To those who worked all day he gave justice, to the rest mercy. Likewise God mercifully accepts people into the kingdom who come to him later in life as well as those who spend their whole lives serving him.

Prayer   *Father, we praise you for your grace, for it is the only hope of each of us. In Jesus' name. Amen.*

Day 290 Read Matthew 21-22

CALLING FOR A DECISION

When we proclaim the gospel, we ought always call the hearers to make a decision regarding the place Christ is to have in their lives. The actions and words of Jesus, as he entered Jerusalem for the last time, called for such a decision.

Previously Jesus had told his disciples to keep quiet about the fact that he was the Messiah. Now by riding into Jerusalem publicly on a donkey, he is openly proclaiming himself as Messiah, for all knew the prophecy of Zechariah.

When Jesus cleansed the temple, again he was challenging the people and especially their leaders to come to a decision as to who he is. The business in the temple was a racket being administered by the high priests. Jesus showed his authority when he chased out those who were doing business there. Now they either had to accept that authority or get rid of him, which they did through crucifixion.

The parable of the two sons and the parable of the vineyard were also challenges requiring the listener to make a decision about who Jesus is. The leaders realized that this was the purpose of these parables (21:45). Sad to say, they made the wrong decision. They wanted to arrest him, but they didn't dare. Instead, they tried to lead Jesus to make statements which would get him in trouble (22:15). In every case Jesus answered them wisely.

Prayer — *Father, help us to graciously challenge people to accept Christ. Cause many to do so. In his name. Amen.*

Day 291　　　　　　　　　　Read Matthew 23–25

PREDICTING THE END

As the Truth, Jesus had to tell people the truth about themselves. He called the religious leaders *hypocrites*. God hates hypocrisy, which is the opposite of genuineness. A hypocrite is different on the outside than on the inside. He makes believe he is more pious than he really is. Other people may or may not realize his hypocrisy, but even worse is the hypocrite who doesn't realize he is one himself. Having thus spoken to the religious leaders, Jesus had signed his own death warrant. Having done so, he withdrew with his disciples and taught them concerning the fall of Jerusalem and the end of the world, two events many centuries apart but having much in common.

Jesus says that certain things will happen before the end of the world. These things have now happened to a sufficient degree that Jesus could return at any time. He warns us not to set dates for the time of his return. Instead, he deliberately keeps that time hidden so that we will always seek to be ready for his coming. He tells the parable of the ten maidens to impress upon us the importance of being spiritually ready at all times.

In another parable, Jesus says that when he comes we will give account of what we have done with our opportunities to serve him. In the parable of the sheep and the goats, he teaches that when he comes we will be judged by our works, for those with true faith in him will do works which are evidence of such faith. Are you ready for the return of Christ?

Prayer　　*Father, may Jesus Christ come to earth soon and give us the grace to be prepared. In his name. Amen.*

Day 292　　　　　　　　　　　　　　　　　Read Matthew 26

NIGHT BEFORE THE CRUCIFIXION

Consider the events which take place during the night before the crucifixion:

(1) The celebration of the Passover, a symbol of belonging to God's people, and rejoicing that God had set his people free from the bondage of Egypt.

(2) The inauguration of the Lord's Supper. Jesus uses some of the elements of the Passover to provide a new symbol of belonging to God's people, a symbol which reminds us of being set free from the bondage of sin through the atoning death of Christ.

(3) The prayer in the garden. Jesus realizes the horror of the cross which he will soon endure. Being truly human, he prays earnestly that some other way be found to save God's people, but he concludes in complete surrender: "Not as I will, but as you will" (v. 39 ESV). May we also be completely surrendered to God's plan for our lives.

(4) The betrayal by Judas, who sees that Jesus is not the kind of Messiah he wants. He feels he has wasted the years in following Jesus and decides to get something out of it, 30 pieces of silver. How sad for Judas. How painful for Jesus. Be careful not to betray him.

(5) The denial of Peter. Peter had been so sure of his own allegiance, but when the pressure is on, he caves in. Yet how different from Judas; when he realizes he has done wrong, he weeps bitterly. Let us not deny our Lord; but if we do, let us weep bitterly in repentance and faith with hope. He forgave Peter. Will he not forgive you, too?

Prayer　　*Father, how grateful we are that our Lord was willing to die for us. Help us to be faithful to him. Amen.*

Day 293   Read Matthew 27–28

CRUCIFIXION AND RESURRECTION

The Jewish leaders did not have the authority to impose the death penalty, so they brought Jesus to Pilate. He tries to avoid making a decision, so he tries to get the Jewish leaders to decide, thinking they will choose to free Jesus rather than a notorious criminal. It doesn't work, so he washes his hands of the affair, which is impossible. We are responsible for our behavior.

Mistreated by the soldiers, Jesus is brought to Calvary (Golgotha). Evidently there was a group of pious Jewish women who had made it their task of love to provide a drugged drink for those about to be crucified so that the pain will not be as great. But Jesus is there to suffer for us, so he refuses the drink.

It is about nine in the morning when they crucify Jesus. At noon the sky grows strangely dark until three in the afternoon. Then Jesus cries out, "My God, my God, why have you forsaken me?" (27:46 ESV). Jesus suffered hell in our place. This was physical torment, but the sense of being abandoned by his loving Father was the worst part of the ordeal. Above all, hell is to have God turn his back on a person.

Having risen from the dead, Jesus appeared to women who had come to the tomb. Consider seriously what he says to all of his followers, including us: "Make disciples of all nations."

Prayer   *Father, we praise you for the death and resurrection of our Savior. Help us to obey him. In his name. Amen.*

Day 294 | Read Mark 1–3

THE BEGINNING OF MINISTRY

It is commonly thought that of the Gospels, Mark wrote first, under the guidance of Peter, and that Matthew and Luke took the work of Mark and supplemented it with other materials. Matthew, Mark and Luke are called the Synoptic Gospels, that is, they look at the life of Jesus from a similar perspective while John takes a different approach.

Possibly because of the impetuousness of Peter, Mark begins with the ministry of Jesus, passing over the first 30 years of his life. Notice how often the word "immediately" is used, perhaps another indication of the influence of Peter's personality.

John the Baptist begins preaching and baptizes Jesus. Jesus is tempted by Satan and, having resisted the temptation, goes forth preaching: "The time is fulfilled, and the kingdom of God is at hand; repent, and believe in the gospel" (1:15). The centuries of waiting for the promises to be fulfilled during the time of the Old Testament and for 400 years afterward are over. The King has arrived, and he ushers in the kingdom. There is only one right response, that is, repentance and faith. Faith in the good news that God has fulfilled his promises in his Son Jesus Christ. This is still the message of the church today and this is still the required response. Jesus demonstrates his powers to show he really is the Messiah.

Prayer   *Father, help us to preach the gospel with urgency; work in hearts by your Spirit as people hear. In Jesus' name. Amen.*

Day 295 — Read Mark 4–6

PARABLES AND MIRACLES

The word *parable* means "to throw alongside." Jesus lays a physical truth alongside a spiritual truth, so the first casts light on the second. He told these interesting stories to the multitudes, and he explained their meaning to the disciples. The parable of the sower shows that though the Word of God is sown, it does not have the same effect on all. The response to the Word is crucial. If we have a heart which is hardened or shallow or absorbed in "the cares of the world, and the delight in riches, and the desire for other things" (4:19), we will not profit from the Word.

The kingdom of God is like a seed which starts small but becomes great. First Jesus had only 12 followers; now he has millions, making an impact on the whole world.

The great words of Jesus were matched by great deeds. He showed he was the Messiah by causing the storm to cease, by healing a man controlled by many demons, by curing a woman ill for many years, by raising a little girl from the dead, and by taking a few loaves and fishes and multiplying them so that 5,000 men plus women and children could be fed.

This great teacher, this great miracle worker, is who he claimed to be, the Son of God, and today he reigns in heaven ready to help all those who come to him in faith.

Prayer *Father, we praise you for the greatness of your Son Jesus Christ. May he help us in our daily lives. Amen.*

Day 296   Read Mark 7–9

JESUS AND PEOPLE

Our calling is to be like Jesus, who was always involved with people, seeking to do what good he could for them. The Pharisees needed to be warned that their hypocrisy could only do harm to them and others, so Jesus gave them the warning they needed. As Christians, we must not only encourage good but also warn against evil.

In dealing with the Syrophoenician woman, he first stretched her faith and then met her need, a foretaste of the fact that the results of his ministry would reach beyond Israel. "He even makes the deaf hear and the mute speak" (7:37 ESV). Whatever the needs, Jesus had the power and the willingness to meet them.

He feeds the hungry. We do not have miraculous power to heal the sick, but we can send medical missionaries to heal and food to feed the hungry. These things should have a higher priority in our lives than surrounding ourselves with increasing luxuries.

Jesus begins to reveal himself to the apostles, for their benefit and for the benefit of those who would be reached by them. He challenges them to consider who he is and elicits from Peter the Great Confession. He reveals to them that he will be a different kind of Messiah than they thought, one who would be killed but rise again. He is transfigured so that this vision will keep them going in the difficult days ahead.

Prayer   *Father, help us to see people not as those from whom we can receive but those to whom we can give. In Jesus' name. Amen.*

Day 297   Read Mark 10-11

THE GOAL OF LIFE

Mark 10 describes Jesus' Perean ministry. Perea was an area on the east side of the Jordan. There the rich young ruler (in Mark called simply "a man") meets him and turns away because following Jesus called for a greater price than he was willing to pay. The lesson for us is surely that nothing should stand in the way of total commitment to Christ. Make riches the goal of your life and you will lose out.

Jesus is heading for Jerusalem to be crucified. The disciples follow him fearfully. Sadly James and John are looking for a place of honor greater than that of the others. Make glory the goal of your life, and you will lose out. Rather we should make service the goal, for then we will be like Jesus who said, "The Son of Man came not to be served but to serve, and to give his life as a ransom for many" (10:45 ESV).

Jesus now arrives at Jerusalem. He uses a donkey, a humble animal which serves him. Usefulness to Jesus and service to others should be the twin goals of our lives. Having entered Jerusalem amidst the acclaim of the common people, Jesus curses the fig tree, the only destructive miracle recorded. But the purpose is to teach an important lesson. Jesus wants to see fruit, and he also wants to see it in our lives. And what kind of fruit does he look for? The gracious qualities which are the fruit of the Spirit.

Prayer   *Father, help us to examine our goals and change to the goals to which you call us. In Jesus' name. Amen.*

Day 298   Read Mark 12-14

THE NOOSE TIGHTENS

Opposition to Jesus mounts. He adds fuel to the fire by telling a parable about the owner of a vineyard who sends servants to collect what is his, and when they fail sends his own son. The religious leaders realize the parable is about them and would have arrested Jesus then and there, but are afraid of how the multitudes would react. So they try to get him to make statements which will cause him to lose his popularity.

They try to get Jesus to make a statement about taxation which will either turn the people against him or make him liable to the charge of tax evasion. He answers by calling on them to give the government what it deserves and God what he deserves.

Then the Sadducees give Jesus a trick question which enables him to turn the tables against them and show their lack of understanding of Scripture. Finally, a scribe asks about the greatest commandment and Jesus shows it is the commandment to love God and neighbor.

They then try another tactic, to bribe Judas to betray him so they can capture him in a secluded place where the multitudes cannot interfere. They conduct a trial full of illegalities. Then Jesus makes a statement in which he admits to being the Messiah. This was true, but they take it as a statement of blasphemy and condemn him to death. The end is near, but it turns out to be a new beginning.

Prayer   *Father, work in the hearts of many today who oppose Jesus and lead them to repentance and faith. Amen.*

Day 299   Read Mark 15-16

CRUCIFIED, HE ROSE AGAIN

It is possible that the first Lord's Supper was held in the upper room in the home of Mark's mother, and that young Mark followed Jesus and that he was the young man who fled leaving his garment behind him (14:51-52). The description of the trials and crucifixion reiterate what we recently read in Matthew. In fact, at many points the accounts are word for word the same, evidence that suggests Matthew, who expands a bit here and there, had Mark before him when he wrote. In any case, each Gospel ends with a detailed account of the crucifixion and resurrection. The Gospels are not biographies; they are proclamations of good news. This is the good news—that Jesus died in our place so that we might be forgiven, that he rose showing he has power over sin and death for our sake, and that he is alive today.

There is great variety in the manuscripts we have of Mark 16, therefore there are shorter and longer endings to the Gospel. However, in every case there is the fact of the resurrection and of the women meeting an angel at the empty tomb. The message of God to them, through the angel, is the directive found frequently in the Bible: "Go." This amazing fact that Jesus Christ though crucified, dead, and buried is yet now alive must be proclaimed to the world. God has provided a Savior. We must go everywhere with that message.

Prayer   *Father, fill us so full of the joy of our salvation that we will be impelled to tell the world of Jesus. In his name. Amen.*

Day 300   Read Luke 1–2

TO YOU IS BORN A SAVIOR

Many stories about Jesus were floating around, so Luke carefully investigates to be sure his account is accurate. It is possible that he interviewed Mary, Elizabeth, and others. He alone provides us with information about the words of the angels who told Zechariah and Mary about the amazing births which were to take place. He alone tells us how Mary said, "My soul magnifies the Lord," and Zechariah, "Blessed be the Lord God of Israel" and tells us of the angels proclaiming the good news to the shepherds.

God first brought the message to shepherds, common humble men, not to kings or priests. How they must have been startled when suddenly the sky was bright and an angel said, "To you is born this day in the city of David a Savior, who is Christ the Lord." How they must have listened in awe as the angels praised God and spoke of his glory and peace.

But then the darkness of night returned, for the angels had departed. This is the crucial moment. What will they do? They make the right decision: they hasten to find this wonderful Child. And seeing him, what do they do? They go quickly and tell others. Our response to the message of the birth of the Savior must be similar. Let us meet him personally, which we can do by faith, knowing many more wonderful things about him than the shepherds did, and then let us tell others of how wonderful it is to meet Jesus.

Prayer   *Father, we thank you that your Son was willing to step out of the ivory palaces into our world for us. Amen.*

Day 301   Read Luke 3-4

WHAT SHALL WE DO?

John the Baptist preached repentance. *Repent* means literally, "change your mind." By nature we think our sin is not so serious; we are to change our mind and realize it is. By nature our lives revolve around ourselves; we are to change our mind and realize our entire life should revolve around God. At about this time, baptism was used as a sign that a pagan was spiritually dirty, and must be washed before he could become one of God's people. To accept baptism involved the humbling admission for a Jew that he was also by nature spiritually dirty in God's sight.

The preaching of John the Baptist led to a question to which all good preaching should lead: what does God want us to do in response to his truth? The multitudes asked and were told that they should share with those less fortunate. The tax collectors asked and were told that they should be honest. The soldiers asked and were told they should not use their power to take advantage of people and should be content with their pay. If you want to know what you should do, the answer is all of the above and more.

John then points the people to the Christ who was to come and Luke in summary said, "So, with many other exhortations, he preached good news to the people." I exhort you to respond in faith and obedience to the gospel of Christ.

Prayer   *Father, help us to apply your word to our specific situations. In Jesus' name. Amen.*

Day 302   Read Luke 5–6

THE PREACHING OF JESUS

Matthew gives us the Sermon on the Mount. Luke gives us a similar sermon but tells us it was delivered on "a level place." There are two possibilities. One is that these were two different sermons. After all, Jesus preached many sermons in many places, and the content in each place very likely had some similarities. The other possibility is that this was one sermon, delivered on a level spot on the mountain.

Both accounts tell of the blessings we will receive if we have the right attitudes. Luke also records the "woes" which come to those who have so much that they yield to the temptation of being complacent.

Jesus stresses the importance of doing good (6:27, 33, 35). We must realize that we are not saved by good works, but only through faith in Christ. We must also remind ourselves that we are saved to live a life of good works, doing all the good we can to all the people we can in every way we can. Jesus reminds us that such good must not just be done to people who are nice to us, but also to those who are not.

Later in the sermon, Jesus says "The good man out of the good treasure of his heart produces good" (6:45). Salvation is a matter of escaping from hell, but it is much more. It is also a changing life that increasingly reflects the very life of Christ himself, who always went about doing good—to people.

Prayer   *Father, we praise you for saving us by grace alone.*
                Enable us to do good as you have commanded us. Amen.

Day 303   Read Luke 7–8

JESUS AND PEOPLE

As we learned yesterday, Jesus was always going about doing good—to people. As someone has said, "How is it then that I am so often satisfied just going about." Wherever Jesus met people, he was a blessing to them. "Go and do likewise" (Luke 10:37).

Jesus met a centurion who had a sick slave, and he made the slave well. He met a widow who was taking the corpse of her only son to the cemetery, and he raised the young man from the dead. He met the disciples of John the Baptist, and he sent them back to their master with words of encouragement. He met a sinful woman, and he forgave her, and in doing so taught a lesson to a Pharisee for his benefit. His disciples were caught in a storm at sea, and he rescued them. He met a man full of demons, and brought him back to normalcy. He met Jairus whose daughter had just died, and he raised her from the dead.

We do not have the power to do healing miracles, except on rare occasions when God chooses to work in that way through us. But there is much good we can do. We can support medical missions in places where people do not have the kind of care we take for granted. We can feed the hungry and teach them to feed themselves. We can be loving and encouraging to the many hurting people who cross our paths. Above all we can invite people to be saved through Christ.

Prayer   *Father, take away any satisfaction we have in living selfishly and enable us to go about doing good. Amen.*

Day 304 Read Luke 9–10

JESUS AND HIS FOLLOWERS

Since we are called to follow Jesus, we can learn about our relationship to him as we note how he dealt with his followers when he was here on earth.

Jesus empowered his followers for the task to which he called them (9:1). When God directly or through his church calls you to a task, do not say you are unable to do it. When Jesus calls us to do something, he will surely give us the ability to do it.

Jesus uses his disciples to help other people (9:16). He wants us to be instruments through whom he will work in the world today. The needs are so great, Jesus wants to use you.

Jesus prayed with his disciples (9:18). He is always praying for us as he is now seated at the right hand of the Father, and when we earnestly pray in his name, he presents our prayers to the Father, who will certainly answer them for his sake.

Jesus calls his disciples to sacrifice (9:23). Salvation is free, but the saved are called to be his followers who pay a price. There will be difficulties, but to those who are faithful there will be a reward well out of all proportion to the sacrifices made for the great cause.

Jesus revealed himself more fully to his disciples (9:29). Why did only three experience seeing the transfiguration? Apparently they were closest to him, and they wanted to know him more fully. Do you?

Prayer   *Father, as we follow your Son, empower us, use us, and give us the courage to pay whatever price necessary. Amen.*

Day 305　　　　　　　　　　　　　　Read Luke 11-12

TO BE AND NOT TO BE

Jesus gives us a great deal of practical advice on how we are to live as well as how not to live if we are ready to listen. Here Jesus gives us five directives:

(1) Be prayerful (11:2). Jesus gives us himself as an example of prayerfulness (v. 1). He gives us a model for prayer, the Lord's Prayer. He gives us encouragement to pray urgently, as the friend who needed food to serve his guest (vv. 5-8). He gives us promises that prayer will be answered (vv. 9-13).

(2) Be not hypocritical (12:1). Do not be as the Pharisees, making believe on the outside that they were more holy than they were on the inside. God looks at the heart; hypocrisy is a hopeless failure.

(3) Be not covetous (12:15). It is tempting to want what others have, to be unhappy if we do not have these things. Material possessions do not bring happiness. Why then do we want them so badly?

(4) Be not anxious (12:22). If we really believe that God is in control and that he loves us, will he not take care of us? Put first things first, and God will take care of the rest, for Jesus says, "Seek his kingdom, and these things shall be yours as well."

(5) Be always watchful (12:36). Christ is coming again, and it will be suddenly. Let us always live in a state of spiritual preparation, so that we will be ready when he comes.

Let Jesus' directives guide you in your life. Surely he knows what is best for us far better than we do.

Prayer　*Father, work in our hearts by your Spirit that we may be the kind of people you want us to be. In Jesus' name. Amen.*

Day 306　　　　　　　　　　　　　　Read Luke 13–15

REJOICE, THE LOST HAS BEEN FOUND

Luke 15 contains three parables with this in common—in each there is rejoicing when what was lost is found. A shepherd has 100 sheep, 99 of which are safe, but one has wandered off and is in mortal danger. The shepherd puts forth the effort to go find that one sheep and rejoices when it is found. There are many people who are wandering sheep, so let us be involved in evangelism, for there is no joy greater than that of having a share in bringing a person to Christ so he or she can experience eternal salvation.

A woman has ten coins and loses one. She does not have adequate natural light allowed by large windows such as are common in homes today and probably hers is a dirt floor. So she works hard to find the coin and when she does, she rejoices. Some people are lost right within the Father's house, the church. Let us do all we can to bring them to Christ, and then let us rejoice.

A father has a wayward son. The young man is greedy and selfish. He is headstrong and lusts after evils readily available in the sinful world. But the father still loves him. When he hits bottom, the son finally realizes what a mistake he has made. He is willing to humble himself. He comes back to his father who goes running out to meet him, rejoicing at his return. God is like that father; be sure not to be like the elder brother.

Prayer　　*Father, bless various methods of evangelism, and we shall rejoice in the wonderful results. In Jesus' name. Amen.*

Day 307　　　　　　　　　　　　　　Read Luke 16–17

MORE PARABLES

Most parables have only one point; therefore we must not press the details but seek that one truth addressed to us. Here we have three parables:

(1) The parable of the unrighteous steward (16:1-9). Jesus is not recommending dishonesty here. We must always seek to be absolutely honest in all our dealings with people. The point is that this steward prepared for the future, and so must we, by shrewdly putting all of our trust in Christ and laying up treasures in heaven.

(2) The parable of the rich man and Lazarus (16:19-31). What was the sin of the rich man? Was it that he kicked Lazarus as he went past him? Was it that he spit upon him? No! The sin was that he passed him, saw his great need, and did nothing. And when he died, he went to hell. The boundary between heaven and hell is fixed. How important then that we be not like the rich man. Let us, realizing our need, place all of our trust in Christ, and go forth to live a life of meeting the needs of other people.

(3) The parable of the servant (17:7-10). What is the point of this parable? It is this: we are to do everything God tells us to do. Having done so, let us not feel that this merits us anything. We have only done our duty. Many people act as if they are doing God a favor if they serve in some capacity in his church. Let us rather serve in humility.

Prayer　　*Father, enable us to understand how to apply these teachings of your Son to our lives. In his name. Amen.*

Day 308   Read Luke 18–20

TAX COLLECTORS

The parable of the publican and the Pharisee was told to "some who trusted in themselves that they were righteous and despised others" (18:9). We must examine ourselves to see if that describes us. Tax collectors, called "publicans" in earlier versions, were hated for two reasons: they worked for the hated Romans who ruled the land, and they took unfair advantage of their position to make money at the expense of their countrymen. On the other hand, the Pharisees were the self-acclaimed religious leaders who were highly respected by most of the population. It was not good to be a publican. But their situation made them much more open to repentance than did that of the Pharisee. It was the repentance of individual tax collectors which Christ praised. It was the spiritual pride and hypocrisy of most Pharisees which Jesus condemned.

In Jericho a tax collector met Jesus. He was a little man named Zacchaeus. He was very anxious to meet Jesus, perhaps because he had heard this was one man who would not despise him. Jesus chose to stay at this man's house, and this led to a decision on the part of Zacchaeus to show his repentance by giving a great deal to the poor and repaying all those whom he had defrauded along with the additional penalty called for in the Old Testament. Let us repent and show it.

Prayer   *Father, forgive us for ways in which we have been like the publican or like the Pharisee. In Jesus' name. Amen.*

Day 309   Read Luke 21-22

THE LAST WEEK

The last week in the earthly life of our Lord was a busy one. Some of the major events were as follows:

(1) Warning of the end. Jesus described to his disciples what would happen before the fall of Jerusalem in AD 70 and what will happen as the end of the world approaches. The purpose is to warn us to be ready at any time for the return of Christ.

(2) Institution of the Lord's Supper. Jesus met with his disciples in an upper room to celebrate the Passover, a reminder of the miraculous way God freed his people from the slavery of Egypt. Jesus then took parts of the meal, the bread and the fruit of the vine, and used them to celebrate the Lord's Supper, a periodic reminder to us of the more wonderful way God has set us free from the bondage of sin.

For Jesus the evening was marred by his knowledge that one of his disciples would betray him and by the argument among the disciples as to who was the greatest. Today it must hurt his loving heart as he sees ways in which we are disloyal to him and the power struggle which still takes place in many churches. Be sure that you are not involved in either.

(3) Prayer in the garden. Jesus is fully human. He pleads with his heavenly Father to find some way to save his people without the cross, but yet he is totally surrendered.

Prayer   *Father, may we be so deeply moved by the events in Scripture that we will have new attitudes. In Jesus' name. Amen.*

Day 310   Read Luke 23–24

THE CRUCIFIED AND RISEN CHRIST

Jesus was crucified between two criminals. One joined the mocking crowd; the other had the amazing faith to see in this dying man one who would be king. The result was that Jesus promised him they would be together in Paradise that very day.

Luke also records for us the dying words of Jesus, "Father, into your hands I commit my spirit!" (23:46 ESV). Unless Christ returns first, each of us will die. Because of our trust in Christ, we can die with peace in our hearts, knowing we are going to be with the Lord.

On Easter afternoon, two people had a great experience. Out for a walk, they were joined by a stranger. They were discussing the crucifixion and the report of the women that the tomb was empty. Jesus showed them what the Old Testament said about the Christ. They did not know who he was until he broke bread. Later that day, Jesus appeared to his disciples and even ate fish as evidence that his was a physical resurrection. Later, they saw him ascend into heaven.

We have historical accounts written on the basis of the testimony of eyewitnesses. Jesus who was crucified is alive! Believe this and you too will live forever. Our faith is based on fact! Later, Luke will give us another volume, which tells us what happened next, how Jesus established his church. Be a part of it.

Prayer *Father, we praise you for preserving these records upon which we can base our faith. In Jesus' name. Amen.*

Day 311   Read John 1–2

THE WORD BECAME FLESH

Probably John had before him the other three Gospels. He is getting old and realizes he is the last eyewitness alive. He knows so many things firsthand which are not recorded in the other Gospels. So he writes with the purpose that those who read may believe in Christ and find true life (see John 20:30-31). He uses the structure of calling upon a series of witnesses who will point to the fact that Jesus is the only Son of God.

He begins with his own witness. He who was so personally involved with Jesus is convinced that the Word (the Logos in Greek, that is, Jesus) is God (1:1). He then lets John the Baptist speak, "I have seen and have borne witness that this is the Son of God" (v. 34). He gives us the testimony of Andrew, "We have found the Messiah" (v. 41). He quotes Nathanael, a man without guile, who upon meeting Jesus cries out, "You are the Son of God! You are the King of Israel!" (v. 49).

John records for us the first miracle Jesus performed, that of turning water into wine, and says that, as a result, "his disciples believed in him" (2:11). He tells us that as Jesus did other miracles (which John always calls signs, for they point to the deity of Christ), "many believed in his name" (v. 23).

If you know some who do not have faith in Christ, urge them to read the Gospel of John. It is written for the purpose of getting people to believe.

Prayer   *Father, as people read this great account of Christ, give them saving faith in him. In his name we pray. Amen.*

Day 312 — Read John 3–4

MEET JESUS

Two very different people meet Jesus, one a scholarly Pharisee, the other an immoral woman. Both testify to the greatness of Jesus. May we also meet him and realize his greatness.

The Pharisee Nicodemus comes at night since he doesn't want anyone to see him. Jesus proclaims to him the necessity of the new birth. The Spirit must work in our hearts causing us who are by nature spiritually dead to become spiritually alive. If there is evidence that you are born again, that you have faith which is beginning to produce fruit, it is because of a miracle produced in your heart by the Spirit. It is all of grace, so be filled with gratitude. Jesus speaks to Nicodemus the words of what many consider to be the greatest verse in the Bible: John 3:16.

The interview of Jesus with the woman at the well teaches us how to evangelize. Jesus arouses her curiosity so that she will listen by offering water which will cause her never to thirst again. He brings her under conviction of sin by asking about her husband when in fact she had had five and now was living with a man who was not her husband. When she tries to change the subject, he refocuses the conversation. Finally, he announces that he is the Messiah (Christ). She goes back to her village and many believed because of her testimony, and over a couple of days many more listen to Jesus, testifying, "This is indeed the Savior of the world."

Prayer — *Father, we praise you for the greatness of your love which gave us your Son to be our Savior. In his name. Amen.*

Day 313   Read John 5–6

THE BREAD OF LIFE

John records one miracle after another, all meant to testify to the fact that Jesus is so great that we should believe in him. There is the miracle of the healing of the official's son (4:46-54), the healing of a man who could not walk for 38 years (5:1-9), the feeding of the five thousand with a few loaves and fishes (6:1-14) and walking on water (vv. 19-21).

But instead of believing in Jesus because of the miracles, most people are only interested in getting more miraculously produced food to fill their stomachs. So Jesus proclaims to them that he is the true bread from heaven and that believing in him will give them eternal life. In proclaiming himself the bread of life, he tells them that they must eat his flesh and drink his blood in order to have eternal life. He is using metaphorical language, which reminds us that believing is in fact taking Christ into our hearts.

This kind of talk was too much for them, and they discontinued following him. Only the Twelve remained. When Jesus asks if they will also leave, Peter testified, "We have believed, and have come to know, that you are the Holy One of God" (6:69). But even among the Twelve, one would betray him.

Believing is not just accepting facts about Jesus; it is a commitment of loyalty which makes fellowship with him real.

Prayer   *Father, give us the grace to cling to Jesus no matter what other people may do. In his name. Amen.*

Day 314   Read John 7-9

JESUS AND THE PHARISEES

Jesus gives the Pharisees an opportunity to come to him as he testifies to them of his uniqueness, but they reject his testimony. Then we have a passage (7:53–8:11) not found in the best (earliest) manuscripts but found in some manuscripts at the end of John's Gospel or after Luke 21:38. Here the Pharisees bring a woman caught in the act of adultery. Interestingly they do not bring the man! Jesus challenges them by saying that whoever is sinless should cast the first stone as prescribed in the law. One by one they slip away, and then Jesus says to the woman, "Neither do I condemn you; go, and do not sin again." Adultery is a serious sin; that of spiritual pride is worse. Let us avoid both.

Jesus testifies, "I am the light of the world" (8:12), which is challenged by the Pharisees. He then gives sight to a man who had been born blind, as evidence of his claim. Still the Pharisees would not accept him. At this point the man testifies that although there is much he does not know about Jesus, this he does know: he had been blind, yet now he sees.

Up to this point, the man believed Jesus was a prophet, which was great but not great enough. Jesus meets him again and tells him that he is the Son of Man, that is, the Messiah. As a result, the man confesses faith in Jesus as the Messiah.

Prayer   *Father, we pray for those who are resisting the gospel that the Spirit may cause them to believe. Amen.*

Day 315 — Read John 10-12

I AM

There are seven great "I ams" in the Gospel of John. We have already considered some of Jesus' claims, "I am the bread of life" (6:35) and "I am the light of the world" (9:5). Later Jesus will say, "I am the way, and the truth, and the life" (14:6) and "I am the true vine" (15:1). Significantly, the great name of God, Yahweh (or Jehovah), comes from the Hebrew verbal root "I am," so these statements of Jesus are also claims to deity.

In the passage today, we have three more "I ams":

(1) "I am the door; if any one enters by me, he will be saved" (10:9). Jesus refers to the door of a sheepfold. The only way the sheep can enjoy the green pastures and find life is by passing through that door. Jesus is the one way for us to experience life.

(2) "I am the good shepherd" (10:14). Significantly, in Ezekiel, God condemns the leaders of Israel for their unfaithfulness as shepherds and promises that he himself will come. Also in Psalm 23, "The LORD [Yahweh] is my shepherd." Now Jesus comes fulfilling that role. Again, a claim to deity.

(3) "I am the resurrection and the life; he who believes in me, though he die, yet shall he live" (11:25). Lazarus lies dead in the grave. Martha believes he will rise at the end of the world, but now Jesus makes this claim and proves it by raising Lazarus from the dead. How great Jesus is!

Prayer — *Father, we praise you that you have come to us in the person of your Son to give us eternal life. In his name. Amen.*

Day 316   Read John 13-16

IN THE UPPER ROOM WITH JESUS

What great teachings Jesus has for us in these chapters. He teaches us by example in the foot washing that we are to rid our hearts of pride and to serve each other gladly. How easy that is to say, how difficult it is to do.

Jesus tells us that our hearts need not be troubled because heaven is like a large house in which he has prepared a room for each of us and to which he will personally escort us when he meets us at death. There is only one way to our Father's eternal house and that is Jesus. We must take that way and tell people everywhere, for it is the only way.

Jesus is the vine, we are the branches. By faith we are joined to the vine. Without that relationship we can do nothing, but as Paul says, with that relationship we can do all the things he wants us to do. Only through that relationship can we produce the fruit of the Spirit, which consists of qualities like those displayed by Jesus in his life when he was on earth.

Jesus teaches us about love. We are not just to love one another, but we are to love one another as he has loved us. How is that? Sacrificially, unselfishly. What a challenge! How difficult! But possible through Christ and yielding wonderful blessings.

Jesus promises that the Spirit will lead us into all truth. Let us study the Word, which the Spirit has inspired.

Prayer   *Father, how wonderful to listen to Jesus speak to us through the Word! Give us grace to trust and obey. Amen.*

Day 317   Read John 17–19

CRUCIFIED

In the high priestly prayer, Jesus prays for his disciples then and today. It includes a definition of life eternal: "This is eternal life, that they know you the only true God, and Jesus Christ whom you have sent" (17:3 ESV). That verse had a transforming effect upon my life. Previously I had thought of salvation as heaven. This verse caused me to realize that salvation and eternal life start now and last forever, and in essence is a personal relationship to Jesus. Do you have that relationship?

In Gethsemane, Jesus is captured and condemned in an illegal trial. In the meantime, Peter denies him. May we not deny him, either in word or deed. Because the Jews did not have the power to impose the death penalty, they brought him to the Roman governor who, to save his own career, unjustly condemns Jesus to the horrible death of crucifixion. May we not sacrifice our convictions to forward our personal plans.

As he died, Jesus said, "It is finished" (19:30). All that needed to be done in order to redeem us from our lost condition in sin had now been done. The perfect sacrifice had been made, sufficient for our complete salvation. But our task is unfinished. Our task is now to tell the world of this Jesus so that people everywhere may come to him to receive eternal life. Having received the free gift of eternal life, let us devote ourselves to spreading the gospel.

Prayer   *Father, we stand in amazement as we think that your Son suffered such agony for us. In his name. Amen.*

Day 318   Read John 20–21

RISEN

Jesus died, but that was not the end. Because of what happened to him on Easter morning, that is not the end for us either. "Jesus lives and so shall I!" Peter and John saw the tomb was empty. Jesus appeared to Mary Magdalene. That Sunday night, he appeared to his disciples. Thomas missed the blessing because he was somewhere else. If your church has evening worship, Jesus is there meeting with his disciples. Don't miss that blessing by your absence.

The next Sunday, the risen Jesus again visits his disciples. This time Thomas is not only present, but seeing Jesus, he breaks forth in a great confession, "My Lord and my God" (20:28). Jesus is God in human flesh; he has risen from the dead. Let us confess our faith in him by word and deed, not only in the church but also in the world around us.

Jesus meets with several disciples who went back to their old job of fishing. These appearances of the risen Lord, along with others mentioned in the other gospels, point to the historical reality of the resurrection. In our Scripture passage for today, we find the reason why the Gospel of John was written: "These are written that you may believe . . . and that believing you may have life in his name" (20:31). The purpose for John's Gospel is evangelism. If you or someone you know is not saved, read or ask them to read the Gospel of John.

Prayer   *Father, as today people read John's Gospel, may its purpose be fulfilled—may they believe and find true life. In Jesus' name. Amen.*

Day 319 — Read Acts 1–3

THE STORY CONTINUES

Acts is the second in a two-volume set of which Luke's Gospel is the first. Thus it continues the story of what happened after the resurrection. After appearing to his disciples over a period of 40 days which gave clear evidence that he really was risen, Jesus ascended into heaven while they watched.

Before leaving, Jesus gave the Great Commission. Acts tells how the disciples began to obey that commission. Jesus made it clear that they could not present that gospel in their own power, so they first had to wait for the coming of the Spirit. After days of prayer, the Spirit came on an Old Testament holiday, Pentecost.

It is evident that the Spirit does give power to witness, for Peter who had denied Jesus now boldly proclaims him, and the result is 3,000 people are saved. Soon after this, Peter by the power of the Spirit heals a lame man and takes the opportunity once again to proclaim Christ in a very public place.

And the story continues. The church must continue to carry out the Great Commission. We must proclaim the message of Christ everywhere. Everyone who experiences salvation through Christ shares in that responsibility. But we will not be successful if we trust in our own strength. We must constantly pray to be filled with the Spirit.

Prayer — *Father, fill us with your Spirit that we may be effective in witnessing for Christ. In his name. Amen.*

Day 320   Read Acts 4–6

PROBLEMS ALREADY

As a result of powerful preaching, the number of believers grows to 5,000. A problem develops. The rulers arrest the leaders of the church. The church then prays, not for protection but for boldness.

The problems from within prove worse than those from without. Though the Spirit has just come, there are problems in the church. In every church there are those who have not been born again, and those who have been born again continue to possess the old sinful nature as well as the new spiritual nature. Therefore we must seek to be godly Christians but also be patient with our fellow sinners in the church as they too grow in grace and need to be patient with us.

One problem in the church is people who are unwilling to surrender completely and yet want to receive honor from their fellow church members. Many people in the church are like that. Ananias and Sapphira have their lives taken away by God as a warning of the consequences of such attitudes.

Another problem is that differences in ethnic background cause bad feelings, as one group of widows is given better care than another. Our oneness in Christ should overcome the differences which naturally divide us. Part of the solution was practical. People were chosen to deal with this problem so the apostles could continue to focus on their task.

Prayer   *Father, cause us to so grow in grace that we can overcome the problems which afflict the church. Amen.*

Day 321   Read Acts 7

THE GREAT DEACON

To solve the problem of food distribution to the widows, deacons were chosen. First on the list was Stephen, "a man full of faith and of the Holy Spirit" (6:5). These are qualities needed by all who serve in the church, no matter what the task may be.

Stephen not only cared for the widows, he began preaching. As a result, he was arrested, and standing before his accusers he preached a powerful sermon. He traced God's dealings with their ancestors, beginning with Abraham. He talked about God's dealing with Joseph and Moses and how their forefathers had rebelled against God again and again. From time to time it is well for us to review our spiritual heritage, how God dealt not only with people in the Bible, but also with people in the early church and in the days of the Reformation. It is well to remind ourselves of how God dealt with our grandparents.

Then Stephen made his application. Every sermon must end with application. As their forefathers had rebelled against God, so had they by murdering Jesus. There is a sense in which we crucified Jesus. He had to go to the cross because of our sin.

This application infuriated Stephen's audience. Stephen said he saw Jesus standing, concerned with what is happening. He gave Stephen the grace to die with a forgiving spirit like his own.

Prayer   *Father, as we consider our spiritual inheritance, help us to pass the torch of faith on. For Jesus' sake. Amen.*

Day 322 — Read Acts 8–9

THE DEACON AND THE DESTROYER

Another deacon involved in evangelism was Philip who carries out the next step of the Great Commission, going to Samaria. There he has a fruitful ministry, yet God calls him from that ministry to meet one man, the Ethiopian official who knew about the true God but needed to know about Jesus.

The Ethiopian officer is reading the Bible but does not understand it. He is reading Isaiah 53, and Philip tells him how Jesus fulfills that passage. The church must explain the Bible to people, being very careful to interpret it aright, realizing that above all we must meet Jesus in the Bible.

Saul seeks to destroy the church. Jesus meets him on the road to Damascus, where Saul (later called Paul) is converted and commissioned to be a missionary. In spite of his past, Jesus said Saul was "a chosen instrument of mine to carry my name before the Gentiles" (9:15). God has chosen every Christian to be an instrument to spread the gospel. What a privilege, what a responsibility! Paul's message was, "He is the Son of God" (9:20). Our message is to tell who Jesus is and what he has done. We must also call people to respond to that message in surrender to Jesus. You know about Jesus. Has that been your response? What are you doing to share the gospel with others?

Prayer — *Father, we pray that many people may be converted and go on to proclaim the truth by word and deed. Amen.*

Day 323　　　　　　　　　　　　　　　Read Acts 10–12

PETER'S MINISTRY

The Acts of the Apostles or acts of the Spirit through the apostles consists in part of the acts of Peter, who is considered for a few chapters, and the acts of Paul, which take up the remainder of the book. Peter needed a vision from heaven to make him realize that God's plan was broader than his. We too need to realize that the gospel is not just for "our kind" of people but for all kinds of people who are to be welcomed on an equal basis in the church.

Having been prepared by the vision to see things this way, Peter preaches to Cornelius and his family, and the result is a Pentecost for Gentiles, so that Peter realizes neither he nor any Jewish believer in Jesus can withhold baptism from believing Gentiles. When he goes back to the church at Jerusalem, he needs to argue convincingly to explain such unorthodox behavior.

The gospel now spreads to Antioch, a city on the coast many miles north of the Holy Land, and there for the first time followers of Jesus are called Christians. It was originally an insulting label given to them by pagans because the most distinctive feature of their lives was their relationship to Christ. But the name stuck. Is that the most distinctive feature of our lives?

In the meantime, Peter is thrown in prison. One miracle is this, the night before his execution he is sound asleep. The other is that an angel brings him out of prison. Those at the prayer meeting on his behalf are surprised their prayer is answered.

Prayer　　*Father, work in our hearts that the name Christian will not just be a name but describe a relationship. In Christ's name. Amen.*

Day 324   Read Acts 13–15

THE FIRST MISSIONARY JOURNEY

Led by the Spirit, the church at Antioch sets aside its best men for missionary work. A Christian young person who is qualified ought not to ask "What occupation will give me most money?" but "Does the Lord want me to be a missionary?" Paul and Barnabas make the island of Cyprus their first stop. There the Roman proconsul is converted. They then sail for the south coast of what is now Turkey. There John (also named Mark, who later wrote the gospel so named) quit the mission and returned home.

At Antioch of Pisidia, Paul preaches in the synagogue, and like Stephen, recounts God's dealings with Israel up to the point where Jesus arrives on the scene. Having preached about the crucifixion and resurrection, he warns his hearers of the danger of rejecting the gospel. It is still very dangerous to do so.

At Lystra the people first want to honor them as gods and, shortly after, stone Paul, apparently knocking him unconscious. They then double back on the cities where they had established churches, "strengthening the souls of the disciples, exhorting them to continue in the faith" (14:22). May the preaching in our churches strengthen each one spiritually. Returning to Jerusalem, a general synod of sorts is held to set guidelines to assure that Gentiles will be accepted in the church on an equal basis with Jews.

Prayer   *Father, bless missionaries whom we have sent forth that their work will result in many converts to Christ. Amen.*

Day 325　　　　　　　　　　　　　　　　　　Read Acts 16–18

ON THE ROAD AGAIN FOR CHRIST

Paul and Barnabas get ready for a second missionary journey. Gracious Barnabas wants to take the quitter Mark along, but Paul refuses. Sad to say, they part company. Tensions have always existed in the church. May God heal those that exist today. God overrules sin, and the result is that two missionary teams go out instead of one. Paul takes Silas along.

An event occurs which changes the course of history. Paul wants to continue to work in Asia, but the Spirit calls him to Europe. He lands in Macedonia, the northern part of Greece. Lydia, a businesswoman, is converted quietly, and the Philippian jailer is converted dramatically. He proves the reality of his conversion by washing the wounds he had inflicted. Have you hurt someone? Do everything possible to compensate for that hurt.

They moved on to Thessalonica, where they are charged with turning the world upside down, which in reality is turning it right side up. At Berea people show the right spirit by "examining the Scriptures daily to see if these things were so" (17:11 ESV). God will bless you as you read the Bible every day seeking to find the will of God. Having had a disappointing experience in Athens where the people thought they were too intellectual for the gospel, Paul preaches at Corinth noted for its immorality.

Prayer　　*Father, help us to reach both up-and-outers and down-and-outers with the gospel. For Jesus' sake. Amen.*

Day 326   Read Acts 19–20

MINISTRY AT EPHESUS

When the New Testament mentions Asia, it does not mean the continent. It means a small province in the western end of what is now Turkey. Ephesus was the major commercial city of that province, the kind of place Paul liked to work, knowing that the gospel would spread from there to many other places. We should seek the leading of the Spirit to fashion the best possible missionary strategy. Words of Hope is doing just that. Based on careful research we are sharing the gospel with many thousands of people each week in Turkey, in the very same places where Paul preached two thousand years ago.

Paul had a productive ministry in Ephesus. "The word of the Lord grew and prevailed mightily" (19:20). The work was so successful it hurt the local idol-making business. The nerve to the pocketbook is most sensitive, so the idol makers brought charges against Paul, causing a riot. Paul left Ephesus, but later had a meeting with the elders of Ephesus, telling them how they should conduct their ministry. According to the New Testament, the elder is the office upon which the government of the church is structured. Elders today ought to listen carefully to the word of Paul: "Take heed to yourselves and to all the flock, in which the Holy Spirit has made you overseers, to care for the church" (20:28).

Prayer   *Father, we pray for the lay leaders of congregations that they may be examples of godliness. In Jesus' name. Amen.*

Day 327   Read Acts 21–23

A PRISONER FOR CHRIST

Paul is now on his way back to Jerusalem, realizing he is headed for trouble, but convinced he is being led by the Spirit. We need to seek the leading of the Spirit each step of the way in life, realizing God has a good plan for us although it may not be easy.

Arriving in Jerusalem, the leaders of the church there are concerned that Paul has lost his Jewishness, so they ask him to take a vow, which brings him into the temple area where he is seized by the Jews and then rescued by the Roman soldiers. When the soldiers arrest him, he asks for an opportunity to address the people, giving him a chance to witness for Christ. He tells of his conversion experience. The people listen with interest until he mentions the word *Gentile*, at which point they riot.

The Roman officer in charge is perplexed and arranges for the Sanhedrin to meet with him. When things start off badly from the get-go, Paul, perceiving that this body was made up of Pharisees and Sadducees who differed on the resurrection, shrewdly states that the reason he is being condemned is his belief in the resurrection. This results in heated debate between the Pharisees who believed in resurrection and the Sadducees who didn't. The following night, after narrowly surviving this dangerous situation, "the Lord stood by him and said, 'Take courage . . . you must bear witness also at Rome'" (23:11). The Lord says to you, "Take courage."

Prayer   *Father, your servants in the past have suffered much.*
           Give me the grace to take up my cross. For Jesus' sake. Amen.

Day 328 Read Acts 24–26

THE WAY

It is too bad that the wonderful term "The Way" has been spoiled because there is a cult with that name. Paul in his defense uses the term several times. And, indeed, Christianity is The Way. It is a faith, not just a body of doctrine; it is also a way of life. Essentially, it is a commitment of one's faith to a person, the One who said, "I am the way, and the truth, and the life." It is following the One who said, "The gate is narrow . . . that leads to life." Are you walking that way?

Paul's capture gives him the opportunity to testify to people in high places, like the Roman governors, Festus and Felix, and King Agrippa. Paul confronts them so clearly with the gospel that, in fact, they are on trial, not he. We must also proclaim the gospel boldly. We must not do so with an inferiority complex, because by God's grace we are on the winning side.

The early Christians out-thought, out-lived and out-loved the sinful world, and so must we. We must, like Paul, "not [be] disobedient to the heavenly vision" (26:19). Like him we must call people everywhere to "repent and turn to God" (v. 20). And like him, we must do so with "the help that comes from God . . . saying nothing but what the prophets and Moses said" (v. 22). As we read of Paul, we must realize we are engaged in the very same work which was his, and we must carry out that task vigorously as he did.

Prayer *Father, rouse up your church to its great task of evangelism. For Jesus' sake. Amen.*

Day 329   Read Acts 27–28

SHIPWRECKED BUT SAFE

Having appealed for a hearing before Caesar, which was his right as a Roman citizen, Paul is taken as a prisoner on a ship bound for Rome. Because they did not heed Paul's warning, they end up in the midst of a violent storm which threatens to sink the ship. This gives Paul another opportunity to testify. In the midst of difficulties, let us be aware of special opportunities to witness for Christ.

Paul had been assured that all aboard would be rescued for his sake. We are to be the salt of the earth, keeping society from crumbling. He tells those aboard that "the God to whom I belong and whom I worship" has said, "Do not be afraid" (27:23-24). How wonderful to know we belong to God, that we are the objects of his love! Let us worship him by our praise in the sanctuary and by our obedient lives throughout the week. Constantly he says to his people, "Be not afraid." May we hear him say this to us every time we are in a difficult situation.

The ship smashes on a reef, but they all get safely ashore on Malta. From there they take a ship to Italy and travel by land to Rome. There Paul is under house arrest, giving him the chance to witness to those who visit him. The book ends with Paul at Rome for two years. Tradition says he was released and had further opportunity to work as a missionary.

Prayer   *Father, you know those things which make us afraid. Take away those fears as we trust in you. In Jesus' name. Amen.*

Day 330 — Read Romans 1–3

ALL HAVE SINNED

Like the Old Testament, the New Testament begins with historical books: the four Gospels and Acts. Also, like the Old Testament, the New Testament then has a series of writings. In the Old, the writings are the poetic Wisdom Literature; in the New, the Letters (the Epistles). The Letters are arranged as follows: first the letters of Paul, not chronologically, but roughly in the order of length, and then the letters of others.

Romans is divided into three sections: sin, salvation, and service; another way to divide it is guilt, grace, and gratitude. The Heidelberg Catechism, a great Reformation document, follows the same order. In the first chapter, Paul deals with the sins of the Gentiles. He points out how pagans began worshiping the creature (in idolatry) rather than the Creator. God then "gave them up," allowing them to fall farther into sin. In the second chapter, he shows how the Jews also sinned. Condemning the sins of the Gentiles, they themselves committed similar sins.

In the third chapter, Paul points out the advantage of being a Jew, yet all (both Jews and Gentiles) have sinned. Those who knew the law of God did not keep it. Therefore, our only hope is not in trying to keep the law, but acknowledging we are sinners, to turn to Christ alone for grace. Through Christ, God can be righteous and yet forgive sinners.

Prayer — *Father, we thank you for Christ. We are sinners. Our only hope is in him. In his name. Amen.*

Day 331 Read Romans 4-7

FAITH

Having shown that every human being is a hopelessly lost sinner, Paul now shows the way for us to be made right with God (justified). Since Christ has shed his blood as an atonement, all who put their trust in him (have faith) will be forgiven and received back into fellowship with God, which is true life.

Is this idea something new? No, already at the beginning of the establishment of God's people, Abraham, our spiritual ancestor, "believed God, and it was counted to him as righteousness" (4:3 ESV).

As a result of being justified by faith, we have peace and joy and hope and the assurance that even the difficulties of this life are working for our benefit (7:1-5). The sin of Adam has had tragic consequences in the lives of all of us, but now through Christ we who believe receive great blessings.

If justification is by faith and not as the result of our good works, does this mean that it does not matter if we keep on sinning? Paul is horrified by such a conclusion, for we are now united to Christ by faith, and such a union can only produce good works.

We are not saved by keeping the law of the Old Testament, for we sinners are unable to keep it perfectly. The law has a different, but important role; it convicts us of our sin so we will flee into the open arms of Christ.

Prayer *Father, we rejoice that though our faith is often weak, it is focused on the right person, Jesus Christ. In his name. Amen.*

Day 332   Read Romans 8-10

LIFE IN THE SPIRIT

What a contrast between Romans 7 and 8. The seventh chapter is one of spiritual defeat. The word "I" is mentioned again and again, but the Spirit is not mentioned. In Romans 8, there is little mention of "I," but note how the Spirit is mentioned again and again. The chapter begins with no condemnation and ends with no separation from Christ. In between we are given the conviction that in all things God is at work for our good—we who love him, whom he has called.

Paul faces the fact that many Jews have not believed. He is deeply concerned for them, but they do not respond. The conclusion is that those only are saved whom God has chosen. If this is so, we realize a startling fact that he has evidently not chosen many Jews, to open the door to the Gentiles.

This emphasis on the sovereignty of God in salvation in no way dampens Paul's enthusiasm for evangelism. He is deeply concerned for his own people, the Jews. "My heart's desire and prayer to God for them is that they may be saved" (10:1). Oh that we might be so filled with love for people that we would give our very best to the task of evangelizing the world. God chooses whom he will save, but he uses one method to do this: we must proclaim the gospel and those who hear must respond with a faith in their hearts which they express by a confession of that faith with their lips. Have you done that?

Prayer   *Father, as your Word goes forth, work in the hearts of the hearers by your Spirit that many may be saved. Amen.*

Day 333   Read Romans 11–13

SAVED TO SERVE

Paul ends the second section of Romans, dealing with salvation by grace, with concluding thoughts on his disappointment that more of his own people are not being saved (chap. 11).

He then begins the final section of the letter dealing with a life of service as the way to show gratitude for salvation by grace. He begins chapter 12 with "therefore," because of all he has said about salvation by grace. "Therefore" we should respond with total surrender to God. "Present your bodies as a living sacrifice, holy and acceptable to God, which is your spiritual worship" (12:1). The sacrifice is not the offering of dead animals as in the past, but giving our living bodies to God's service. Spiritual worship is expressed by what we do with our physical bodies!

One version translates Romans 12:2, "Do not be conformed to this world," by saying "Do not let the world squeeze you into its mold" (Phillips). We are to dare to live differently than the sinful world around us. God has given each of us different abilities; we are to use them. We must never seek vengeance but seek to live in peace. We must realize we have responsibilities to the government. Good Christians are good citizens.

Love has a prominent role in this life of gratitude. Such love must be genuine and is our obligation toward others.

Prayer   *Father, we have been saved by grace. Help us to show our love for you and our gratitude for all you have done for us by our service toward people. In Jesus' name. Amen.*

Day 334   Read Romans 14–16

DEALING WITH PEOPLE

The Bible says that the way to show that we love God is to love people created in his image. Therefore, we are to welcome people into our churches, though they differ with us on "secondary issues." One problem, of course, is deciding what is secondary. Certainly right belief regarding the deity of Christ and salvation by faith in him alone does not fall in that category, while issues like diet and how to celebrate religious holidays do. If we think people are weaker in the faith than we are, we are to be especially gentle with them.

A basic Pauline principle is "let each of us please his neighbor for his good, to edify him" (15:2). We are not to be concerned about pleasing ourselves. That is easier said than done. The question which is to control our behavior is, "Does this edify (build up in the faith of) the other person?" The spiritual growth of others must take priority over pleasing ourselves.

It is not enough to have the right principles; we must put them into practice in dealing with the flesh-and-blood people with whom we come into contact. In the final chapter, Paul mentions individuals for whom he has concern. He assumes a fellowship of believers in which each one is encouraging the other. He ends with the theme "to God be the glory." To glorify God is to show publicly how great he is. We do that by expressing in action our love for others.

Prayer   *Father, give us the grace no longer to have as our goal personal pleasure but rather the good of others. Amen.*

Day 335   Read 1 Corinthians 1-4

IS THERE HARMONY IN YOUR CHURCH?

Corinth, a city in Achaia (southern Greece), was known for its immorality. In that environment Paul had planted a church and left. Now he hears that they are struggling with problems, so he writes this letter giving solutions to these problems, one by one.

The first problem was lack of unity. One characteristic of a healthy church is a spirit of harmony. Is your church characterized by harmony? If not, a top priority ought to be to work for such unity. In the Corinthian congregation, instead of being united in Christ, some people considered themselves followers of Paul, some of Apollos, the pastor they had after Paul left. The Corinthian Christians considered themselves very "spiritual," but Paul tells them that this forming into cliques proves they are very unspiritual. All must realize that, while God used Paul to found the church and Apollos to nurture the church, it was God himself who caused many good things that happened among them.

The one foundation upon which to build the church is Christ. Each one who works in the church must build on that foundation. The judgment day will reveal how effective that work has been, and God will give rewards accordingly. Our abilities have been given by God and we are accountable to him.

Prayer   *Father, give us love and wisdom to deal with the problems that exist in our congregation. In Jesus' name. Amen.*

Day 336   Read 1 Corinthians 5-7

SEX AND MARRIAGE

The Greeks believed the soul was so important it did not matter what you did with your body. As a result sexual immorality was rampant. A member of the Gentile church there was sleeping with his stepmother and the church treated the matter with indifference. Paul insists this man should be excommunicated to show that the church cannot accept such behavior.

Such a problem must not be handled in the civil court but in the church. No matter how common sexual immorality may be, God's Word says, "Do not be deceived; neither the sexually immoral, nor idolaters, nor adulterers, nor men who practice homosexuality, nor thieves, nor the greedy, nor drunkards, nor revilers, nor swindlers will inherit the kingdom of God" (6:9-10 ESV). What a message for us!

Because sexual temptation is so powerful, it is best that each man have a wife, and that husband and wife seek to satisfy each other's sexual appetites (7:3-5). However, Paul believed that the end of the world was coming soon and, therefore, a single person could best remain single, like himself. Besides, persecution was coming, which could be handled more easily if one was single. If a person chose to get married, it was "only in the Lord." The other person must also be a Christian. This is a point which we should stress to our children at an early age; it is essential that they choose a true Christian as a spouse.

Prayer   *Father, give wisdom and courage to do your will in the important area of sex and marriage. In Jesus' name. Amen.*

Day 337   Read 1 Corinthians 8–11

CONCERN FOR OTHERS

As Paul deals with one problem after another, a common theme runs through his writings —concern for others. Idols represent gods which do not in reality exist; so if meat has been dedicated to them in the market place, what difference does it make? But if a church member has been so steeped in idolatry that he cannot separate the meat from the idol, then he shouldn't eat meat, lest he shake his fellow believer's faith. We do not have that particular problem so much today, yet our desire must be not to satisfy our appetites, but rather to be concerned with the impact of our actions on others.

If we are to evangelize people, we must be sensitive to where they are spiritually. We must not compromise principles, but we must be flexible in order to share the gospel in a way in which they can really hear it. As Paul says, "I have become all things to all people, that by all means I might save some" (9:22 ESV). The concern is not with our convenience but for the spiritual welfare of others.

The inconsiderate Christian says, "All things are lawful" for me (10:23). But Paul replies, "Let no one seek his own good, but the good of his neighbor" (v. 24). This is to be the guiding principle for all our actions. The rich who arrived at the church potluck first with a basket full of food were to be considerate to the poor who came later.

Prayer   *Father, help us to forget ourselves and do all we can to meet the needs of others. In Jesus' name. Amen.*

Day 338   Read 1 Corinthians 12–14

GIFTS OF THE SPIRIT

In the Corinthian church, the gift of speaking in tongues was being given too great a place of prominence, so Paul gently emphasizes that other gifts, ones much less spectacular, are more important.

The church is like a human body. As the body has different parts, so members of the church have different gifts. A person with one gift is not to look down on a person who has a different gift. A person with one gift is not to be jealous of those who have other gifts. A body is only healthy when it has different parts all functioning for the sake of the others. So with the church. We need to help each other.

In the two lists Paul gives in chapter 12, he places the gifts of being able to speak helpfully in ordinary language near the top of the list, the ability to speak in tongues near the bottom. He then says that they should have a greater desire for the gifts near the top, but that there is something more important than gifts; it is love. Love is unselfish action for the benefit of others. It will last forever, while even the most important gifts pass away. May your life and your congregation be dominated by love which is "patient and kind . . . not jealous or boastful" (13:4).

In chapter 14, Paul returns to the theme of how much more important is helpful speech than that which cannot be understood.

Prayer   *Father, help us to lead the church to an attitude of unity in diversity, where love abounds. In Jesus' name. Amen.*

Day 339   Read 1 Corinthians 15-16

RAISED FROM THE DEAD

Greek philosophers thought of the body as a prison from which the soul needed to be freed. They had difficulty with God's plan, that the soul should inhabit a perfect body forever. Even after becoming Christians, many Greeks had a problem with this.

Paul tries to convince them by reminding them that the resurrection of Christ is the foundation for our salvation. Resurrection, therefore, must be good. While the new body will in many ways be like the old, it will also be much more wonderful. When Christ comes, Christians yet alive will have their bodies transformed into these wonderful new bodies, and those dead will be raised with these bodies. Thus death will be completely conquered.

It is typical of Paul that one moment he is talking about the great doctrine of resurrection and next he is asking for funds for a worthy cause. Since we will be raised from the dead, we are to abound "in the work of the Lord, knowing that in the Lord your labor is not in vain" (15:58) and a good way of doing that is to gather on Sunday, the day of the resurrection, to have an offering for hungry people.

Paul's closing words to this church with so many problems was, "Be watchful, stand firm in your faith, be courageous, be strong. Let all that you do be done in love" (16:13-14). That is God's Word to you.

Prayer   *Father, we thank you for our present experience of salvation, knowing the best is yet to come. In Jesus' name. Amen.*

Day 340   Read 2 Corinthians 1–5

PROBLEMS CONTINUE

After writing 1 Corinthians, Paul sent Timothy to straighten out the problems. Hearing that they persisted, he made a quick visit himself. He then probably sent a severe letter to them, followed by a visit from Titus. Having heard from Titus that there was improvement, he writes 2 Corinthians. Problems in churches do not disappear easily; they require much loving patient work. Let us commit ourselves to such work that truth and love may abound in the church for which Christ shed his blood.

Because of the problems, in writing to Corinth Paul expresses much about himself and his feelings. He wants the Corinthians to respect his message, so he gives reasons why they should respect his apostolic authority. He tells them how they have given him joy and sorrow because of his great care for them. As their founding pastor, they should consider what he says. He is aware that he has his frailties, for he is a "jar of clay" (4:7 ESV), but that vessel contains a great treasure, the gospel. He knows his true motivation, "for the love of Christ controls us" (5:14), and he hopes they will accept him because of that motive.

We are ambassadors for Christ (5:20). An ambassador does not make up his own message; he simply delivers the message of his government, but he does so with authority.

Prayer   *Father, help us to be humble and gracious in working with people in the church, for the sake of Christ. Amen.*

Day 341　　　　　　　　　　Read 2 Corinthians 6–10

GIVING TO THE CAUSE OF CHRIST

Paul was a great missionary and theologian; he was also a great fund-raiser. Christians in Jerusalem are starving, and Paul seeks to raise funds to help them. After speaking about his feelings for them, he tells them of this need. They are in Achaia (southern Greece). He tells them of the generosity of the Christians in Macedonia (northern Greece). He sees this fund as an opportunity for the Corinthian Christians to show that they love Christ as much as do the Macedonians. He assures them that safeguards will be taken to ensure the fund will not be misused. He reminds them that God richly blesses those who give generously. When the needy receive the gift, they will glorify God, which is our goal. He concludes with the words "Thanks be to God for his inexpressible gift!" (9:15). This is to be the final motivation; we are to give to God because of whom he has given us, a gift beyond human description: Jesus Christ!

Today there are so many opportunities to spread the gospel. If we have experienced abundant life through Christ, and we have his love in our hearts, we will want people everywhere to know how to be saved for eternity. We must witness personally. But there are many whom we can only reach through others. One way is through Words of Hope broadcasts. Let us give generously for the cause of Christ.

Prayer　　*Father, give us the grace to express our love through generous giving to proclaim the gospel. In Jesus' name. Amen.*

Day 342   Read 2 Corinthians 11-13

PURE DEVOTION TO CHRIST

Paul is concerned that his readers have a "pure devotion to Christ" (11:3). He himself is an example of such devotion to which each of us is called.

Such devotion leads us to share God's Word with the world: "We have made this plain to you in all things" (11:6 ESV). Such devotion calls for paying a price. Paul tells of the price he paid in terms of the dangers and sufferings he endured. We may not be called to pay that price, but we should share his concern for the condition of every Christian congregation. "There is the daily pressure upon me of my anxiety for all the churches" (v. 28). Do we have such a care or are we indifferent to what is happening in other congregations?

While pastors need to be paid so they can devote all their time to the work of the church, devotion to Christ will make pay secondary: "It is you I want—not your money" (12:14, Phillips). Devotion to Christ should be the ultimate motive in the service of both pastors and lay people: "My only reason for so doing is to help you in your spiritual life" (v. 19 Phillips). Devotion to Christ will motivate us to pray urgently for others, "What we pray for is your improvement" (13:9 RSV). May Paul's closing words to the Corinthian church speak to us today, "Mend your ways, heed my appeal, agree with one another, live in peace" (v. 11).

Prayer   *Father, work in our hearts that devotion to Christ may motivate us in all we do. In his name. Amen.*

Day 343 — Read Galatians

BY FAITH ALONE

Galatia was an area in what is now Turkey, which included such churches as Lystra and Derbe. After Paul founded them and left, others came along insisting Gentiles had to adhere to the law of Moses, including circumcision. Paul writes this letter to counteract this false teaching and to reemphasize that we are saved by faith in Christ alone. Galatians was one of the biblical sources which caused Luther to emphasize that central truth and thus begin the Reformation.

While we are not saved by good works, such faith leads to a life lived according to the highest ethical standards. Although we are free from keeping the Old Testament law, "Be careful that freedom does not become mere opportunity for your lower nature. You should be free to serve one another in love" (5:13 Phillips). The lower nature is the sinful nature with which we are born, and which struggles with the new nature to dominate our lives. The works produced by this old nature are things like "sexual immorality . . . rivalries . . . drunkenness," concerning which Paul added that "those who do such things will not inherit the kingdom of God" (vv. 19-21 ESV).

We are to be filled with the Spirit, who will cause us to abound in "love, joy peace, patience" (5:22). Let us examine our lives to see that we are trusting in Christ alone and controlled by his Spirit.

Prayer — *Father, give us grace that, trusting in Christ, we may abound in the fruit of the Spirit. In Christ's name. Amen.*

IN CHRIST

Notice how often the term "in Christ" is used in this passage. It was "in him" (1:4) that God chose us from before creation that we might be "holy and blameless." Therefore the grace that has been "freely bestowed on us" is "in the Beloved" (v. 6). God's whole great plan is "set forth in Christ" (v. 9). Our hope (v. 12) and our faith (v. 15) is in him. God showed his great power "in Christ" (v. 20) by raising him from the dead.

While we are yet on earth, there is a sense in which we are in heaven "in Christ Jesus" (2:6). In the ages to come, God will show "the immeasurable riches of his grace in kindness toward us in Christ Jesus" (v. 7). We were "created in Christ Jesus for good works" (v. 10). We who are not Jews have been joined together with believing Jews to be brought near to God "in Christ Jesus" (v. 13). God's eternal plan has been "realized in Christ Jesus" (3:11). The glory of God is thus manifested "in Christ Jesus" (v. 21).

Beside all this, notice how often Christ is mentioned in these chapters. We cannot exalt Christ too much. Someone has said, "Christianity is Christ." How true. We who believe are now in a new position; we are "in Christ." He is to be the center of our lives. He is to be the focus of the life of the church. We must not let anything else distract us. What about you? What place does Jesus Christ have in your life?

Prayer *Father, we praise you that through Christ and him alone we have abundant life. In his name. Amen.*

Day 345 — Read Ephesians 4–6

NEW LIFE IN CHRIST

Believing the truth about Christ must lead to new life in Christ. Paul always begins with doctrine and ends with ethics. This section begins with the words, "Lead a life worthy of the calling to which you have been called" (4:1).

Since the church is the body of Christ, it must be united, which is only possible when we have "all humility and gentleness, with patience, bearing with one another in love" (4:2 ESV). The talents God has given the leaders of the church are "to equip the saints for the work of ministry, for building up the body of Christ" (v. 12). Living the new life means forsaking the old life, that of the pagans (vv. 17-19).

Christ must have a profound effect on how we treat our marriage partner. "Husbands, love your wives, as Christ loved the church and gave himself up for her" (5:25). If we really believe that Christ loved us sacrificially, that is the way in which husbands and wives are to love each other. Is that the kind of love you have?

Likewise, our faith will affect the way children treat their parents and the way parents treat their children. How much happier so many people would be if they put these teachings into practice. And our faith must affect the way employers and employees treat each other. Some of the final directives are "be strong," "put on the whole armor of God," and "pray at all times."

Prayer *Father, give us the grace to live lives consistent with the great things we claim to believe. In Christ. Amen.*

Day 346   Read Philippians

REJOICE

As was the case with many of Paul's letters, he was in prison when he wrote this one. Yet his theme is "Rejoice!" Focusing on Jesus Christ, we can have joy in the midst of affliction.

Paul has this joy because he knows that even if he is killed for his faith, he is the winner. "For to me to live is Christ, and to die is gain" (1:21). Dying is gain, because it will mean experiencing a fuller measure of Christ. The result of such an outlook on life should be "let your manner of life be worthy of the gospel of Christ" (v. 27).

Another cause of rejoicing is if we can see that the people with whom we are trying to share Christ respond by doing "nothing from selfishness or conceit" (2:3) and thus reflecting the spirit of Christ who "emptied himself, taking the form of a servant" (v. 7). We can rejoice because we have the assurance that such humility will lead to blessing.

We can also rejoice in our fellowship with those who share our dedication to Christ, especially if they can tell us of good things that are happening in the church of Christ (2:28).

Another reason for rejoicing is that God helps us look at life from a new perspective, to be content whether we have much or little. He also will give us the strength we need for everything. So, rejoice!

Prayer   *Father, fill our hearts with joy as we consider the many reasons Christ gives us to have such joy. In his name. Amen.*

Day 347   Read Colossians

CHRIST ALONE

In Colossians, Paul is combating a heresy which threatens the church, the idea that Christ was just one of a series of mediators between God and man. Paul's response is that Christ is all-sufficient.

Christ must be given the one central place in the plan of salvation because of who he is, God in human flesh, "for in him all the fullness of God was pleased to dwell" (1:19). He must be given the central place because of what he has done: he created all things, the earth as well as the angelic beings in whom the heretics were putting their trust. Besides, Christ is the head of the church and the first to rise from the dead "that in everything he might be preeminent" (1:18 ESV).

Because salvation is in Christ alone, our lives must be "rooted and built up in him" (2:7 RSV). Again, what we believe ought to transform how we live. Because "Christ . . . is our life" (3:4), "put to death therefore what is earthly in you: sexual immorality, impurity," and the like (3:5). But the emphasis is on the positive, "Put on then, as God's chosen ones, holy and beloved, compassion, kindness . . . forgiving each other . . . and above all put on love" (3:12-14). First of all, you need a strong relationship to Christ by trusting his promises and feeding on his Word, and then you need to develop qualities like his. The family resemblance to Jesus will become apparent as these changes occur in your character and conduct over time. Again, this will affect your family relationships and your business practices.

Prayer   *Father, give us grace that all of life may center around your Son Jesus Christ. In his name. Amen.*

Day 348 — Read 1 Thessalonians

CHRIST IS COMING AGAIN

The New Testament places great emphasis on the fact that Christ is coming back to this earth. Today churches either neglect the subject or place their emphasis on the details of his coming, many of which are not based on solid biblical interpretation. In any case, we've lost nearly all sense of urgency about Jesus' return.

Christ is coming again. The church at Thessalonica was "an example to all the believers" (1:7), and one of its characteristics was "you turned to God from idols . . . to wait for his Son from heaven" (vv. 9-10). Paul also is waiting for the coming of Christ as he looks forward to standing in the presence of Jesus with them "at his coming" (2:19). It is for this reason that he is concerned about the quality of their Christian life and sends Timothy "to establish you in your faith" (3:2). As with the previous two chapters, this one also ends in a reference to the second coming of Christ. Because we must all stand before Christ at his coming, it is important that our hearts be established "unblamable in holiness" (v. 13).

In the fourth chapter, Paul details such holiness of life and then also gives some description of what the second coming will be like. Our loved ones who have died will also share in that glorious event, "therefore comfort one another with these words" (4:18). Christ will come suddenly, therefore our task is to build one another up (5:11).

Prayer — *Father, may your Son return soon. Work in our hearts by your Holy Spirit so we will be ready. For Jesus' sake. Amen.*

Day 349   Read 2 Thessalonians

WHAT'S DONE FOR CHRIST WILL LAST

The belief of the Thessalonian Christians in the truth that Christ is coming again led them to false conclusions. In this letter, Paul reaffirms belief in the second coming but points out that it will not happen until after the powers of evil have manifested themselves for some time. Only then will victory come. It is difficult to know exactly what Paul is speaking about when he talks of "the lawless one" (2:8). Beware of those who think they have the only answer to such difficult questions. There have been great manifestations of evil throughout history and especially in our day. The point to emphasize is that the struggle will be over and the victory complete when our Lord returns. The truth should have practical results; in the light of the truth of the second coming, "may our Lord . . . comfort your hearts and establish you in every good work and word" (vv. 16-17).

A misunderstanding of some of the Thessalonian Christians was that since Christ was coming soon, they might as well quit their jobs and wait in laziness. Paul says the opposite should be true. Let them work while they wait. The fact that Christ may come soon should cause us to labor diligently.

> Only one life, 'twill soon be past,
> Only what's done for Christ will last.

Prayer   *Father, not knowing how much time we have left, help us to work hard in spreading the gospel. In Jesus' name. Amen.*

Day 350   Read 1 Timothy

GOOD PASTORS

The letters of 1 and 2 Timothy and Titus are called the "Pastoral Epistles" because in them Paul gives advice to his helpers on how to be good pastors.

The addressee named Timothy must be prayerful and teach the people to whom he ministers to pray diligently (2:1-4). They should not focus on clothing but rather on inner beauty (vv. 9-10). They must be careful to choose good leaders who have the right qualities and practices (3:1-12). The word "overseer" (or "bishop" in other translations) is another word for elder. Elders have responsibility for the spiritual oversight of a congregation, and its members should recognize this.

Timothy is to focus on Scripture reading, preaching, and teaching (4:13). People in different categories in the congregation (older, younger, men, women) are each to play an appropriate role in the life of the church. The importance of teaching is emphasized (6:2b-10). A healthy church is one having a strong teaching ministry based on Scripture. Members of all ages should be enrolled in this educational program. We must continue to be learners all our lives. Are you in some Bible study group in your church?

Pastors must guard against the "desire to be rich" (6:9). For "the love of money is a root of all kinds of evils" (v. 10 ESV) and has led to the downfall of some but "as for you, man of God, flee these things. Pursue righteousness" (v. 11 ESV).

Prayer   *Father, help both pastors and laypeople to guard themselves from the love of money. In Jesus' name.*

Day 351   Read 2 Timothy

MORE ADVICE FOR PASTORS

In this second letter, Paul continues to tell Timothy how to be a good pastor. Apparently, Timothy tended to be too timid, for Paul reminds him that "God did not give us a spirit of timidity [or fear] but a spirit of power" (1:7). As servants of Christ, we should all have a humble boldness. We should not be ashamed to speak of him and live for him (v. 8).

Again, Paul emphasizes the importance of a teaching ministry. He is to teach so that his pupils will in turn become teachers (2:2). Through the church, is God calling you to be a teacher? Be willing to do this for Christ and at the same time keep learning. We are to learn from the soldier, the athlete, and the farmer how to work in the service of Christ (vv. 3-7). Our focus on Jesus Christ is to be our great inspiration as we work in the church (vv. 8-13).

The world gets worse (3:1-9), but we are to follow the example of Paul (vv. 10-17). We are to believe that "all Scripture is inspired by God" (v. 16a). But this is not enough. We must use Scripture for its intended purpose, for it is "profitable for teaching, for reproof, for correction, and for training in righteousness" (v. 16b). We must not only have a thorough knowledge of the Bible—we must do what it says. These words of Paul should be taken seriously, for he is soon to be killed for his faith.

Prayer   *Father, help every Christian to realize we are each called to serve faithfully in your church. In Jesus' name. Amen.*

Day 352 — Read Titus

GODLY LIVING

Titus was a Greek convert serving as pastor in churches on Crete. In this letter, Paul emphasizes the importance of godly living. A lay leader of the church is to be "a lover of goodness, master of himself, upright, holy, and self controlled" (1:8). In a day when shame has been brought to the church by the immoral lives of some of its prominent leaders, it is important that we show the world that these are exceptions and that Christians are people of integrity.

The pastor is to be an example of such integrity. Paul says to Titus, "Show yourself in all respects a model of good deeds, and in your teaching show integrity, gravity, and sound speech" (2:7-8). The church needs pastors who will preach the gospel of grace clearly and passionately and who will back up that preaching by a life which is above reproach.

All Christians are to be reminded "to be gentle, and to show perfect courtesy toward all men" (3:2). A rude Christian is a poor advertisement for Christ. This way of life is possible, not in our own strength, but through "renewal in the Holy Spirit" (v. 5b). We must seek to live the new life, but at the same time, we must rely on the work of the Holy Spirit in us to make us like Jesus: holy. There is also to be a concern for helping people in need, "Let our people learn . . . to help cases of urgent need" (v. 14).

Prayer — *Father, give all Christians the grace to live a life which will bring honor to our Savior. In his name. Amen.*

Day 353   Read Philemon

SOCIAL JUSTICE

Slavery is a horrible violation of the law of love. The Christian faith did not make a frontal assault on this evil institution but undermined it so that in time it collapsed. This letter of Paul illustrates how this happened. Philemon had a slave named Onesimus, who ran away and probably took some of Philemon's money. Paul was in prison in Rome and apparently Onesimus sought him out and was converted.

Now Paul sends Onesimus back to his master with this letter. In the letter Paul urges Philemon to treat Onesimus no longer as a slave but as a brother in Christ (v. 16). Paul urges Philemon to see the whole event as the providence of God through which Onesimus was led to Christ. He promises to repay Philemon for the financial loss he had suffered, but at the same time reminds him that since Philemon himself had been led to Christ by Paul, Philemon owes Paul a great debt. Making wise use of psychology, he tells Philemon that he expects that he will do more than Paul asks. He tells him he hopes to get out of prison and visit him, thereby reminding him of his accountability.

Some Christians emphasize evangelism, some social justice. If we would be biblical, we must emphasize both. The two should complement each other, as they do in this letter. Let us be the salt of the earth and the light of the world.

Prayer   *Father, give us a passion for evangelism and for justice in the structures of society. In Jesus' name. Amen.*

Day 354 — Read Hebrews 1–7

WORTH DYING FOR

Throughout the first century, a number of Jews had become Christians. Now they were beginning to suffer great persecution and were beginning to wonder if it would be better to return to Judaism, which was still the worship of the true God. This book, whose author is unknown, was written to tell them that Christ is so central to our salvation that to believe in him is worth dying for. One can only really live to the fullest who has committed himself to something worth dying for, and the truth is that the something is a someone, Jesus Christ.

The writer points out that Jesus is greater than the angels (chaps. 1–2). Jesus is greater than Moses whom God used to establish the old covenant with Israel (chap. 3). He is also greater than the priests of the Old Testament; therefore "let us hold fast our confession" (4:14).

Jesus is a high priest of a higher order than that of the sons of Levi. He is a high priest like Melchizedek who is shown to be greater than Levi, because Abraham, the father of Levi, paid tithes to him. The Levitical priests had to offer sacrifices every day, not only for the sins of the people but also for their own sins. Christ, the sinless one, only had to offer himself once. This sacrifice is sufficient to give complete salvation to those who believe in him. Therefore, he is worth dying for, if necessary.

Prayer   *Father, may Christ be so important in our lives that we will live for him every day. In his name. Amen.*

Day 355   Read Hebrews 8–13

FAITH

The Old Testament had predicted that the old covenant with Israel would pass away and be replaced by a new, better covenant. As Moses was the central person in the old covenant, Jesus is the central figure in the new covenant. He has made a better way possible by which we can come to God with assurance of being accepted. "Therefore . . . let us draw near with a true heart in full assurance of faith . . . Let us hold fast the confession of our hope without wavering" (10:19-23).

Then more about that faith follows. It is not simply accepting facts with our heads. It is such a trust in the promises of God that it produces action. "By faith Abel offered to God" (11:4). "By faith Abraham obeyed" (v. 8). There were a host of others "who through faith conquered kingdoms . . . stopped the mouths of lions" (vv. 32-33). We are saved by faith in Christ alone, but faith is not just saying we believe; it is acting in accordance with God's will because we do believe.

We have a host of faithful Old Testament people who witness to us about what faith really means; "therefore, since we are surrounded by so great a cloud of witnesses . . . let us run with perseverance the race that is set before us, looking to Jesus" (12:1-2). Have you made a wholehearted commitment to Christ? Are there pressures which are tempting you to back down? Have faith and be faithful!

Prayer   *Father, produce genuine faith in many hearts by the work of your Spirit. For Jesus' sake. Amen.*

Day 356   Read James

FAITH PRODUCES WORKS

James was probably a half brother of Jesus, who had not believed in him during his earthly life but came to faith as a result of the resurrection and became the leader of the congregation in Jerusalem. There is a tradition that he was nicknamed "camel knees" because of the calluses produced by spending so much time on his knees in prayer.

At first glance James seems to contradict Paul. Paul says we are justified by faith alone; James says we are justified by works (2:21-22). But they were dealing with two different problems which we still have today. Paul was concerned with those who thought they could save themselves by their good works. Such people must be told that they can only be saved by Christ and that their good works in no way make them right with God. James was concerned with those who just say they have faith and think that as a result they are saved. He tells such people that the genuineness of faith is proved by the lives they live.

James puts his finger on ways in which we are inconsistent. The same mouth must not praise God and curse (3:10). Our prayers may not be answered if we want the wrong things (4:3). We are not in control, so when we make plans we must add "if the Lord wills" (v. 15). The rich better be careful that they do not take advantage of the poor (5:4).

Prayer   *Father, give us grace to put all our trust in Christ and show our faith is genuine by the way we live. Amen.*

Day 357 — Read 1 and 2 Peter

GODLY LIVING

As we live our daily lives, we are to be inspired by the assurance of our future, "an inheritance which is imperishable, undefiled, and unfading, kept in heaven for you" (1 Peter 1:4). Because of such hope, we are to "be holy yourselves in all your conduct" (v. 15). Peter shows us that we who trust in Christ now hold the privileged position once held by the people of the Old Testament: "you are a chosen race, a royal priesthood, a holy nation, God's own people" (2:9). This is a description similar to that in Exodus 19:5-6. Again, the privileged position is to motivate us to live godly lives and "maintain good conduct" (v. 12).

Like Paul, Peter teaches us to respect the government. He tells servants to serve their masters faithfully. He tells husbands and wives to treat each other well "since you are joint heirs of the grace of life, in order that your prayers may not be hindered" (3:7). You cannot expect your prayers to be heard if you are not treating your spouse lovingly!

In the second letter, Peter urges us to let faith produce a number of qualities culminating in godliness, brotherly affection, and love (2 Peter 1:7). The sudden return of Christ is to be a powerful motive for personal godliness. "Since all these things are thus to be dissolved, what sort of persons ought you to be in living lives of holiness and godliness" (3:11).

Prayer — *Father, in the midst of an immoral world, give us the strength to live godly lives. For Jesus' sake. Amen.*

Day 358   Read 1, 2, and 3 John

ASSURANCE OF SALVATION

In his gospel, John told us he wrote that we might believe in Christ and as a result have real life. In his first letter, John tells us he wrote so that we might have assurance of such salvation. He urges us not to sin, yet our assurance comes not at all from our attempt to live a sinless life but from knowing we have One who represents us in God's presence, Jesus (1 John 2:1).

What does he mean when he says that "no one who abides in him keeps on sinning" (3:6 ESV)? This is best understood as saying that although we are not sinless, we will not continue to wallow in sin (habitually) as does the lost world. Assurance comes as we see the fruit of the Spirit, which is love, growing in our lives, for "he who loves is born of God" (4:7). We show that we love God by loving our fellow sinners (v. 21).

The second letter emphasizes the importance of the truth (2 John 1-2). Therefore John is made happy when he sees those whom he has led to Christ "following the truth" (v. 4).

In the third letter, John deals with a sticky situation in which Diotrephes is pushing his weight around in the church. Much better to be like Gaius of whom John can say "I know that it is well with your soul" (3 John 2). This inspired the hymn "It Is Well with My Soul." Another good example is Demetrius whom everyone knows is a good man (v. 12).

Prayer   *Father, so fill our hearts with love for you and people that we may have assurance of our salvation. In Jesus' name. Amen.*

Day 359 — Read Jude

OPPOSING HERESY

Jude was probably another half brother of Jesus like James. The similarity between this book and part of 2 Peter indicates that Peter had Jude's work or the other way around. Both share a concern about heresy, which leads to immoral living. When people have the wrong doctrine, they live the wrong way. Having rejected the God of the Ten Commandments, people today wallow in all kinds of unethical and immoral behavior.

In the midst of a world of people "following their own ungodly passions" (v. 18), Jude urges Christians to "build yourselves up on your most holy faith; pray in the Holy Spirit; keep yourselves in the love of God" (vv. 20-21a). The best safeguard against the evil around us is to constantly nurture our faith. The stronger we grow in the Lord, the more protection we have against falling into the sin so prevalent.

This little book closes with one of the most beautiful benedictions found in the Bible: "Now to him who is able to keep you from falling" (v. 24). In the Reformed faith, we speak of both the *preservation* of the saints and the *perseverance* of the saints. On the one hand, we must persevere, we must remain faithful year after year, and we must guard against sin. On the other hand, God will keep us in the hollow of his hand so that, with such protection, the evil one cannot take away our salvation.

Prayer — *Father, in the midst of a world of sin, give us grace to live holy lives as we feed on your Word. In Jesus' name. Amen.*

Day 360　　　　　　　　　　　Read Revelation 1–3

STRENGTH FOR SUFFERING

There are three basic ways to interpret the book of Revelation, and devout Christians differ by holding each position. One is the futurist view, in which most of the book deals with events near the end of the world. Another is the historic view, which sees the book as a prediction of events throughout history. The third is the preterist view, which holds that most of the book deals with what would happen shortly after the time the book was written, as Christians were faced with persecution by the Roman empire. I interpret the book on the basis of this last view since we read in 1:1, "what must soon take place" and in 1:3 "for the time is near." In this view, the purpose of the book is not to give details regarding the end of the world, but to give courage to Christians who would soon suffer persecution at the hands of Rome and to Christians today who face suffering.

John is in exile on Patmos. Jesus Christ comes to him giving him a revelation which begins with seven letters addressed to churches in what is now western Turkey. Each letter follows a similar pattern and assures the church that Jesus is aware of their situation. "I know your works" (2:2), "I know your tribulation" (v. 9), and so on. What an encouragement in the midst of suffering. Jesus knows what is happening to us and he cares. He also offers reproof and discipline as needed because of his love for the church (3:19) but overall urges us to remain faithful to him.

Prayer　　*Father, speak to us through this book which is so difficult for us to understand and yet promises a blessing for those who read, hear, and obey you. For Jesus' sake. Amen.*

Day 361   Read Revelation 4–7

CHRIST CAN DO IT

To understand Revelation we must realize that in terms of its type of literature it is mostly a form of writing called apocalyptic. Narrative writing, such as the description of what Christ did as found in the Gospels, must be taken literally. But apocalyptic literature must not be taken literally, although it must be taken seriously. It consists of visual descriptions which are meant to stir the whole person, rather than simply the mind. It uses metaphorical language which is misunderstood if taken literally.

John now has a vision of heaven. At the center of heaven sits God in all his glory. The physical eye may see the Roman legions marching through the streets, but Revelation shows true reality. It is not Caesar but God who has all power. Therefore to remain faithful to God even though it means death is far wiser than rejecting God as Caesar demands. O Christian, visualize the unseen reality of the throne of God in all his glory, and as a result, get your priorities straight.

Someone is needed to carry out God's great plan (5:2). No one is found until Christ appears on the scene, he who is both like a lion and a lamb (vv. 5-6). Only he can open the scroll, that is, carry out the plan of God. As he opens it, there appear four horsemen, representing the various forces which God uses to unfold history. The section ends with a song of praise to God, who wipes way our tears.

Prayer   *Father, how good it is to know that our Savior is in control of history. Wipe away our tears. In Jesus' name. Amen.*

Day 362   Read Revelation 8–11

GOD PUNISHES A SINFUL WORLD

The world dared to persecute faithful Christians. God in heaven will not let this go on forever. He will pour out his wrath upon such a world. When the seventh seal of the scroll that only Christ can open is loosened, seven angels blow their trumpets, and as they do God punishes the world in ways similar to the plagues on Egypt. The message is: although it seems prudent to deny your faith to save yourself from persecution, that denial will put you on the losing side. Temporarily wrong seems strong, but God is the ruler, and wrong will be punished.

Revelation picks up many figures of speech from the Old Testament, especially from the apocalyptic sections. As God made measurements in the days of Ezekiel to separate those who were his own from their adversaries, so he continues to do here (11:1-2). As Zechariah has a vision of a lampstand supplied with oil by olive trees, so also here. Those who are faithful witnesses, though they suffer much (vv. 7-8) will in the end be victorious (v. 11). This is God's way of working. He does not promise that we will not suffer, but he does promise that in the end we will be victorious.

There is a song in heaven (11:17-18), a song of thanks to God. Although the sinful world is able to hurt Christians, the final word is judgment for the world and reward for God's servants.

Prayer   *Father, give us the faith to believe that "although the wrong seems oft so strong, God is the ruler yet." Amen.*

Day 363   Read Revelation 12-15

THE ENEMIES OF GOD'S PEOPLE

Here we have a new vision in which the woman represents God's people (first Israel, then the church). The child represents Jesus. The dragon represents the devil. The devil tries to pounce upon Jesus, but he ascends to heaven. The devil then turns his attention to the church which is protected by God.

An ally of the devil is the beast from the sea (13:1). Rome is across the sea from Turkey, so this beast apparently represents the persecuting power of Rome (v. 7). Under such persecution, Christians are called upon to remain faithful to Christ (v. 10b). Another ally of the devil is a second beast from the land, probably representing the persecuting power of the local officials. The infamous number 666 probably comes from giving a numerical equivalent to the name Nero Caesar. It thus was a code word describing Rome as the enemy but in a way that would not lead to the arrest of a Christian possessing a copy of the book of Revelation. Likewise, Babylon (14:8), the ancient enemy of God's people, is used as a code word for Rome, the contemporary enemy. Although Rome still had great power at that time, God's far greater power assured Rome's defeat with such certainty that it could be described as past: "Fallen, fallen is Babylon."

The section ends with a song in heaven. "Great and wonderful are your deeds, O Lord God the Almighty!" (15:3).

Prayer   *Father, as today also we are confronted with the wiles of the devil, help us to remain faithful. For Jesus' sake. Amen.*

Day 364   Read Revelation 16-19

LORD OF LORDS AND KING OF KINGS

Seven angels pour the wrath of God upon a world which dares to persecute Christians. The harlot represents Rome, the city of the seven hills (17:9). One after another of her emperors persecute Christians, but they will be defeated by Christ "for he is Lord of lords and King of kings" (17:14). One may have to pay a great price to be on the side of Christ, but in the end it will pay; therefore be faithful! That is the constant message of the book of Revelation, first to Christians of that day persecuted by Rome and now to us today as in many subtle ways we are tempted to be unfaithful to Christ.

Babylon represents Rome, for both had been powerful and prosperous and hurtful to God's people. As Babylon was destroyed because of this, so will Rome. Rome was destroyed by barbaric tribes, but the church continued on. As we sing "Onward, Christian Soldiers," we sing the line "Crowns and thrones may perish, / Kingdoms rise and wane, / but the Church of Jesus, / Constant will remain."

Christ will conquer his enemies (19:15). His side will win, so pay the price however personal, whatever the cost, to be on his side. Sorely tempted Christian, remain faithful to him. He is "King of kings and Lord of lords" (v. 16) and he wishes to reign in your heart.

Prayer   *Father, you have revealed to us unseen reality. Help us to make our decisions in the light of this truth. Amen.*

Day 365   Read Revelation 20–22

THE GRAND FINALE

Many people talk a great deal about the millennium. The only place where a thousand-year millennium is mentioned in the Bible is in Revelation 20. Sincere Christians have held three different views, the premillennial view which says Christ will come to earth before the millennium, the postmillennial view which says Christ will come after the world gets better and better, and the amillennial view which says there is no literal millennium because Revelation is a book of symbolism.

Christ defeated Satan at Calvary. Since then he no longer has the place he held when he deceived all nations with paganism. After a period in which the Christian faith has had great success throughout the world, Satan will be loosed for a little while. Perhaps this post-Christian era of history is that "little while."

While sincere Christians disagree about the events leading to the second coming of Christ, we can all agree that the final chapter is a new heaven and a new earth for eternity. Whatever you may have to suffer in this life, be it from persecution or some other source, know this: if you belong to Jesus Christ, you will spend eternity in that glorious heavenly city, and the most wonderful thing will be to live in the presence of the Lamb of God. But you can begin experiencing eternal life here and now through fellowship with him in the assurance that the best is yet to come.

Prayer   *Father, for me to live is Christ and to die is gain, for it will mean a fuller measure of Christ. In his name. Amen.*

About the Author

The Rev. Harry Buis served as a Reformed Church in America pastor for 41 years, serving six congregations. He had a consuming passion for the Word of God, preached and written, and would take up his pen to share that passion at a moment's notice. His enthusiasm for God and the Bible was his signature. Rev. Buis edited the Words of Hope daily devotional for twenty years, and wrote several books and numerous articles. He also taught as an adjunct at Hope College, Western Theological Seminary, and Kuyper College. He served the church in many capacities, and was elected President of General Synod of the RCA in 1980. Rev. Buis died of cancer in 2001, but his teaching ministry continues in this book.